The Pale Abyssinian

THE PALE ABYSSINIAN

A LIFE OF JAMES BRUCE,
AFRICAN EXPLORER AND ADVENTURER

Miles Bredin

HarperCollins*Publishers*

HarperCollins*Publishers*
77−85 Fulham Palace Road,
Hammersmith, London w6 8jb

Published by HarperCollins*Publishers* 2000
1 3 5 7 9 8 6 4 2

A catalogue record for this book is
available from the British Library

ISBN 0 00 255671 5

Set in Bembo by
Rowland Phototypesetting Ltd,
Bury St Edmunds, Suffolk

Printed in England by Clays Ltd, St Ives plc

For my father, James Bredin

In memory of James Bredin, Carlos Mavroleon
and Giles Thornton

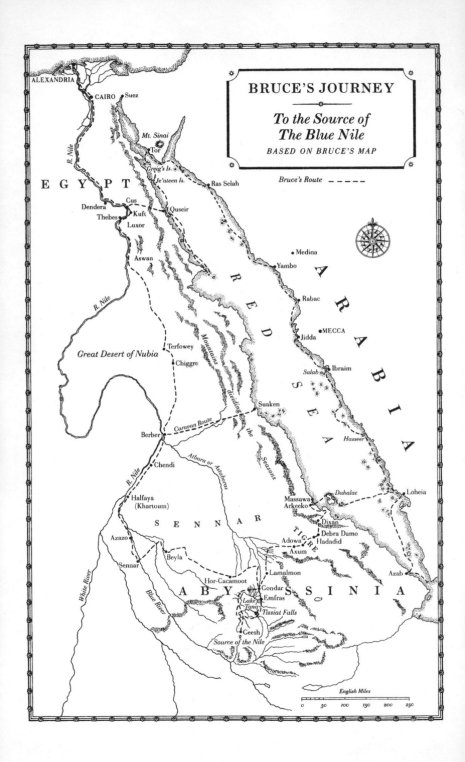

BRUCE'S JOURNEY

To the Source of The Blue Nile

BASED ON BRUCE'S MAP

Bruce's Route — — — —

ALEXANDRIA

CAIRO • Suez

Mt. Sinai
Tor

Greig's Is.
Je'ateen Is. Ras Selah

EGYPT

Cus
Dendera   • Quseir
Thebes Kuft
Luxor

Aswan

• Medina

• Yambo

• Rabac

Great Desert of Nubia   Terfowey

Chiggre

• MECCA
Jidda •

Salab Ibraim

Suaken

Hasseer

Caravan Route

Berber

Chendi

Halfaya
(Khartoum)

Dahalac   Loheia

Massawa
Arkeeko

Dixan
Debra Damo
Hadadid

Adowa
Axum

ARABIA

RED SEA

Hunting the Seasons

Atbara or Astaboras

SENNAR

Azazo

Beyla

Sennar

Hor-Cacamoot

Lamalmon

Gondar
Emfras

Azab

ABYSSINIA

TIGRE

White River

Blue River

Lake Tana
Tissiat Falls

Geesh
Source of the Nile

English Miles

0   50   100   150   200   250

CONTENTS

ACKNOWLEDGEMENTS

Firstly, I must reserve a special thanks to the Yale Center for British Art and its benefactor, the late Paul Mellon. By awarding me a fellowship it allowed me to study Bruce's letters and journals in exquisite and intellectually fertile surroundings. To be able to pick up the internal telephone and speak to the world's expert on whatever small discovery I had just made was of incalculable assistance to my research.

Chapter 5, 'All Points Quest', would not have existed without Graham Hancock's biblical research and writings on James Bruce, leaving me little to do but to check it.

Hundreds of people have helped Jim Stephens and myself research this book over a long period. Some provided breakfast or alcohol when they were most needed, others mended cars; others offered more cerebral but equally useful assistance. Thank you to all and to the many others who helped along the way: James and Virginia Bredin, John and Penny Horsey, Goshu Fisseha and Yemani Assemu at FATCO, Ruth Burnett, Alex Renton, Emma Campbell in Nairobi, Edward Ullendorf, Charles Beckingham, Neil Warner, Chris Field, Mengist Gebra Selassie, Lucy Hannan, Joanna Stephens, Gillon Aitken, Ben Parker, Catherine Bond, Gordon Turnbull at the Boswell Papers; Liza Campbell, Lucy Soutter, Johnny Stephens, Glenn Adamson, Tseggaye Hiwet, Geraldine and Glyn Maxwell, Ivo Phillips, Jan and Alex Meddowes, Charlie Phillips, Guy and Eileen Nicolson, The Earl of Elgin and Kincardine, Lechum Maru, Elisabeth Fairman at the British Art Center, Laura Campbell, Elisabeth Road at the court of the Lord Lyon, Andrew Sinclair, the staff of the London Library, Lucy Warrack, Katherine Stephens, Phillip Winterbottom at Drummonds Bank, Robbie Browne-Clayton, Annabel Heseltine, Tim Deagle, Alison Aylen, Simon Cox, Ingrid Mason, Carlos Mavroleon, Zara d'Abo, Colin and Isabella Cawdor, Hugo de Ferranti, Aidan Hartley, Jojo Primrose, Sue Fusco, Richard Wheaton, Mike Fishwick, Kate Johnson, Annie Robertson, Richard Collins, Lili Schad, Toby Young, Ammanuel Mehreteab in Asmara, Dhafi Khateeb, Quentin Keynes, Don Young, Halvor Astrup, Kath Lyall, Rob Sawyer, Roland and Zoe Purcell, Lengai Croze, Tony and Robina Duckworth, Michael Stan Stavrides at Focus, Mark Jones, Sam Kiley and Malaya.

List of Illustrations

INTRODUCTION

James Bruce was one of the world's greatest explorers. A full century before the age of Stanley and Livingstone, he ventured deep into the African hinterland and added vast tracts of country to the map of the known world. His greatest achievements were in Abyssinia where he discovered the source of the Nile, a riddle that had preoccupied the world since the ancient Egyptians began to wonder where all the water came from. In his success, however, lay his failure. It was the wrong Nile – the Blue rather than the White – and he was so far in advance of any other African explorers that no one believed him anyway. It was another hundred years before Speke and Burton made their discovery of Lake Victoria and finally solved the 'opprobrium of geographers' that had for so long obsessed the world. Bruce was of course not the first to discover the source of the Nile; the Ethiopians were, from ancient times, well aware that the source lay in their country.

Bruce has an undeserved and unenviable reputation. He is generally remembered, if at all, as ill-tempered and a liar. And whilst there is a certain amount of truth in both accusations, they also leave a great deal unsaid. He *was* foul-tempered but only towards the end of his life when, his reputation in tatters, he was suffering from myriad illnesses; and he *was* a liar, but only in a small way, as were all the explorers who followed him. The main accusation against him – that he never went to Abyssinia – was proved to be a fallacy fifty years after he died, by which time it was too late to restore his reputation. In this book I hope to do that and more. Bruce was a colossus of his age. He inspired Mungo Park to trace the Niger, Samuel Taylor Coleridge to write 'Kubla Khan' and generations of scholars to learn about the ancient culture of Ethiopia. He should be remembered for that and not for the envy he inspired in others.

Bruce could not have achieved half that he did had he been the vicious old curmudgeon described in popular folklore. In fact, in his heyday he was considered charming and handsome as well as extraordinarily large: he was six foot four and immensely strong. Women everywhere adored him, from the harems of North Africa to the salons of Paris and the court of the Abyssinian Emperor. Men too loved him, but only a certain kind of man; in them he inspired an almost fanatical loyalty. He could ride like an Arab, shoot partridge from the saddle at the gallop and faced danger with icy calm. These particular manly virtues were all very well in the East where they won him friends and influence but in the eighteenth-century world of Horace Walpole, Samuel Johnson and James Boswell they were of little use. His bluff, no-nonsense attitude won him few friends at the court of George III and his rage at having his word doubted only made him seem the more ridiculous.

It is through the eyes of those three men – Walpole, Johnson and Boswell – that most is known about Bruce, and it is their opinions and viewpoints that I hope to redress. Bruce lived for sixty-four years; the first thirty and last twenty were spent in Britain. He was in his prime during the fourteen or so years in between, exploring the unknown world with a sword in his hand and a pistol at his side, leaving weeping women and vanquished enemies in his wake. The painter Johann Zoffany met him soon after his return to the West. He saw Bruce as he should be seen: 'This great man; the wonder of his age, the terror of married men, and a constant lover.' This is the Bruce about whom I have written: brilliant intellectual, talented diplomat and fearless explorer but, above all, a magnificent man.

CHAPTER I

THE JACOBITE HANOVERIAN

On a damp evening in April 1794 James Bruce sat gazing from the window of his Stirlingshire dining-room and saw a woman walking unaccompanied to her carriage. Having levered his considerable bulk from a chair, he rushed to her aid to perform what would be his final chivalrous deed. On the sixth step of the staircase, he slipped, fell on his head and was dead by morning. It was an ignominious end to a life of rare adventure.

During the previous sixty-four years, Bruce had crossed the Nubian Desert, climbed the bandit-bedevilled mountains of Abyssinia, been shipwrecked off the North African coast and sentenced to death in Sudan. He had lived with the rulers of undiscovered kingdoms and slept with their daughters, been granted titles and lands by barbarian warlords and had then returned – more or less intact – to the place of his birth, a small town near the Firth of Forth where very few believed he had done what he claimed and many pilloried him as a liar and a fraud. Decades after his death, it began to emerge that most of the time he had been telling the truth. He had travelled in Abyssinia and the Sudan, he had been to the source of the Blue Nile and he had charted the Red Sea. But by then he had lapsed into obscurity and his successors had outdone him in both fame and infamy.

Bruce had great charm but he could also be utterly brutal and cantankerous. He was generous to strangers but they crossed him at their peril. He could tumble down African mountainsides and cheat death at the hands of jihad-inspired potentates, yet in the end his demise was caused by a trivial accident. In the early nineteenth century a few commentators wrote about his life by glossing over its inconsistencies and showering him with praise. His own, five-volume *Travels to Discover the Source of the Nile in the Years 1768, 1769, 1770, 1771, 1772 & 1773* is packed with invaluable information but should have been published as at least three different books. It has not been published in full for decades.

In spite of his prolixity, it is the things that Bruce left out of his life's work that make him so fascinating. There are many detectable errors in the book (carelessly, he failed to consult his notes) but there are also eloquent omissions and deliberate evasions which contributed to his not being believed on his return. He failed to address the rumour that he had killed the artist who accompanied him and indeed scarcely refers to him in the book. He makes almost no mention of the Ark of the Covenant when one of the few things then known about Abyssinia was that it was claimed to be guarding the Ark. It was, though, his manner which did the greatest damage to his credibility.

Haughty and proud (the portmanteau word 'paughty' might almost have been coined for him), he once forced a visitor to eat raw meat after the unfortunate man had expressed doubt at its being the Abyssinians' favourite dish. Bruce brooked no criticism and eventually refused to discuss his work with anyone except an adoring audience. He was prickly even to his disciples. Too great a display of amazement at his astonishing stories was often interpreted as disbelief and no one was allowed to accuse Bruce of lying and walk away. An expert swordsman from a long line of pugnacious ancestors, he gained notoriety after challenging his former fiancée's husband to a duel. It was understood that the same treatment would be handed out to what he called his 'chicken-hearted critics'.

He was born in 1730, with the blood of the Hays and the Bruces, both families famous for their martial history, coursing through his veins. In a century of almost continuous warfare, however, 1730 was a surprisingly peaceful time to arrive. The Treaty of Seville between France, Spain and England had been signed the year before and had produced a temporary lull in the Catholic–Protestant wars that dominated the period. James's father, David Bruce of Kinnaird, was a Hay of Woodcockdale (a scion of the better known Hays of Errol), a family that fought with honour at Bannockburn and still one of the oldest in Scotland. David's father had been forced by contract to adopt his wife's name – Bruce – which can be traced in a moderately straight line to Robert the Bruce, in order to inherit the estate of Kinnaird. The two great Scottish families had been inextricably linked since before Bannockburn and the marriage was merely another link between them.

For a young Scot with such a surname, born so soon after the Act of Union of 1707, it would seem inevitable that James should support the Jacobites, but this was not the case. His father, David, had endured an extremely close brush with death in the aftermath of the 1715 uprising with which he had been intimately involved. He had been sentenced to death and had only escaped the gallows because of the reluctance of Scottish judges to execute Scots accused of breaking English laws. This had been a chastening experience and he was adamant that his son should not follow in his rebellious footsteps. Having died of a 'lingering illness', probably tuberculosis, before James's fourth birthday, his mother Marion had no influence on his upbringing. Whilst Bonnie Prince Charlie was being brought up in exile, so too was James, the former in Catholic France, the latter in staunchly Protestant England. The Young Pretender and his army actually marched past Kinnaird on the way to the final showdown at Culloden but the young James was not there to witness it, nor the Battle of Falkirk which was fought a few miles away. Instead he was in London being raised as an English gentleman. He was forever to remain one.

Well before the '45 uprising, David Bruce was showing a vulnerability to the charms of women that his son was to inherit. Having fathered James with Marion Graham, he went on to father six more sons and two daughters with his second wife, Agnes Glen. Preoccupied by this frenzied period of procreation and fearful that his son would be caught up in the Jacobite machinations of their Stirlingshire neighbours, the laird of Kinnaird contrived to send his son as far away from their influence as possible. At the age of eight, James was sent to London where for the next few years he lived with the family of his uncle, William Hamilton. From 1738 he was taught both by Counsellor Hamilton and by a Mr Graham who had a small private school in London, but by 1742 it was decided that he needed more formal education. He was sent to Harrow, where he excelled.

In the eighteenth century Harrow was still outside London and it was a respected school. The few hundred boys with whom James was educated would go on to be ministers, courtiers and landowners. Much more so than today, Harrow and the few schools like it were of immense importance to a child's future. The really important families like the Cecils, Pelhams and Caven-dishes had just started sending their sons away to school rather than having them educated at home by tutors. They sent them to one of five schools – Charterhouse, Eton, Harrow, Winchester or Westminster. By 1800, three-quarters of the English peerage (who comprised the court and the House of Lords and largely controlled the House of Commons) had been educated at one or other of the latter four. James and his two greatest friends, William Hamil-ton and William Graham, were all first-generation Harrovians. By breaking with family tradition and sending James away, David ensured that his son would always be a member of the British ruling classes rather than the obscure Scottish laird he was otherwise destined to become.

James was an excellent student and soon learned the basic necessities for a young gentleman in the eighteenth century – Latin, Greek, French, philosophy and arithmetic. He also developed a wide circle of friends which he would retain throughout his life and which would become extremely important to him in later years. By all accounts he was a paragon of virtue. In 1744, his stepmother's brother described him thus: 'What I wrote to you about James, is all true, with this difference only, that you may say, as the Queen of Sheba said to Solomon, the one half has not been told you, for I never saw so fine a lad of his years in my life.' His headmaster at Harrow, Dr Cox, praised him in even more glowing terms: 'He is as promising a young man as ever I had under my care, and, for his years, I never saw his fellow.'

This was no pandering to wealthy parents; James was neither grand nor well off compared with his fellow pupils. Dr Cox reinforced his claims by asking James to give the annual pupils' address to the school, which he did brilliantly in Latin, as was the custom. This was heady tribute to any boy at one of England's best schools, but as his mind grew his health began to fail him. A weak chest, inherited from his mother, combined with his great height (in an age when the average was five feet seven) contrived to make him very ill in his teens. With dark red hair and a body shaken with coughing, at fifteen he must have been a bizarre sight, resembling a victim of the rack.

David's plan to keep his son James away from their rebellious neighbours had worked well and it became more likely that James would be operating the rack rather than lying upon it. Indeed he became a fanatical Hanoverian, making firm alliances with his new English friends, whilst losing contact with the acquaintances of his Scottish childhood. William Graham (who, interestingly, was also his uncle) and William Gerrard Hamilton were in fact born Scottish but they were enjoying the same privileged English education as he and soon became English too.

The distance between England and Scotland was not only cultural. Travel between London and Stirlinghsire was a dangerous and arduous business over roads that were scarcely worthy of the name. Before the advent of the railway and when turnpikes were still used mainly for connecting rivers, much of the journey would be along rutted drove roads which in even quite mild weather frequently became impassable. Presuming he was not intercepted by a highwayman (Dick Turpin was hanged in James's second year at school), it would have taken the young Scot at least two weeks to return home. John Macadam, who would eventually transform Britain's roads, had not even been born and for at least another fifty years Englishmen would only journey far into Scotland for adventure – more exploration than tourism. It was still the subject of gripping, incident-filled travel books in the nineteenth century. The young boy therefore spent his holidays far from his place of birth, staying with his Hanoverian guardian, Counsellor Hamilton, which only served to deepen the division from his Scottish family. It was not the most stimulating of environments: the lawyer was reputed to be one of the dullest men in the union. The inveterate letter writer Horace Walpole described him as 'the first Scot who ever pleaded at the English bar and as it was said of him, should have been the last'.

This environment, designed specifically to cut the boy off from his Scottish roots, had the required effect on James. Throughout his life, although he became very proud of his ancestry and used it unashamedly when necessary, he described himself as an Englishman. On his later travels, he always had an eye open for any way his exploits might benefit the crown. In the Red Sea he would forge treaties; in Spain he would make invasion plans before admiring the sights. This adoption of England was not as odd as it seems; conditioning and distance from home apart, he was born a Lowland Scot rather than a Highlander. Highlanders were generally more interested in independence than Lowlanders and viewed their more southerly countrymen with contempt. In those days 'Sassenach' was not a term of abuse used by Glaswegians to describe Englishmen. It was instead used by Highlanders to describe Glaswegians and other Lowlanders. Lowlanders were often terrified of their savage neighbours who lived far more primitive lives and spoke what many considered a strange, unintelligible language. Not until Bruce was in his fifties was the legend of the proud Highlander created by his much younger acquaintance, the novelist Sir Walter Scott. When Bruce was fifteen the Highlanders were actually fighting the English and any book extolling their virtues would have been seditious.

In April 1746 James completed his studies at Harrow but the Highland purges continued in his homeland and it was deemed unwise for him to return. He was thus sent briefly to a finishing school. By April 1747, Bonnie Prince Charlie had completed his dash through the Highlands and had effected his escape to France; the bloody Duke of Cumberland had entered London as Handel termed him the 'conquering hero' and northern Britain was safe once more. James was able to return to Kinnaird and attempt to insinuate himself into the bosom of his father's new family. He spent the summer hunting, a sport at which he excelled, and which would become a lifelong love. He thrived on the fresh air and his health saw a marked improvement. For six months he roamed the fields around Kinnaird, indulging his passion for blood sports; at the age of only sixteen he departed, revived, for Edinburgh University to study for the Bar.

James's first preference had been to become an Anglican priest.

Although it was a vocation for which he became entirely unsuited
– he became far too combative – at this time his guardian believed
him well suited to the cloth. Writing to David Bruce in 1746,
William Hamilton had said:

> He very modestly says, he will apply himself to whatever profession
> you shall direct; but he, in his own inclination, would study divinity
> and be a parson. The study of the law, and also that of divinity,
> are indeed both of them attended with uncertainty of success. But,
> as he inclines to the profession of a clergyman, for which he has
> a well-fitted gravity, I must leave it to you to give your own
> directions, though I think, in general, it is most advisable to comply
> with a young man's inclination, especially as the profession he
> proposes is in every respect fit for a gentleman.

James's ancestor, the Rev. Robert Bruce, had been a guiding
light of the early Kirk; indeed in Scotland he still receives a great
deal more recognition than his descendant. It would not have been
seemly if the Rev. Robert's great grandson had become a cleric of
an opposing faith. This, when combined with the fact that James's
maternal grandfather was the dean of the law faculty at Edinburgh,
probably led to David's decision to overrule James and make him
study for the Bar. Law – and Scottish law at that – seems an
unlikely career but it was essential that James did something that
would support him in later life. The family's wealth was too thinly
spread for James to live off the proceeds of the estate and, if it was
necessary for him to work, the law was one of the few respectable
options.

So it was that James spent the next few months reading up on
the law and attending dry lectures at the university rather than
studying the lives of the saints and learning how to deliver sermons.
As the heavily annotated margins of the law books which he was
supposed to be studying testify, he spent rather more time in the
extra curricular study of Italian than on his articles. By the spring
of 1748, however, he was too ill to continue. This was to mark
the end of his formal education but the lust for knowledge that
his studies had instilled in him would be a lifelong preoccupation.
Due to the state of medical learning in the eighteenth century it is
hard to know what was actually wrong with him: this was still an age

when bleeding was considered a cure-all. He could have had asthma, he could merely have been growing too fast, but the symptoms which eventually led to his being forced to leave the university were a constant weakness, wheezing and shortness of breath.

In 1747, at the age of seventeen, he retired to the country and went back to his former pastimes of hunting and shooting. For five years, the weak young man wandered the moors slaughtering the local fauna, reading the Bible and teaching himself modern Romance languages. It was not until 1753 that his sojourn with nature came to an end and his character began to change. He had been heading speedily towards a life of indolent dilettantism but his physical recovery fed his ambition. At last he began to take on some of the characteristics that would help him survive in later life and to behave in a manner more suited to a man destined to become one of our greatest explorers. He recovered his health and filled out. Towering above his contemporaries and with a burly chest to match, he decided to seek his fortune in India. Though brave (fewer than half the writers who went to India returned) this was not particularly unusual. With Robert Clive in his prime, the subcontinent was already well-trodden ground. It was, however, at least a step in the right direction.

Just before he left Edinburgh on 1 August, he and William Graham were initiated into Canongate Kilwinning Lodge No. 2. The smart Edinburgh branch of the Mother Lodge at Kilwinning, Canongate – despite its secondary title – was the most influential masonic lodge in the world, a fertile sanctuary of the Enlightenment which would soon be frequented by Robert Burns, the Adam brothers, James Boswell and Sir Walter Scott. This was a significant moment in James's career. From it stemmed his great intellectual interest in astronomy and the Arab world, his remarkable ease with foreign bankers and his almost encyclopaedic knowledge of obscure biblical works. For the time being, though, it gave him access to a vast and influential network of people who could help him in his career. He set off for London full of good intentions.

He was by then too old to join the East India Company by the traditional route as a Writer (a clerk with prospects) but had influential acquaintances and money enough to become a licensed trader. He petitioned the directors for a free trader's permit but before it was granted he fell in love and the course of his life was once more changed. Meeting Adriana Allan, the beautiful daughter of a London wine merchant's widow (who came with an excellent dowry), was to set him on the route which would eventually lead him by a much meandering course to 'the coy fountains' of the Nile.

In the mid-eighteenth century London was an influential capital but it had not yet taken on the glorious trappings of Empire. There was not a square foot of pavement in the entire city; indeed, there would not be until after Bruce returned from his travels. William Hogarth was at the height of his powers and the streets of the capital were much as he depicted them. The sale of gin had only just been restricted and rakes progressed down streets lined with harlots and steeped in ordure. The inhabitants of the city were debauched, diseased and for the most part mired in the most hideous poverty. Even extreme wealth – which at that point Bruce did not possess – could not protect the visitor from the horrors of everyday life.

When Bruce arrived in 1753 (he had by then become Bruce and left the James of his youth behind) London was on the very cusp of its most glorious years. The city was changing daily after the political upheavals of the forties. The process began that very year with the founding of the British Museum, initially to house Hans Sloane's collection. Rivers were still crooked but were slowly being forced to straighten and become canals, industry was ripe for revolt and minds both in London and Edinburgh were yearning for Enlightenment. Samuel Johnson had published his dictionary but had not yet met his biographer, James Boswell. It would be another fifteen years before Sir Joshua Reynolds founded the Royal Academy. James Watt had yet to improve the steam engine, the burgeoning iron industry was still reliant on charcoal and the innovations which were to transform the country were still largely restricted to agriculture. The boom years of the 1760s, the canal mania of the 1780s and the mixture of intelligence and patronage that exploded into the Enlightenment all lay ahead. Bruce was one of the first of an extraordinary concentration of Scots who would transform the country and, with the outward looking attitude of which Bruce was a pioneer, the world.

In 1753 Great Britain was still a country unsure of itself. It had only been ratified by the Act of Union in 1707 and was still ruled by a German king who was more fond of his home town than his kingdom and was not entirely comfortable on his throne; he could scarcely speak English. Britain was an acknowledged power but it was still only great in name. Even among the electors of Hanover, our royal family was not in the forefront. Frederick the Great was the successful member of the family, not George II or his young grandson and eventual successor.

It was in this world of as yet unfulfilled promise that Bruce was introduced to the elegant and witty young Adriana Allan. They fell in love and on 3 February 1754 were married. For a few months they lived happily in London. All thoughts of India were discarded and Bruce settled down to learn about the wine trade; part of Adriana's substantial dowry had been a partnership with her brother in the Allans's successful wine importing business. Bruce threw himself into his new occupation with gusto but, just as when he studied law at Edinburgh, he soon became preoccupied with learning other, less profitable things. He was fascinated by different languages, countries and peoples and would spend hours studying subjects in which he was interested. His restless curiosity encouraged him to explore many diverse areas of learning: military architecture became a great interest at this point. The study of wine led him to a broader understanding of botany; astronomy led to geography and both became passions. Fast evolving into a man of the Enlightenment, his only lack of interest was in working for a living. What he really needed was a good private income. He was now paying the price of his father's virility: his small inheritance was dwindling by the day. Indeed he had often been forced to plead with his father to increase his allowance, before the opportunity of becoming a wine merchant arose.

In September 1754 Adriana, now pregnant, set off with her mother for France. Bruce planned to meet them at Boulogne. Adriana was suffering from as yet undiagnosed tuberculosis, and they planned to spend the winter in Provence where Bruce would look at vineyards and Adriana would recover her health. They had spent much of the past few months taking the waters in Bath and Bristol (then a fashionable spa) in the vain expectation of curing Adriana's consumption. Bruce hoped that a winter spent in the beneficial climate of Provence would effect a similar cure to the one which had strengthened him after leaving university. It was not to be. Healthy living and plenty of exercise was no cure for TB: Adriana died within a week of their arrival in Paris. It was a blow that fell particularly hard on the young Bruce. Motherless, he had spent years away from home while his father produced a new family; he had been sick and had found it hard to indulge his ambitions. At the age of twenty-four he had at last found some happiness and human warmth only to see it taken from him a few months later. Writing to his father in November, Bruce was feeling justifiably downcast.

> If I could be susceptible of more grief, I should have been much concerned for my good friend Mr Hay [a recently deceased cousin]; but my distress at present does not admit of augmentation. Death has been very busy among my relations of late. My poor wife, my kind uncle [Counsellor Hamilton had died in March], who had always been a tender father to me, both gone in eight months! God almighty do with me as he sees best!

Adriana's death had a gruesome aspect. The manner of her demise and the events following had been particularly appalling and had rekindled Bruce's hatred of Catholics. As Adriana had coughed Gemellus-like in their Parisian rooms, the couple had been assailed by 'Roman Catholic clergy hovering about the doors'. And when his pregnant love died, Bruce discovered that it was illegal to bury his Protestant wife in consecrated ground. He was only saved from resorting to common land by the intercession of Lord Albemarle, the British ambassador. Eventually Bruce was allowed to conduct the funeral at midnight in the embassy's private plot.

For an Englishman to harbour a particular malevolence against Catholics in the eighteenth century, over and above that which was normal, was in itself remarkable. The vilification of Catholicism was at its height, helping to gather the country around the Protestant king, and was one of the founding principles of the still new Great Britain. Strangely, however, Adriana's death did nothing to instil any anti-French feeling in Bruce's Protestant bosom.

Throughout the century and beyond, there was an aristocratic truce between warring nations. In the years to come, Bruce travelled all over Europe not so much as an Englishman but as an aristocrat (he was always known as *le chevalier Bruce* in France, *Signor Cavaliere* Bruce in Italy, even by those who understood the British class system and knew that he was a laird and not a knight). He corresponded with French friends, he used French agents, dressed *à la mode Française*, drank French wine and, like many of his peers, he spoke French with his friends. There were laws banning the import of French lace because it was so expensive that it affected the balance of payments, not because wearing it was unpatriotic. For those who could afford it, imported lace remained *de rigueur* until the 1850s. Despite his unhappy memories of Paris and indeed his later travels in the lace-making provinces of the Netherlands and Italy, Bruce wore French or Brussels lace when wishing to look smart and would do so all his life.

Immediately after Adriana's funeral in the early morning of 11 October, Bruce left his mother-in-law in Paris and headed for the coast in a fit of sorrow:

> From thence, almost frantic, against the advice of everybody, I got on horseback, having ordered the servant to have post horses ready, and set out in the most tempestuous night I ever saw, for Boulogne, where I arrived next day without stopping. There the riding, without a great coat, in the night time, in the rain, want of food, which, for a long time, I had not tasted, want of rest, fatigue and excessive concern, threw me into a fever.

He eventually arrived back in London a few days later, sick and miserable. 'Thus ended my unfortunate journey, and with it my present prospect of happiness in this life.'

He had just cause for lapsing into depression. Almost everyone to whom he was close – his mother, uncle, brother and wife – had died and left him with a permanent sense of impending loss. In spite of or perhaps because of this he became profoundly self-sufficient and was genuinely content when on his own. As more of his close friends and relatives died in his twenties, he developed a kingly arrogance that would win him few friends but went a long way towards keeping him alive when he was travelling in parts of the world where unbounded self-confidence was a pre-requisite for survival. Bruce developed a bravado in the face of danger which would often tip the balance in his favour at hostile foreign courts. Mungo Park, who was sent to discover the course of the Niger, directly as a result of Bruce's journeys in search of the Nile's source, suffered many dangers but combated them with a contrasting subservience:

> Though this trough was none of the largest, and three cows were already drinking in it, I resolved to come in for my share [wrote Park in his first book] and kneeling down, thrust my head between two of the cows, and drank with great pleasure, until the water was nearly exhausted, and the cows began to contend with each other for the last mouthful.

This may have been acceptable and successful behaviour (until his untimely death in 1806) in Mungo Park's West Africa but in more sophisticated Abyssinia and Sudan, Park's method would have labelled Bruce an expendable slave. Hard though Bruce's youth was, rather than weaken him it helped him to develop an emotional carapace that little could crack.

In London, he at once dedicated himself to learning, leaving most of the running of the wine business to his brother-in-law. In the next two years he became fluent in Spanish and Portuguese, brushed up his Greek and Latin and learned how to draw. At Harrow, he had been taught basic drawing skills but he wanted to be able to paint the sights he was planning to visit. His interest in the wine business would give him the opportunity to do a Grand Tour like so many of his contemporaries but he wanted to make his journey worthwhile. His constant friend, the artist and engraver Robert Strange, found him a teacher, Maître Jacob Bonneau, whose duty it was not only to teach Bruce how to draw but also to instil in him what the editor of the second edition of Bruce's *Travels* described as 'a correct taste in painting'. The midnight ride after Adriana's death had done nothing but worsen Bruce's health and had caused a recurrence of his childhood bronchial problems. For two years he kept himself one part removed from society, coughing and spitting blood whilst studying astronomy, art and architecture and dealing as little as possible with the wine business. It was not until 1757 that he believed himself sufficiently recovered and well enough prepared for informed tourism.

In July of that year, Bruce set sail from Falmouth to embark on a tour of Spain and Portugal, justified by doing some business with the British port families in Oporto. It was an eventful journey. Britain was again fighting with France – indeed, they were set upon by two French ships during the voyage. Bruce was not one to panic. 'My fellow travellers Messrs Stevenson [sic] and Pawson went down and put each of them on two shirts in case we were taken. I made no preparation,' he told his commonplace book. He would maintain his courage in the face of danger for the rest of his life but he would change his mind about preparation. By the time he set off on his real travels he would be almost obsessive in his planning.

They landed at La Corunna on 15 July. Bruce and Matthew Stephenson immediately set off to inspect the harbour at Ferrol. Pawson was worried that they might be arrested for what today would be the equivalent of taking photographs of a strategic air-port. Bruce, though, had been horrified by a Spanish captain they had met in the port who seemed to know far too much about the state of the British fleet. Imbued with a new talent for military engineering, he wanted to carry out some freelance intelligence work. They mapped the harbour, inspected the fortifications and took copious notes before setting off to do some more traditional sightseeing. Bruce and Stephenson were to spend much of the next few months together, touring through Spain and Portugal, where Bruce's interest in martial architecture and Masonry would both have been satisfied, for the area they travelled through was rich in Templar history. The castles of the Ordem de Christo, Santiago and Calatrava, built by warrior monks whom Bruce believed to have been the forefathers of Freemasonry, were scattered about the countryside. There was much too of artistic interest, although Bruce did not hold orthodox views on everything he saw:

> In the evening we went to see the famous church of Santiago di Compostella the outside is elegant enough . . . the inside has

nothing in it worth notice ... The paintings are executed with
about as much judgement as they were plann'd. Considerably worse
than the worst daubing I ever saw on a country signpost or with
a burnt stick upon a wall.

His studies in art history at least qualified Bruce to criticize the
church's otherwise admired *portico della glori* by Mateo and its
renowned carvings. It was not the only thing he disliked; the entire
region offended him: 'We now took our leaves of Galicia one of
the most disagreeable countries ever I saw, upon all accounts the
whole face of the country is hideous.' So did Portuguese inns:
'We were lodged in one of the worst inns in Portugal which is
saying one of the worst inns in the world.' And indeed the Portuguese themselves: 'There are many particular customs in Portugal,
all of which may be known by this rule, that whatever is done in
the rest of the world in one way, is in Portugal done by the
contrary.'

Though Bruce loathed Portugal and the Portuguese he was
forced to spend some time there inspecting the vines and sampling
the vintage for his wine business. His irritation was relieved only
by the English people he met. In fact he was being overly harsh
on the Portuguese who had just suffered a devastating earthquake
that had left the country in ruins. The effects of that great earthquake can still be seen in Lisbon today where the few buildings
to survive from before 1750 are those that were built on marshy
ground which absorbed the tremors. Unfair or not, Bruce's was
to remain an abiding hatred. Thirty-five years later he would
devote a substantial part of his book on the Nile to criticizing
and discrediting the Portuguese and Spanish missionaries who had
visited the country before him. Throughout his life, he bore
grudges with a long-lasting and peculiar malevolence, long after
the time when most people would have forgotten the original
slight. In later life, he took three separate court cases, involving
property disputes, through the entire judicial system to the House
of Lords; his extended introduction to the *Travels* contained a
sustained and virulent attack on critics who had offended him
fifteen years previously, which he was well aware was likely to
work against him. Weakness offended Bruce and he would be

blind to the enfeebled Portugal's merits for the rest of his life.

By November he had shaken the dust of Portugal from his feet and arrived in Madrid. On his way he had learnt how to deal with customs men, a lesson that was to serve him well. He wrote at the border: 'Here you are asked for your passport by the governor and your baggage undergoes a strict search. If you have no letters to the administrator you must be particularly careful of having no snuff either French or Portuguese not even in your snuff box.'

His writing style was becoming increasingly eccentric. He sounds as though he was writing either a guide book or a letter to a friend. He was in fact merely taking notes in his commonplace book. 'At the Caldas the Inn is very bad. I would advize all English travellers to go from Aleobaca to St Martinho which is very little out of their way.'

Bruce later formed a policy of never writing for publication unless it was on a subject not previously noted and never, as far as we can tell, showed any inclination to publish a book of his European travels. One wonders, therefore, for whom he was writing these handy travellers' tips.

Spain, despite being full of Catholics, was fascinating territory for Bruce. He was intrigued by the Moorish and Templar castles of Andalusia and resolved to learn more about them. He started to learn Arabic in the markets of the region and contrived to gain entry to the renowned library of the Escorial (the sixteenth-century monastery built by Philip II for his warrior monks). He made friends with and was even offered a job at court by Don Ricardo Wall, an Irish courtier of the king, but was still not allowed into the Escorial. He thus continued his tour of Europe with his interest in the world beyond it aroused but unsatisfied.

Bruce had left England on an extended business trip but from Christmas 1757 he was travelling solely for pleasure and education. In Bordeaux he became a temporary member of French society – hunting, going to parties and attending the fashionable salons. It was not unheard of for Englishmen to travel in France at times of animosity between the two countries nor vice versa, but it was generally done with the approval of both governments. Bruce was on no government mission yet was allowed to travel regardless.

Given that France was at war with Britain at the time and Bordeaux was one of France's principal ports, this indicates considerable charm on Bruce's part in addition to his better known curmudgeonliness. He soon, however, tired of polite society.

Bruce resolved to continue his journey through much of France, Strasbourg and up the Rhine to Frankfurt and thence to Brussels, then the capital of Holland. There he bought some books which would transform his life – the works of Job Ludolf, a German, the father of Ethiopian scholarship. They had been written in the sixteenth century when Ludolf – then resident in Rome – had met Gregorius, an Ethiopian monk, and had been fascinated by his stories of his homeland. Their collaboration formed the foundation of all foreign knowledge of Ethiopia and, to this day, Ludolf is still consulted by students of Ethiopic. The books contained a précis of known Ethiopian history, a grammar of the Ethiopian liturgical language, Geez, and a description of Ethiopia's unique Christian religion. Whilst in Brussels, Bruce also bought many Arabic books from which he managed to teach himself to read the language that he later perfected on his travels.

While nourishing his intellectual interests, Bruce also attended to his more basic instincts. In the next few months he contrived to witness a battle and to fight a duel, challenging his as yet little tested courage. Happily both conflicts were resolved with no loss of Bruce blood. They did though give the budding explorer his first taste of danger. The history of the duel is rather murky, probably due to the absurdity of the episode. In the 1750s duelling was going out of fashion in Britain, and yet more so on the Continent. Two decades later he faced ridicule for challenging someone to a duel; at this time, however, it was deemed only slightly silly. F. B. Head, who had the story from Bruce's daughter, described the incident in his otherwise laudatory *Life of Bruce*:

> On the second day after his arrival [in Brussels] he happened to be in the company of a young man, a perfect stranger to him, who was rudely insulted. Bruce foolishly remonstrated with the aggressor, who sent him a challenge, which he accepted. They met; Bruce wounded his antagonist twice, and in consequence left Brussels immediately.

He took advantage of this forced departure (he feared a man-slaughter charge) to see an army in action.

For at least another fifty years war was to remain a spectator sport which could be watched with relative impunity, even by citizens of the warring factions. In fact, it was a popular pastime for people who wanted a taste of adventure and danger without incurring too much risk to their person. Though of course fictional, it did not seem strange to Tolstoy's readers when Pierre in *War and Peace* observed the Battle of Borodino (1812) from his grassy knoll:

> Pierre wished to be there with that smoke, those shining bayonets, that movement, and those sounds. He turned to look at Kutuzov and his suite, to compare his impressions with those of others. They were all looking at the field of battle as he was, as it seemed to him, with the same feelings. All their faces were now shining with that latent warmth of feeling Pierre had noticed the day before.

And thus it was nothing out of the ordinary when Bruce and several shiny-faced fellow Englishmen, then serving with the Dutch army, embarked on a short trip to northern Germany where they watched the Germans and French fight each other at the Battle of Crevelt.

Soon after the excitement of the battle, Bruce received in Brussels the worst of news from home. His father had died in May, joining the long list of Bruce's recently dead friends and relatives. The twenty-eight-year-old was left with a much reduced inheritance and myriad responsibilities. His many half siblings had drained the family coffers and, coupled with the complications of dividing the estate, Bruce found himself unable immediately to fulfil the ambitions to travel that his Grand Tour had inspired. It was not until December 1762 that he finally resolved the issue by settling with his half-brother, David, who had joined the army. He did well out of the arrangement for it soon emerged that his land was a great deal more valuable than had previously been believed. Kinnaird – 'a house to be lived in not looked at' (according to Nimmo in his *A General History of Stirlinghsire*. The house no longer exists) – was built upon a rich seam of coal that was to make Bruce's life a financially comfortable one. He was extremely fortunate, however. But for an extraordinary coincidence the money would not have flowed until the next generation.

If, in 1759, coal had been found almost anywhere else in the world it would have languished for another fifty years and thus have been of no use to a hard-up young adventurer. The Bruce family miners (there was an almost serf-like class of people who mined coal in Scotland and were bought and sold with land) had been digging in a desultory way for years but no one had made a decent profit out of the excavations. The Industrial Revolution was not yet under way and there was none of the insatiable demand that was so to enrich such later mine owners as the Lowthers just over the border in Westmorland. In nearby Carron, however, there was a small company part-owned by one of the most brilliant practical scientists of the age. John Roebuck was the first partner of James Watt and had set up a firm at Carron with the businessman Samuel Garbett. The Carron Company was to pioneer a method of smelting iron ore that would transform industry. It involved coke made from coal rather than charcoal and Bruce was the closest supplier of coal. The Carron Company became major cannon makers in an era with an enormous demand for arms and Bruce made a fortune supplying them with fuel. Today, one can still see iron letter boxes made by the Carron Company on the streets of Britain.

It was a heaven-sent opportunity for the young Scot and, although he behaved extraordinarily badly in all his dealings with the company, suing them and disputing their every action on his return from his travels, this association more than any other allowed him to travel the world at his own expense and to have all the adventures that make up the most interesting part of his life. Without the discovery of this new use for coal and the accident of Bruce having it on his land, he would have been compelled to retire to Scotland and live the life of a Scottish laird.

By now almost thirty, Bruce was at last in a position to do something with his life. Since leaving Harrow fifteen years earlier he had amassed a great store of knowledge which he constantly supplemented. Botany had become an interest through his work as a vintner and friendship with the dilettante and patron of naturalists, Daines Barrington; he had studied law, military architecture, astronomy, the Bible, art, Arabic and masonic lore. A great talent for languages meant that he was not confined to English reading matter and this had aroused in him a thirst for news of the world outside Europe. The death of his father and the resulting inheritance would enable him to use all his learning to a more productive end. Thus it was that Bruce embarked on his thirtieth year, prepared for informed exploration but still lacking a mission. One was about to present itself.

CHAPTER 2

THE CALAMITOUS CONSUL

One man was to be the catalyst for Bruce's new life – the politician, civil servant and former traveller, Robert Wood. Wood had the ear of all the great men of the age. Pitt, Egremont, Halifax, Bute, Grenville and the king himself, all listened to the man who had explored the ruins of Palmyra and Baalbek before going on to forge a brilliant career in the service of the crown. As eighteenth-century political alliances were made and dissolved, as administrations rose and fell, Wood, who purposely avoided great office, was one of the few men who consistently kept close to power. Ministers came and went but he managed to outstay them all until his death in 1771. His first significant job had been as Pitt's secretary at the Irish office where he soon became known as 'Mr Pitt's Wood', but from there he had moved on to greater things, always managing to keep out of the way when governments fell and always reappearing when the new ones arose. It is not certain how the two men met but, although there are no records of either claim, Wood said that he had been to Harrow and Oxford. Although they were not contemporaries, Harrow may well have been the link between him and Bruce. Wood recognized the spark of talent in the unfulfilled Scot and ensured that it was kindled and fed. It was through Wood's efforts that Bruce's abilities were put to more productive use than that of enlightened land owning.

The two were already friends when British relations with Spain declined drastically once more and it occurred to Bruce that the scribblings he had made in Ferrol a few years earlier might be of some use to the country. He formulated a plan for the capture of

Ferrol; from this seemingly impregnable port where he had spent a few days with Matthew Stephenson in July 1757, an invasion could be launched. The plan offered two things Bruce sought: advancement and the opportunity to wage war upon a Catholic country. He wrote to Wood and 'offered to fix an ensign upon the landing place in the first boat that went on shore'.

Wood took the plan from Bruce and arranged an interview with William Pitt. Secretary of State Pitt – who had yet to become either Prime Minister, Chatham, or elderly – was impressed by Bruce but was unable to accept the scheme since war with Spain, let alone invasion of one of its principal ports, was a catastrophe he was then trying to avoid. Already embroiled with Frederick the Great of Prussia against France, Russia and Austria, another front was the last thing he desired. He would, however, take note for the future, he said. France was by now the principal enemy and Spain was becoming of secondary importance.

It must have been a galling time for Bruce; his contemporaries were making names for themselves whilst he had only just managed to extract himself from the wine business in which he was no longer interested. His affairs in Scotland were still not settled to his satisfaction and until that was done he was unable to plan his future. He returned north invigorated by his flirtation with power but still having achieved little. He threw himself into re-organizing the estate, attempting to remove some tenant farmers and coal miners who were spoiling the view from Kinnaird. He had great plans for the house and park so at the same time ensured that the new collieries being planned to supply the Carron Company would not provide additional eyesores.

Months later, he heard from Wood again and was summoned to London. His Ferrol plan was being revived by Pitt but in a modified form that Bruce believed would doom the project to failure. It was intended that the attack on Ferrol should coincide with an invasion of France through Bordeaux. Swiftly, Bruce composed a memorandum in which he begged the government not to pursue such a course. It had some effect and the original plan was once more adopted and championed by Pitt. Ferrol would be invaded as Bruce recommended and an army landed. It was, however, almost immediately abandoned due to objections from the Portuguese ambassador who, as the representative of Britain's oldest ally, could not be disregarded. Bruce could not understand why he was being consecutively ignored then fêted by the great men of the day and in high dudgeon he decided to return once more to Scotland and find himself a wife. His ego was not the most important casualty of the plan's rejection: a furious Pitt went to Bath and resigned over the issue.

As Bruce made his preparations to leave, however, one of his conspicuously more successful friends – William Hamilton – contacted him and, acting as Lord Halifax's secretary, asked Bruce to come and see the great statesman. Hamilton and Bruce had remained friends since Harrow but, while Bruce had battled with illness and spent rather too much time hunting and changing careers, Hamilton had only deviated once. He had trained as a lawyer and then changed course to become a politician. By this time, he even had a nickname – 'Single Speech' Hamilton – an epithet he had earned following his spectacular fifteen-hour maiden speech in the House of Commons in 1754. The speech was said to have been written by Samuel Johnson but, since Hamilton rarely spoke in public again, this charge was never proved. His reticence, however, earned for him a great reputation as a thinker, although perversely he also retained his standing as an orator. Hamilton was thus by this time – seven years after the speech – an important player in the corridors of power. (This would be the apex of his career. He would later be described by Lord Charlewood as 'a man whose talents were equal to every undertaking; and yet from indolence, or from too fastidious vanity, or from what other cause I know not, he has done nothing'.) Lord Halifax sympathized with Bruce – who had wasted much time commuting between Scotland and London only to be left languishing in anterooms by busy ministers – and told the industrious laird that he had work for young men of initiative. Acting under Wood's influence, Halifax offered Bruce the consulship at Algiers. It was just the kind of employment that he both wanted and needed.

The two men talked long about the possibilities that the posting could offer a man of Bruce's enterprise. Halifax expected Bruce to perform his consular duties but he also hoped that he would use the post as a platform from which he could explore and record what he saw for the benefit of the new Britain. Robert Wood had discovered and recorded many of the art treasures of the ancient world but there were hundreds of other sites that required classification. Algiers would be the perfect place from which to mount expeditions and his role as consul would give Bruce the authority to travel in style and safety. The menial work, claimed Halifax, would be handled by a vice-consul, who could stamp all the forms and deal with the day-to-day running of the consulate. Then as now, embassies and consulates in Africa were rather more involved in promoting trade than extending the hand of interracial friendship. Someone more knowledgeable would engage in affairs of business whilst Bruce would appear at official functions and travel. Halifax's plans, however, were foiled and Bruce was compelled to learn the art of diplomacy on the hoof. Algiers was an important, though unprestigious, posting where angering the ruling Dey could result in the enslavement of many British sailors and merchants who sailed in the Mediterranean under a protective treaty with the city state. The Dey was considered little more than a pirate by Britain yet he was in a position to be a serious threat to trade. Bruce would later be condemned for his diplomatic ineptitude although he had been employed for a completely different purpose.

Halifax's principal wish, claimed Bruce, was 'that I should be the first, in the reign just now beginning [George III had become King in 1760], to set an example of making large additions to the royal collection, and he pledged himself to be my loyal supporter and patron, and to make good to me, upon this additional merit, the promises which had been held forth to me by former ministers for other services.' (Bruce claims to have been offered a baronetcy and a pension for his plan to attack Ferrol. There is no record of this but it would have been a perfectly natural offer.) He continued:

> The discovery of the source of the Nile was also a subject of these conversations; but it was always mentioned to me with a kind of diffidence, as if to be expected only from a more experienced traveller. Whether this was but another way of exciting me to the attempt I shall not say; but my heart in that instant did me the justice to suggest, that this, too, was either to be atchieved [sic] by

me, or to remain, as it had done for the last two thousand years, a defiance to all travellers, and an opprobrium to geography.

The deal struck, Bruce headed back to Scotland with a new spring in his step. He was at last a man with a purpose. But he must first settle his affairs. The estate had to be put into the hands of lawyers and factors, the bank must arrange for him to be able to draw money in Cairo and other points east and he must prepare himself for what was destined to be a long journey. On 18 February 1762, he received official notice from Robert Wood that the consulship was his, and moreover, Wood had managed to arrange matters such that Bruce would be able to spend time in Italy on the way. There he would finish his artistic education in order that he might be able better to appreciate the antiquities of the ancient world.

At the age of thirty-two Bruce's professional life had at last come together. His love-life followed suit: he had fallen head over heels for a sixteen-year-old neighbour – Margaret Murray – who promised to wait for him whilst he was in foreign parts. (We know nothing of his relationships with women between the death of his first wife and his engagement to Margaret. He never wrote about this period, but judging by his later behaviour we can presume that he had mistresses and women friends.) Prepared and cocksure in both his private and public lives, he went to London where he was presented at court and given details of the task that awaited him.

The king had, in fact, initially objected to Bruce's appointment. With the good sense which he would retain, for the most part, until much later in his reign, he had ventured to Halifax that it might be wiser to appoint a consul who knew something of the Barbary States. It was true that Bruce spoke Arabic, an unusual accomplishment, but since none of his predecessors had done so, and all consuls were provided with an interpreter, this was not seen as an advantage. Other than this, Bruce had no qualifications for the job. The appointment was, and was intended to be, a sinecure. Wood, though, had not only the ear of the prime minister, but also that of the king. Only two years later he would be made Groom Porter to the Royal Household, a role which had nothing to do with brushing or carrying and everything to do with influence. Already, in 1762, he was in a position to calm the king's anxieties and ensure that his protégé was well-received. In April Bruce, by then 'a man of Herculean physique and more than ordinary strength of mind' (according to Nimmo in his *History of Stirlingshire*), left Britain for France. It would be twelve years before he returned.

In his baggage he had hundreds of books and instruments to which he would add on his travels. Ludolf's *History of Ethiopia* would have been near the top of the pile with Herodotus, Cosmas Indicoplustes and his mentor Wood's 1753 publication *The Ruins of Palmyra*. These would come to a sad end in Cairo:

> To reduce the bulk as much as possible, after considering in my mind what were likeliest to be of service to me in the countries through which I was passing, and the several enquiries I was to make, I fell, with some remorse, upon garbling my library, tore out all the leaves which I had marked for my purpose, destroyed some editions of very rare books, rolling up the needful parts, and tying them by themselves. I thus reduced my library to a more compact form.

Bruce had measuring rods, three telescopes from François Watkins in Charing Cross, another made for Edward Wortley Montagu by Adam, quadrants and charts of the stars so he could use them correctly. (Edward Wortley Montagu, the supremely eccentric son of Lady Mary and a later critic of Bruce, had been unable to collect his telescope for at the time he was penniless in Italy, reeling from the news that his mother, who had just died, had left him only a guinea in her will.) Bruce was extremely interested in astronomy but would also be using the equipment for navigational and charting purposes. He did not merely wish to discover the source of the Nile; he wanted to put it on the map. The telescopes had been troublesome to obtain since all the worlds's astronomers were preparing for the transit of Venus expected in June 1769. Captain Cook and Joseph Banks had set off to view it from the South Seas and their European counterparts were preparing to go to Armenia where it was expected to be especially visible. Bruce also wanted to see the phenomenon but was not sure where he would do so. He had guns aplenty with which to fight and bribe his way around

Africa. Most came from Heriot Row – some 'silver mounted and richly wrought', others, like the three ships' blunderbusses, more practical than attractive. He had snuff boxes and shoes from London, ammunition and swords, wine and cutlery and £66 worth of new clothes from one shop alone. He was as well-prepared as Evelyn Waugh's William Boot in *Scoop* in all but one respect: he had no cleft sticks, for it was Bruce who discovered that they are used in the Ethiopian highlands by message bearers.

The putative consul had managed to receive permission to travel through France despite it being the sixth year of the Seven Years War. None the less, fuelled by pride in his new office, he rushed directly to Rome to receive his orders. The king had given him a mission in Malta so Bruce was able to visit Italy rather than embark immediately for the Barbary States. King George believed himself to have been slighted by the Catholic Grand Master of the chivalric island state, who had been far too friendly to the French. Knowing that diplomacy moves slowly, Wood had already arranged that Bruce should deliver the ultimatum, before it had even been decided upon, let alone written. When it was completed it would be delivered by warship to Bruce in Italy. Wood's purpose was to allow Bruce time in Italy to learn about antiquities. Neither of them, however, realized quite how long the visit would be. Bruce eventually had to kill time for eight months before he continued on his way, a period that he spent profitably, improving his mind and making contact with people who would later be of assistance.

In Rome Bruce studied the paintings and sculptures in the Vatican and in the houses of the fashionable set. Doubtless, he was inspired by his surroundings as he walked around the ancient capital which, millennia earlier, had sent out its own adventurers to seek the head of the Nile. Writing only two years before Bruce's arrival, the German art historian and resident of Rome, Johann Winckelmann, had said of Bernini's Fountain of the Four Rivers:

> The unknown sources of the Nile are ingeniously represented in the figure of this river on the fountain in the Piazza Navona in Rome by a garment with which he seems to be trying to conceal his head. This symbol is still true today, for the sources of the Nile still have not been discovered.

Bruce observed the ancient ruins and continued his studies but still no news came from England. He whiled away his time seeing friends at the Caffè degli Inglesi and sitting for the fashionable painter Pompeo Batoni in an expensive bid to make sure Margaret Murray did not forget him:

> I begin sitting to-morrow to the best painter in Italy; but as he only paints in oil, I am obliged to sit for a head, as it is called . . . and the miniature is to be copied from that picture by the best painter of miniatures in Italy, who is a lady [the society artist Veronica Stern]. This is as certain a way of your having as good a picture as the subject will admit of

In the absence of instructions, most of August was occupied with the strenuous task of sitting still in the studio of the eighteenth-century's equivalent of Snowdon.

For six months he travelled around the various nation states of pre-unification Italy on a short but busy Grand Tour. Bruce took his visit seriously; according to his first biographer, Alexander Murray, who edited the second edition of the *Travels*, much of Bruce's time in Florence was spent attending art lessons.

Although amateur archaeology had been enjoying a great vogue among Britain's Grand Tourists since the 1747 discovery of Pompeii, Bruce also studied the ruins in more detail than was the norm. At Paestum he made some architectural drawings which he even hoped to publish but the project never progressed further than the plate-making stage. The then British Resident and Walpole's correspondent Horace Mann (later to delight in the title of Envoy Extraordinary and Plenipotentiary to the court of the Grand Duke of Tuscany) had him to stay in Leghorn (Livorno) and Florence where Bruce, like many other visitors had an audience of the Grand Duke. In Bologna he met the artistic patron the Marquis di Ranuzzi and renewed friendships with his distant cousin Andrew Lumisden and with Robert Strange.

These last two were great Jacobites who were in cautionary exile but eventually returned to Britain before Bruce. Strange and Lumisden – as exiled brothers-in-law – were extremely close. They used to reply to each other's letters and eventually merited a joint biography. Lumisden had been the Young Pretender's private secretary; Strange, a fine artist, was denied membership of the Royal Academy because of his Jacobite leanings and thus did not receive his deserved knighthood until 1787. His exile was expensive and it stifled his real artistic leanings by forcing him to concentrate on the more profitable task of making engravings of the classics, which sold in huge numbers. He is now more famous for his financially necessary engravings, particularly his Stuart bank notes which would have become the currency of Scotland and England had the '45 rebellion succeeded. Strange, more of a thinker than a fighter, had been coerced by love into fighting for the Jacobites at Falkirk and Culloden. Had he not, he would never have won the hand of Andrew's sister, the fervently pro-Stuart Isabella Lumisden. Even then, the romance did not truly blossom until Strange found himself being hounded around the Highlands by Cumberland's soldiers. He escaped detection only by hiding under Isabella's skirts, whilst she steadfastly insisted to the officers searching the building that she had not seen the fugitive. Brought together in adversity, they had a long and happy marriage and were charming enough to overcome Bruce's Hanoverian instincts. The Stranges became Bruce's closest lifelong friends.

It was January of 1763 before Bruce was ordered to Naples, where his very arrival prompted the Grand Master of the Knights of Malta to send an ambassador to the Court of St James's, seeking absolution for appeasing the French. Sadly for Bruce, the ambassador in Naples was still Sir James Grey rather than the great collector, dancer and cuckold Sir William Hamilton but he did not have to stay long. The apologies of the Maltese Grand Master were promptly accepted and in February Bruce received orders to proceed to his posting aboard the British warship *Montreal*. These were the days of scurvy, powder monkeys, imprecise longitude measurements and colossal, top heavy, wooden sailing ships – dangerous enough for sailors but especially miserable for Bruce who suffered severely from seasickness. We know this from the letters of friends. James Turner, a trader in Cyprus, wrote to him in 1767 saying, 'the calms you had at sea must have been disagreeable to you who suffers so much at sea'. Bruce's willingness to jump on and off boats in the *Travels*, never mentioning his acute discomfort, is admirable. One wonders what other rigours he silently endured.

On 20 March 1763 Bruce arrived in Algiers as His Majesty's
Consul and Agent to Algier'. One senses that Bruce had been all
but forgotten in the preceding eight months and that it had taken
the prompting of his friend Wood to have him sent to Algiers at
all. It would not be long before Whitehall had to sit up and pay
attention. The world's most unsuitable diplomat had just arrived
on station in a posting that he was most unlikely to understand
and was even less likely to tolerate. The historian of the Barbary
States, Sir Godfrey Fisher, later lambasted Bruce:

> Official indifference at home, complicated doubtless by naval wars,
> corrupt practises at Gibraltar and Minorca, and the active hostility
> at Algiers of Aspinwall [Bruce's predecessor] and Bruce, contributed
> to the extinction of British interests, commercial and maritime
> along the southern shore of the Mediterranean.

The Barbary States on the northern littoral of Africa were a motley
conglomeration of city states, separated by warring tribes who
relied almost entirely on systematic piracy for their livelihoods. In
their glory days the city's corsairs had performed such memorable
feats as the sack of Barcelona, but by this time in their history –
nominally under the control of the crumbling Ottoman Empire
– they were in precipitous decline. They were still known, however, as the 'Scourge of Christendom'. Bruce's job in Algiers was
to maintain the treaty that had been forged in 1682 which allowed
Britain to trade in the area without fear of molestation by the
pirates of Algiers. Occasionally he would be asked to intercede on
behalf of people who had been captured and taken into slavery
but his main role – and the most important one in the eyes of his
government – was that of maintaining the treaty. This was something that he managed to overlook in his treatment of the Algerians
and it was to land him in a great deal of trouble. Believing, as he
did, that Britain was the greatest country in the world, he tended
to ignore the importance of maintaining the treaty when he was
petitioning for the release of slaves or the compensation of widows
(something that took up more and more of his time). To the
British government the treaty was all, but to the inadequately
briefed Bruce, the recipient of constant begging letters from
the relations of enslaved Europeans, the treaty was of secondary

importance to his humanitarian role. Moreover, he and the equally unprepared vice-consul William Forbes had no one to show them the ropes. An Irish merchant, Simon Peter Cruise, the man who should have been most helpful, had been consistently defrauding the unfortunate petitioners for years. As soon as Bruce discovered this, the pair became mortal enemies. For the first year, though, all was relatively peaceful.

The new consul kept himself occupied by perfecting his grasp of the Arabic language and Arabic customs. He gave the occasional dinner party for Aga Mahomet, the Dey's brother, and his then friend Mr Brander, the Swedish consul. He also learned modern Greek from Father Christopher, a Greek Orthodox monk, who, having fallen upon hard times, came to live in the consulate as a chaplain-cum-tutor. He met with the traders to whom he had special access through Masonry (Algiers would become even more of a hotbed of Masonry in the early nineteenth century). Now and again he sued an Algerian for the return of enslaved Englishmen. It was a pleasant start to his term of office. He wrote long, chatty letters to his friends Strange and Lumisden and even to Mr Charron, a caterer in Leghorn who kept Bruce's larder stocked with cases of wine and huge quantities of Parmesan cheese. It was not long before he forgot young Margaret Murray. Indeed, he seems to have made no contact with her in all his travels. Within a few months of his arrival, he was complaining to Charron about the lack of women, a predicament with which Charron sympathized:

> I am sorry that you are so badly off for your carnal callings [replied the victualler] but comfort yourself in your thoughts to make it up with interest when you return to Christendom. But if you should tarry longer in that cursed country then you ought to write to your friends to send you a pretty housekeeper.

To Bruce, this seemed a magnificent idea and soon came news of just such a housekeeper wending her way towards Algiers. Amazingly she had the same name as his former mother-in-law – Bridget Allen – but judging by the 'fondest wishes' that are sent to her by Bruce's many correspondents with whom she stayed on her way to Algiers, she was somewhat more winsome. Her presence was brief. She died in childbirth (we can only guess who had fathered the child), in November 1765, and Bruce was once more left on his own.

He devoted the time to preparation. Dr Richard Ball, the consulate's surgeon, spent many hours teaching his ever-curious superior the rudiments of medicine so that he would be able to look after himself in the interior. Bruce also decided that he was going to need someone to help him record the things he saw. Accordingly he wrote to Andrew Lumisden and Robert Strange – the latter having just been made an academician in Bologna – asking them to find a suitable young artist who could accompany Bruce on his travels. A search began throughout Italy for someone willing to drop everything to go travelling with an irascible Scot in unexplored country. Unsurprisingly, it took a long time. Meanwhile, Bruce was encountering problems in Algiers. He had intended to put the consulate in 'the hands of a vice-consul, who is very able, and much esteemed', but Forbes never had the opportunity, for Bruce was never given permission to travel whilst still consul, a source of great irritation to him since that was his sole purpose in accepting the £600 a year position in the first place. The only real difficulty in his first year would be his relations with his predecessor.

Simon Peter Cruise had been acting consul in the years between the departure of the previous office holder and Bruce's arrival. Most of the community had united behind Cruise in his opposition to Bruce and he spent his days persuading friends to lobby for Bruce's removal in London and spreading rumours about him in Algiers. Bruce received little support for he refused to indulge in the corruption that had enriched Cruise and the other merchants. This was a society where everyday corruption oiled the wheels of business: Bruce's moral stance thus had a stagnatory effect on trade and met with a hostile reception from almost everyone. He took on Cruise over what most would have regarded as a trifle: a debt owed to the widow of a merchant captain which had gone missing during Cruise's period of office. Cruise tried to fend off Bruce's ever more virulent letters on the subject.

I said, and now repeat it to you, that if you do not furnish me with an account, or if you furnish a false one, the consequences will fall upon yourself or, as it is oftener called, upon your head. The consequences of false accounts, Mr Cruise, are not capital, but whatever they are, do not brave them. Remember what your behaviour has been to His Majesty's consul, and to every British subject here in Algiers. In consideration of your family, I give you warning not to begin shuffling with me.

In one of Cruise's many replies, he revealed that Bruce had challenged him to a duel: 'I receiv'd your letter which you may believe surprised me much, as it contains nothing less than a challenge to fight you at your or my garden.'

Worse was to come. The previously peaceful posting was about to dissolve into anarchy.

As has been mentioned, Algiers was ruled by a Dey – on behalf of the Turks – and under him was a divan (a type of cabinet of advisers). In previous centuries, the Dey had been an all-powerful figure – obeyed on pain of death and utterly ruthless in his dealings – but as the strength of the city state began to ebb away, so too did the power of the office. By Bruce's time the Dey was as good as subject to the wishes of the divan and the divan, whilst still high-handed, was at least conscious of the wishes of the people. At this time, the people – already victims of famine – were growing increasingly angry with the British. Britain conducted a great deal of trade in Algiers and the Mediterranean but by virtue of the treaty of 1682 they paid very little for the privilege. British ships were issued with passports (known as passavants) that were recognized by the Algerian corsairs. Any ship that could not produce a passport was legitimate bounty for the pirates. The French and Spanish, however, had found a way around this and thus the people of Algiers, who survived primarily on piracy, were earning less and less every year.

In 1756, the French had briefly captured Mahon, then a significant British port. Admiral John Byng was executed for failing to hold it, thus inspiring Voltaire's joke in *Candide*: *'il est bon de tuer de temps en temps un amiral pour encourager les autres'*. The French captors discovered some passavants in the commander's office, copied them and gave them to their own and their allies' ships.

Spanish and French sailors had been sailing unmolested under British passavants ever since. Each time a French or Spanish ship was stopped by pirates or boarded in port they would produce their British passavants and the Algerians would grudgingly have to let them through. It was soon noticed, though, that none of them spoke English.

One such ship was brought to Algiers under tow and Bruce told the Algerian corsairs that indeed they were right, this was not an English ship, thereby condemning the entire crew to slavery. This he described as a 'disagreeable necessity' but it was not disagreeable enough to stop him from repeating it twice. His actions drew the attention of the Algerian mob – already irritated by the little revenue they were earning from the British – and conflict loomed. Not comprehending the depth of the enmity between France and Britain, the Algerians suspected that the British were giving passports to anyone. At the same time the British Admiralty decided to act. Their solution was to change the design of the passavants and issue British ships with new and different ones. It had not occurred to the sea lords that the old ones were recognized by sight rather than by being read by the illiterate corsairs. With the famine crazed mob baying for blood and the divan divided as to what should be done, Bruce swaggered upon the scene, behaving as though, should the Algerians not obey his wishes, the entire might of the British Navy would be brought down upon their unfortunate heads.

There were two schools of thought within the divan: the doves were led by Aga Mahomet, who liked Bruce and realized that challenging the British was not a very safe course of action even if he did suspect that the consul was all bluster and no bellows. The Dey himself, with the backing of the mob, was hawkish. The merchants in the European community at Algiers were also less than helpful, having been manipulated by the embezzler Cruise, and soon Bruce was mired in trouble. In May 1764, Bruce had asked leave to resign and been turned down: he could therefore not be dismissed. In June the Dey pricked Bruce's pride and gave him the impetus to carry on. The Dey, Bruce was informed, had appointed a slave to act as British consul and had sent a pithy missive to Mr Pitt in which he insisted that Bruce be replaced:

'Your consul in Algiers is an obstinate person and like a b——; and does not regard your affairs,' it said.

Bruce dared not walk the streets, and the Foreign Office, preoccupied with rather more important matters, gave him no guidance. In July the situation became worse when the Dey announced that all British shipping would now be subject to pillage and the crews enslaved. Bruce managed to get messages to the other ports in the Mediterranean, warning British merchants not to approach Algiers, but it was too late for one ship. He wrote to Halifax, pleading for instruction:

> This morning early, the master of the above-mentioned vessel, and the supercargo, were carried before the Dey, and in order to extort a confession if they had secreted any effects, were bastinadoed over the feet and loins in such a manner that the blood gushed out, and then loaded with heavy chains: The captain, it is thought, cannot recover. I have likewise received from a friend some insinuations, that I am in danger and advice to fly; but as it was not the prospect of pay, or want of fortune, that induced me to accept of this employment, so will I not abandon it from fears or any motives unworthy a gentleman. One brother has this war already had the honour of dying in his Majesty's service [Robert Wood had told Bruce in a letter to Horace Mann's consulate at Leghorn that 'I am sorry to acquaint you that Mr Bruce died of his wounds at Havanna'], two more are still in it, and all I hope is, if any accident befall me, as is hourly probable, his Majesty will be favourable to the survivors of a family that has always served him faithfully.

Still no word came from Whitehall despite repeated letters in which Bruce called for task forces to be dispatched and a decision to be made about the new passavants. A month later, on 15 August, the Dey ordered Bruce to leave on pain of death, no idle threat in a state where the prime minister had been strangled in front of Bruce on the orders of the divan and consuls of less favoured countries were often whipped and made to pull carts through the streets.

Bruce was, however, soon restored to his post. The consul's bluster combined with Aga Mahomet's lobbying on his behalf produced a change of heart in the divan. Aga Mahomet was not convinced by Bruce's threats but he was aware that the city state was vulnerable to attack from the powerful British Navy and convinced the allies of the danger.

> After their prayers, the whole of the great officers went to the king, and openly declared to him that the dismissing of me was a matter of too great consequence to be determined without their consent; all of them put him in mind of the constant good behaviour of the English, and of their inability to resist our force, and the impossibility of thinking of peace after I was gone.

In September Bruce received a letter from Halifax commending him on his conduct of the crisis. With better communications, the proud diplomat would undoubtedly have been fired for putting such an important trading route in jeopardy but instead he managed to save his skin – literally – and solve the problem before he could be dismissed. Halifax would allow Bruce to resign as soon as a replacement could be found and the relationship between the two could remain cordial, even affectionate. Halifax went so far as to write the letter himself rather than dictating to a secretary.

> I cannot close my letter without giving you the satisfaction of knowing, that the prudent and judicious manner in which you have conducted yourself throughout the whole of the disagreeable circumstances you relate in your several letters, and the measures you took to prevent the ill consequences that might have resulted from them, have met with the king's gracious approbation; and it is not doubted but you will continue to exert your utmost diligence and abilities for his majesty's service.
>
> I have not omitted to lay your request before the king [to resign], and shall not fail to provide for your return to England as soon as it can be done consistently with the good of his majesty's service.

This episode was really the last time Bruce had to act on behalf of the crown. It was almost a year before he left Algiers but, soon after Halifax's letter of September, Bruce received notice that he would be replaced by Robert Kirke who would answer – unlike Bruce who had been neglected by him – to Captain Cleveland, the ambassador to all the Barbary States. Another treaty would be drawn up but Bruce would not be invited to help formulate it.

Slighted and beginning to believe the rumours that Cruise's friends and Consul Duncan, the Dey's representative at St James's, had succeeded in blackening his name at home, Bruce devoted his days to hunting, training his gun dogs and getting himself properly equipped for the travels upon which it seemed he would now have to embark in a private capacity. He spent many hours interviewing traders and sailors, trying to find out all he could about the Red Sea and, when possible, Abyssinia. He studied his books and wrote to the Foreign Office seeking leave to depart his post, but even his most sycophantic letters received either no reply at all or replies that ignored his requests. By November he was engaged in undignified begging:

> But as I hope your lordship thinks, from my attention to late transactions, I am not wholly unworthy of a small vacation, so I know it not to be unprecedented. Mr Dick, consul at Leghorn, received this permission while I was in Italy, though his journey had no other motive than that of pleasure, and I hope mine will not be unprofitable to the arts. There is, in this country, ruinous architecture enough to compose two considerable volumes. If, after obtaining this leave of absence, I could obtain another favour from your lordship, I should beg that I might have the honour to dedicate the first volume to the king, and that, from your lordship's further goodness, I might have liberty to inscribe the second volume to your lordship.

He must desperately have been seeking leave to depart to have written so uncharacteristic a letter. But by now he was longing for travel and – rich enough to attempt it alone – he was as prepared as he ever would be. Throughout his time in Algiers he had acted in a dignified and resolute manner. It may not have been to the Dey's liking from a commercial point of view but he could not help but admire the bluff Scotsman who refused to be bribed or intimidated. Thus he gave Bruce letters of introduction to his counterparts around the region which would make his tour of North Africa a great deal easier. Bruce's friends Strange and Lumisden had also come up trumps: after much searching an artist had been found who would accompany Bruce for a year (he eventually stayed for six). Two others had considered the job but

Lumisden had found it hard to persuade someone to 'depart an easy life' and embark for unknown shores. Strange wrote to say that Luigi Balugani – a fellow academician at Bologna – would accept the job.

> This young man will be able to serve you in your present under-
> taking. He is certainly the best qualified of any I can find here. He
> has lived several years in Rome in the house of Conte Ranuzzi of
> Bologna. This gentleman gives him the best of characters to private
> life as well as diligence [an excellent recommendation since Bruce
> had met and liked Ranuzzi in Rome] . . . Balugani engages to serve
> you a year at the rate of 35 scudi a month. What he seems most
> defective in is figures, in which you must assist him yourself or
> have them afterwards retouched.

Balugani arrived in Algiers in March 1765 and in April Bruce was relieved of his duties. Cleveland came to Algiers with Robert Kirke and the pair ignored all Bruce's advice to them, declining to meet him and even reappointing Cruise as vice-consul. It was a humili-ation for the proud consul but he could not protest overmuch as it was what he himself desired. George Lawrence, the consul at Mahon, wrote to him: 'Congratulations on getting rid of an employment which had so long become disagreeable to you.' He had not been a very good consul though later commentators have been unnecessarily harsh.

> The consulate was conferred on James Bruce solely to study antiqui-
> ties in Africa [said Godfrey Fisher] and he was sent through France
> under a safe conduct to examine classical remains in Italy before
> reaching Algiers after the war. In spite of some likeable qualities,
> he was arrogant and irascible and, judging by his letters there may
> be some reason to question his mental stability. While he frantically
> summoned warships to his aid, he speaks in high terms of the Dey's
> treatment of him . . . his successor complained that he had left
> 'everything relative to publick affairs in much confusion and
> strangely neglected'.

This may be true although the British government, which had sent Bruce to study antiquities, surely had some share of the res-ponsibility for his failure in a task he was neither trained for nor inclined to do. At least he was treated somewhat better than his predecessor and did well enough to get paid. The previous consul, Stanhope Aspinwall, spent five years in penury before he secured his pension, writing to Egremont (Halifax's predecessor) in 1763:

> Having been removed from being the King's agent and consul at Algiers (in reaction to a letter from the Dey that I was unacceptable to him) without any the least previous notice, and left to get home as well as I could with a wife and numerous family, in winter and in time of war, I was many months in England soliciting the Earl of Bute but in vain . . .

Those following fared little better, for Algiers was a notoriously difficult post. The Dey often contrived to have consuls dismissed so as to leave him free to appoint his own. Kirke was soon recalled to Britain after Commodore Harrison, the Commander-in-Chief of the Mediterranean, reported him for corruption and dereliction of duty. Sir Robert Playfair (consul general in Algiers 100 years later and a Bruce enthusiast) wrote of the fate of Kirke's successor, LeGros, who was driven to suicide by the difficulty of the posting: 'He "met with a misfortune that made it impossible for him to execute that employment", and the last we hear of him is that "he was sitting on a bed, with a sword and a brace of pistols at his side, calling for a clergyman to give him the Sacraments that he may die contented".'

Bruce made sure that Halifax knew what he thought of his treatment: 'I only very heartily regret with shame to myself that with my utmost diligence and attention I have not been able to merit of your Lordship the same marks of confidence constantly bestowed upon my predecessors in office,' and in August he gave up diplomacy for good to set off on his travels. It was a chastened Bruce who left Algiers to record the ruins of ancient civilizations in which Halifax and the king had shown such interest: the merchants of Algiers heaved a collective sigh of relief.

The erstwhile consul first made for Mahon − just opposite Algiers, in the Mediterranean − where he had to attend to some 'business of a private nature'. If, as seems likely, this was to do with Bridget Allan's child it would have required all of his meagre diplomatic skills. His 'housekeeper' having died in quarantine on a visit from Algiers to Minorca, a man called Giovanni Porcile, who had been looking after the child, was demanding payment. Bruce was soon on his way back to Africa where he visited only a few ancient sites before going on to Tunis. He had learned the advantage of establishing credentials whilst in Algiers and wanted to meet the Bey before he started his exploratory tour. Carthage only occupied him for a few hours, since he knew he would be able to return with the Bey's help whenever he wished. In Tunis, Barthélèmy de Saisieu, the French consul, provided him with a guide and ten 'horse-soldiers, well armed with fire-locks and pistols, excellent horsemen, and, as far as I could ever discern upon the few occasions that presented, as eminent for cowardice, at least, as they were for horsemanship'. This small army proved to be quite useless when it was actually needed a few weeks later.

> It was a fair match between coward and coward. With my company, I was enclosed in a square in which three temples stood [at the ruins of Spaitla], where there yet remained a precinct of high walls. These plunderers would have come in to me, but were afraid of my firearms; and I would have run away from them, had I not been afraid of meeting their horse in the plain. I was almost starved to death, when I was relieved by the arrival of Welled Hassan and a friendly tribe of Dreeda.

Bruce also had ten servants, two of whom were Irish slaves – Hugh and Roger McCormack – given him as a going away present by the Dey of Algiers (though formerly soldiers in the Spanish army, he was still referring to them as slaves a year later). He was also given a covered cart in which to put his astronomical instruments and other equipment; it was quite a caravan that made its way from Tunis inland, back towards Algiers. Bruce's plan was twofold. He wanted to test his safari equipment – amongst which he doubtless included the artist Balugani – and he wished to record as many ancient ruins as he could. Thomas Shaw – an adventurous Oxford don and author of *Travels or Observations Relating to Several Parts of Barbary and the Levant* – had written about some of the ruins on the north coast of Africa but had missed out a great many others. Bruce wanted to venture where Shaw had not, paint pictures and then present the whole to the king, thus satisfying his own curiosity and simultaneously securing a peerage or a baronetcy for his dotage. They had permission to travel anywhere and took full advantage of it. They had two camera obscura, mirrored boxes, used contemporaneously by Canaletto, which by reflecting the scene on to paper allowed artists inside to trace exactly the outlines of the ruins they observed. It is astonishing how many paintings the two made: three bound volumes were given to George III on Bruce's return. He kept some and gave others to friends. He quarrelled constantly with Dr Shaw's artistic opinions: 'There is at Thunodrunum a triumphal arch, which Dr Shaw thinks is more remarkable for its size than for its taste of execution; but the size is not extraordinary; on the other hand, both taste and execution are admirable,' and criticized his work: 'Doctor Shaw, struck with the magnificence of Spaitla, has attempted something like the three temples, in a style much like what one would expect from an ordinary carpenter or mason.'

Always contrary, Bruce was happy to have differences of opinion but he went out of his way to defend Shaw's honour in the *Travels*, relating a story he knew would not be believed in order to show solidarity with his peer. At Sidi Booganim he came across a tribe which ate lions' flesh. At the first opportunity, he tucked in: 'The first was a he-lion, lean, tough, smelling violently of musk, and had the taste which, I imagine old horse-flesh would have . . . The third was a lion's whelp, six or seven months old; it tasted, upon the whole, the worst of the three.'

Bruce was being deliberately provocative when he wrote about this in the *Travels*. Shaw had told a similar story when he had returned to Oxford twenty years earlier and no one had believed him. Now Bruce was doing the same. By the time of writing Bruce had also been severely criticized by those who did not believe him and, although he disagreed with Shaw on points of taste, he wanted to show solidarity on points of belief. This was an age when most people did not know what a lion looked like, save possibly in heraldry. Twenty-five years later Stubbs was to portray male lions stalking and tearing chunks out of horses – anatomically correct but not behaviourally so. Lions were still more mystical than real – they could only be seen by prisoners at the

Tower of London – and no one could believe that men would or could eat the king of beasts. Thus, no one believed Bruce when he returned. Some of his stories – which seem unremarkable to us now – were judged too outlandish to be true. Bruce thus laboured the point in his book: 'With all submission to that learned university, I will not dispute the lion's title to eating men; but, since it is not founded upon patent, no consideration will make me stifle the merit of the Welled Sidi Boogannim, who have turned the chace [sic] upon the enemy.'

They continued their march up and down the Medjerda valley, through wheat fields that had fed ancient Rome, visiting Hydra and Constantina across lands which had seen Caesar and Hannibal, the Ptolemies and Pompey. Greeks, Romans, Egyptians – all had been there before him and left impressive traces in what, though described in ancient texts, was now the unknown world. Bruce noted all the ruins until the great amphitheatre at El Gemme, confident that the king would be grateful to his loyal subject. After all, it was not long ago that court painters and sculptors had been in the habit of depicting their kings in the guise of Roman emperors. Given the royal preoccupation with the lives of the ancient emperors and the current fascination with archaeology, these were ruins in which regal interest should be guaranteed and, accordingly, he did a thorough job: 'I believe I may confidently say, there is not, either in the territories of Algiers or Tunis, a fragment of good taste of which I have not brought a drawing to Britain.'

They continued along the coast to Tripoli through territory that was disputed between the Basha of Tripoli and the Bey of Tunis. It was Bruce's first taste of real desert travel and the journey, full of incident, was good training for the years ahead. In Tripoli they were met by one of Bruce's myriad distant cousins:

The Hon. Mr Frazer of Lovat [After the débâcle of the suicidal consul at Algiers Archibald Campbell Fraser would eventually suc- ceed Bruce.], his Majesty's consul in that station, from whom I received every sort of kindness, comfort and assistance, which I very much needed after so rude a journey, made with such diligence that two of my horses died some days after.

Interestingly, whilst Bruce writes only about the death of two horses in his book, in a letter to Robert Wood he claimed that on the 'night of the third day we were attacked by a number of horsemen, and four of our men killed upon the spot'. The version in the book is probably closer to the truth for in the letter (which he knew was not only for Wood's eyes) he wanted to show what hardships he had suffered whilst painting the king's pictures. He was no longer travelling on official business, of course, but he wanted the king and others to know that he had suffered for his art. Either way, the journey had been hard but also productive. They were not yet in uncharted territory but this was country where travellers had to look after themselves, thriving or withering according to their talents rather than their riches. On the expedition, Bruce learnt the rudiments of command, the dangers of travelling when the sun was high and had the need to be sufficiently prepared reinforced. They had encountered trouble because of Bruce's impatience in not waiting for a letter of introduction to a tribal chief. He would not make the same mistake again.

From Tripoli, Bruce had to return by boat to Tunis where he stayed with the British representative, Consul Charles Gordon, another distant cousin. He doubtless saw his good friend Maria – an Italian in Tunis – about whom we know little but who continued to write her *carissimo* love letters for years afterwards. This was a convenient relationship for Bruce since Maria wrote that she had a jealous father and that Bruce should therefore never reply to her letters. He received the correct introductions to the Basha of Tripoli before setting off once more in August 1766 for Tripoli and Benghazi. Before doing so, however, he made sure that his paintings and notes from the first part of his journey were sent to Smyrna (Izmir) in the care of an English servant. He was now embarked on strenuous travels and did not want the extra burden of the hundreds of pictures he had completed. The future Libya was in a pitiable state: internecine warfare and famine made it a much more formidable destination than Tunis and Algiers. In Benghazi 'ten or twelve people were found dead every night in the streets, and life was said in many to be supported by food that human nature shudders at the thought of'.

The general lawlessness exacerbated by famine meant that travel was not easy and Bruce only managed to see the principal sites of ancient Pentapolis, the ruin-bedecked area around Tolmeita and Benghazi that borders the Mediterranean. They too were recorded and written about with his usual fierce debunking of myth and legend. Soon, however, it became too hard to travel for so little reward – the ruins were more ruined even than those he had visited hitherto – and so in November they 'embarked on board a Greek vessel, very ill accoutred' for nearby Crete. It soon emerged that it was the captain's first voyage and that he had no idea what he was doing. Within a few hours they were wrecked. Bruce described the mishap in his *Travels*: 'We were not far from shore, but there was an exceeding great swell at sea.' They tried to reach safety in a tender but that was soon swamped so Bruce threw himself into the sea crying, 'We are all lost; if you can swim, follow me.'

'A good, strong and practised swimmer', he soon reached the surf but that was only the beginning of his problems; there was a riptide and he was beaten about by the waves for a good few minutes before he finally trod ground.

> At last, finding my hands and knees upon the sand, I fixed my nails into it, and obstinately resisted being carried back at all, crawling a few feet when the sea had retired. I had perfectly lost my recollection and understanding, and after creeping so far as to be out of the reach of the sea, I suppose I fainted, for from that time I was totally insensible of any thing that passed around me.

Having prevailed against the sea and storm, he now had to prevail against the inhabitants who, like their Cornish contemporaries, saw a good shipwreck as manna from heaven, particularly when the victims were Turks as they suspected Bruce and his bedraggled, but miraculously alive, servants to be. Roasting in the hot sun, the semi-conscious Bruce had been stripped and bastinadoed before it occurred to him that he could speak his captors' language – Arabic. As soon as he explained that he was a Christian doctor he was given succour by the local sheikh. It was, however, a sick and disconsolate Bruce who arrived back in Benghazi two days later. He was lucky that he had sent his earlier paintings on to Smyrna but even then it looked like his travels would be finished before he had even started. Much of his most essential equipment had been lost in the wreck.

> I there lost a sextant, a parallactic instrument, a time-piece, a re-flecting telescope [for astronomy], an achromatic one [for terrestrial observation], with many drawings, a copy of M. de la Caille's ephemerides down to the year 1775, much to be regretted, as being full of manuscript marginal notes; a small *camera obscura*, some guns, pistols, a blunderbuss, and several other articles.

Without all these instruments Bruce would become the kind of traveller that he despised. He needed the equipment to legitimize his wanderings and give a purpose to his travels. In the age of Enlightenment it was no longer thought desirable to discover places unless they could be given co-ordinates and drawn on a map.

CHAPTER 3

THE ENLIGHTENED TOURIST

Disgruntled and frustrated, Bruce arrived in Syria a few months later. His brush with death on the Barbary coast in 1766 was still bothering him the next year: he had done himself more harm than he had initially realized and the weak chest of his childhood was beginning to affect his life again. When he had eventually arrived in Crete on a more reliable vessel, he had been confined to his bed for months. Malaria, near drowning and the terrible buffeting he had received in the African surf were all conspiring to undermine his physical health. His mental state was none too good either. In the past few years he had failed as a diplomat and foundered as an explorer; if things did not look up soon he would have to steal back to England and marry Margaret Murray, then a child, now a mature woman, whom he had left behind with a miniature of himself for solace. He knew that Margaret was still waiting for him since he received the occasional letter from his friends in Rome giving him independent information about the lovesick girl. 'I shall only add that little Murray and all your friends here remember you most affectionately,' he had been told in a recent letter from Robert Strange.

In between bouts of ill health, he made the occasional trip with Balugani to see the sights of Syria, Cyprus and Turkey though most of the time he was seeing places already well-documented by others. This was, after all, Latin Syria where crusaders, pilgrims and latter-day knights had been living for centuries. His expeditions could do little other than satisfy his own curiosity and add more pictures to his already bulging portfolio. None of this adventuring was really worthwhile without the appropriate scientific instruments and they were very hard to come by. He had written to all his friends in France and England but they all encountered the same difficulty: 'Everybody was employed in making instruments for Danish, Swedish, and other foreign astronomers; that all those which were completed had been bought up, and without waiting a considerable and indefinite time, nothing could be had that could be depended upon.'

This was depressing enough but he also received news that wild rumours about his travels were doing the rounds in England. It seemed he had become a laughing stock in his absence. To a man as proud as Bruce, this was worse than failure. 'One thing only detained me from returning home; it was my desire of fulfilling my promise to my Sovereign, and of adding the ruins of Palmyra to those of Africa, already secured and out of danger.'

If he had known how completely uninterested George III was in the pictures he had been promised, he would have taken the first boat back to Dover. There were more important matters on the royal mind: this was the year when Clive departed India, leaving it in a state of complete chaos. Paintings would not have been uppermost in George's thoughts. Bruce embarked for Syrian Tripoli where he went shooting and bought two hunting dogs – Juba and Midore – which, when not kennelled with Consul Charles Gordon, were to become devoted companions. In Tripoli he was told that to visit Palmyra he should approach from Aleppo which advice he immediately followed. After every journey he relapsed into ill health, but thankfully Aleppo was the best place in the Levant to do so, for there lived Patrick Russel, an English doctor who cured him, taught him medicine and became a lifelong friend. A plague specialist who had spent many years living in the Levant, he was well-versed in tropical illnesses and prepared a vast medicine chest for Bruce, which he then instructed him how to use. Russel and his brothers were excellent violinists who would play long into the night, and as Bruce danced with the local consuls, the French merchants and their wives, he began to recover. He also struck up new acquaintances: the Bellevilles and the Thomases, who were local traders, became firm friends. Bruce left Aleppo 'in perfect health, and in the gayest humour possible'.

Palmyra had been visited before, most notably by his friend

Robert Wood, but there was more work to be done both there and at nearby Baalbek, so having arranged the appropriate letters of introduction he set off to more adventures in the desert. He had an enjoyable and instructive time – it was 'all classic ground' – but he wrote little about it for fear of repeating the work of earlier travellers. More importantly, he disagreed with Wood. Not wanting to contradict his friend, he therefore set up his camera obscura, made some very beautiful paintings with Balugani, and returned to Aleppo two months later. Whilst he was away, exciting news had arrived from Europe. Patrick Russel's brother Alexander had found him 'an excellent reflecting telescope' in London and also an achromatic one. Two time-pieces needed for taking longitude measurements had been sent from Paris to await Bruce's arrival in Alexandria. They were not as good as his original Ellicott – a copy of Harrison's 1760 chronometer which, through its ability to maintain accuracy over long periods, transformed navigation – but they would do. (Ellicott was one of the greatest clock-makers of the day, and among other things horologist to Catherine the Great.) This was great news indeed but Bruce recorded that it 'still left me in absolute despair about obtaining a quadrant, and consequently gave me very little satisfaction'. In spite of this he decided to go to Egypt to visit the pyramids. The pyramids – a powerful image on all Masonic paraphernalia – were of special interest to him. It is a central tenet of Masonic lore that their founders built the pyramids.

Before he left, however, he received news he could never have anticipated. Abandoned by officialdom in his own country, it seemed that France was anxious to provide him with the necessary instruments to continue his travels. The fact that France and England were scarcely friends seems to have been overlooked when set against the aristocratic and masonic links that encouraged Bruce's friends to help him and the lust for Enlightenment which was so much more entrenched in France than in Britain. His principal benefactor – the naturalist the Comte de Buffon, who was a member of the same lodge as Voltaire – managed to persuade the French government that the discovery of the source of the Nile was more important than whether the feat was achieved by an Englishman or a Frenchman.

The Comte de Buffon, Mons. Guys of Marseilles, and several others well known in the literary world, had ventured to state to the minister [the Duc de Choiseul who became a friend and had provided Bruce with his *laissez-passer* to travel through France on his way to Italy], and through him to the king of France, Louis XV, how very much it was to be lamented, that after a man had been found who was likely to succeed in removing that opprobrium of travellers and geographers, by discovering the sources of the Nile, one most unlucky accident, at a most unlikely time, should frustrate the most promising endeavours. That prince, distinguished for every good quality of the heart, for benevolence, beneficence, and a desire of promoting and protecting learning, ordered a military quadrant of his own military academy at Marseilles, as the nearest and most convenient port of embarkation, to be taken down and sent to me at Alexandria.

Bruce now had all he needed. In fact, he was rather better equipped than he had been in the first place, for he had just been given one of the best quadrants available – 'reputed to be the most perfect instrument ever constructed in France'. He could straightaway devote himself entirely to discovering the source of the Nile; he had the money and the knowledge and he now had what money could not buy, the equipment with which to record his anticipated discoveries. He spent the winter with his friends in the Levant, preparing for his first venture into uncharted territory. He had learned the error of his ways and would not leave until he had all the permissions he could possibly need. His friend Murray, the ambassador to the Sublime Porte at Constantinople, managed to secure a firman (a letter of recommendation similar to a passport) from the Grand Signor at Constantinople which would prove invaluable; Bruce even acquired a letter to the Khan of the Tartars in case he became really lost. He had to solicit firmans for every eventuality and obtain letters of credit from his bankers in London as well as learn as much as he could about this momentous undertaking. He would still have difficulties if his firmans were not recognized or if he could find no one to honour his letter of credit, but the Arabic banking system was sophisticated and he could rely on it until he arrived in Abyssinia. His former colleagues, the British and French consuls in the area, were extremely helpful in this regard. He thus spent much of the winter writing bread and butter letters whilst others prepared the way for him.

Bruce planned to visit Alexandria, pick up his equipment and take it on a trial run to the pyramids. Then he would set off for Abyssinia through Massawa. Abyssinia's littoral, including the Red Sea port of Massawa, was loosely under the control of the Sublime Porte. The only other way to reach the country was a long march via Sennaar in present-day Sudan. Having heard what had happened to the French ambassador du Roule in 1705, he was shy of going by way of Sennaar. Du Roule, the last man ever to have attempted an unannounced visit to the court of the King of Kings, took the Sennaar road and was murdered in the capital of the Fung kingdom. Massawa was an unknown quantity, unvisited by Europeans for 150 years, and Bruce would not go there until he was exhaustively prepared. As Bruce sat, dressed in the costume of a Barbary Arab, in the prow of a boat en route to Alexandria via Cyprus, he saw a high bank of clouds that he conjectured had come from the mountains of Ethiopia and would water the Nile. He was well-satisfied with his precautions.

> Nothing could be more agreeable to me than that sight, and the reasoning upon it. I already, with pleasure, anticipated the time in which I should be a spectator first, afterwards an historian, of this phenomenon, hitherto a mystery through all ages. I exulted in the measures I had taken, which I flattered myself, for having been digested with greater consideration than those adopted by others, would secure me from the melancholy catastrophes that had terminated those hitherto unsuccessful attempts.

He first must needs make friends with the rulers of Egypt – the Mamelukes. Egypt was nominally ruled by the Turks but, under the recent onslaught of Catherine the Great, and after centuries of decadent rule, the Ottoman Empire was slowly crumbling. The Mamelukes were originally installed as a slave caste by rulers too lazy to govern themselves and as such had fought nobly against the crusaders and their descendants, but they had enjoyed greater and greater autonomy over the previous centuries. Indeed, Ali

Bey, the present ruler, would declare himself an independent sultan the following year. Bruce was to be disappointed in the Mamelukes: 'A more brutal, unjust, tyrannical, oppressive, avaricious set of infernal miscreants there is not on earth, than are the members of the government of Cairo.'

On 20 June 1768, after a five-day voyage, he made his first acquaintance with the Nile. At the mouth of the delta, by the ancient port of Alexandria, he was initially impressed by the near legendary city: 'It is in this point of view the town appears most to advantage. The mixture of old monuments, such as the columns of Pompey, with the high Moorish towers and steeples, raise our expectations of the consequence of the ruins we are to find.'

To a man who had devoted so much of his life to learning about ancient civilizations, this must indeed have been a wonderful sight. He was at last seeing the things that he had heard and read described so many times by the ancients. Warming to his task, he surveyed the old port and gazed at the magnificent ruins. It was not long, however, before he resumed his customary sang-froid. Before he had even set foot on Egyptian soil, Alexandria had disappointed him.

> But the moment we are in the port the illusion ends, and we distinguish the immense Herculean works of ancient times, now few in number, from the ill-imagined, ill-constructed, and imperfect buildings, of the several barbarous masters of Alexandria in the later ages . . . There is nothing beautiful or pleasant in the present Alexandria, but a handsome street of modern houses, where a very active and intelligent number of merchants live upon the miserable remnants of that trade, which made its glory in the first times.

Dressed as an Arab so as to be allowed where Europeans dared not tread, Bruce walked around the town, imbibing the atmosphere and providing inspiration for Richard Burton, who a century later would follow his example by donning Arab dress to visit Mecca and the Abyssinian Muslim stronghold of Harar. Despite being a very tall, red-haired man, Bruce managed, by wearing a turban and speaking perfect Arabic, to convince everyone that he was a peasant from the Barbary States. He was in good spirits.

Two days before he arrived, an epidemic of the plague had petered out and, a few weeks earlier, Bruce's astronomical instruments had been delivered. The Nile beckoned and at last he was able to respond: 'Prepared now for any enterprise, I left with eagerness the thread bare enquiries into the meagre remains of this once famous capital of Egypt.'

With his entire band of servants dressed, like him, as Arabs, Bruce set off towards Rosetto on horseback – 'We had all of us, pistols at our girdles'. Rosetto, midway between Alexandria and Cairo, was the embarkation point for travellers venturing up the Nile. The delta was dangerous and 'besides, nobody wishes to be a partner for any time in a voyage with Egyptian sailors, if he can possibly avoid it'.

He arrived in Cairo on one of the Nile's typical small sailing boats, a felucca, which were then known as canjas. Despite his appearance, he immediately set up house with a trader, M. Bertran, in the French quarter. By night he would dress as an English gentleman; by day he would venture, disguised, through the large gates which enclosed the foreign merchants' street and patrol the bazaars of Cairo, buying manuscripts at Arabic prices and trying to find as much information about his route as was possible: 'I never saw a place I liked worse, or which afforded less pleasure or instruction than Cairo'.

He did not have to stay in the source of his displeasure for very long, for yet again he was uncommonly lucky. The governance of Cairo lay all in the hands of one man, Ali Bey, whose closest confidant was an astrologer called Maalem Risk. The secretary of the Bey was 'a man capable of the blackest designs' but he was also most impressed by Bruce's telescopes and quadrants. He passed Bruce's baggage through customs, charging no duty, and intro-duced him to the Bey – 'his turban, his girdle and the head of his dagger all covered with fine brilliants'.

Here Bruce's expertise at dealing with Eastern rulers – learned at some risk in Algiers – came triumphantly into play. The correct amount of haughty arrogance combined with respect for the office and person of his host always seemed to come naturally to him. This and subsequent meetings allowed Bruce to make a few astro-logical predictions (something he did not believe in and usually disapproved of), and, by using Western medicine, to cure the Bey of a stomach upset, thus disposing the potentate towards him. Within a few weeks, he had been given his own house in the grounds of the seventh-century St George's monastery outside the city and had been supplied with letters to the Naybe of Massawa, the King of Sennaar and the leaders of all the tribes he would encounter on his journey up the Nile. The Sardar of the Janissaries – chief of the mercenaries who policed the Turkish sultan's vast empire – and the Greek Orthodox patriarch both gave him introductory letters also. It was a well-satisfied Bruce who cast off from Cairo on 12 December with his large retinue of servants and his friend Father Christopher, the former chaplain from Algiers, who had reappeared unexpectedly as an aide to Patriarch Mark of Alexandria.

Bruce had spent an unaccountably long time in Cairo considering he claimed to dislike it so. This goes unexplained in either his book, letters or journals. If he looked at the pyramids, he wastes less than a page on them in his book and feigns disinterest. They had, of course, been previously described by other travellers but even the most disenchanted tourist tends to write more than a postcard's worth about them. His only comment in the *Travels* is that he thinks the stones for building them came from a more local source rather than the Libyan mountains, as was usually claimed. This is an odd omission and a mysterious, lost six months.

Bruce had rented himself a very beautiful felucca with 'an agreeable dining room, twenty foot square' for his cruise up the Nile. It did not quite rival that of the Ptolemies 2000 years earlier which boasted five restaurants, but it had an excellent captain, Abou Cuffi, who had been threatened with all sorts of horrors by the Bey if anything should happen to the good Hakim Yagoube (Doctor James). He had been made to leave one of his sons with the Bey 'in security for his behaviour towards us'. Bruce's successful treatment of the Bey had made him more ready to practise his medical skills and they became invaluable to him, not just for keeping himself and his servants healthy but also for gaining favours. He still acknowledged their value in his published thanks to Patrick Russel twenty years later – 'My escaping the fever at Aleppo was not the only time in which I owed him [Russel] my life.' From this point on, he always travelled as a doctor who practised for no payment – thus winning many friends – and in the words of the sultan's firman as 'a most noble Englishman and servant of the king'.

The voyage up the Nile was by necessity a leisurely one. Abou Cuffi, though skilled, was often drunk and the wind was, at that season, ill-suited to their journey. Many mornings they had to employ people to tow them against the current. Bruce was enjoying himself, however. He made friends with the Sheikh of the Howadat, a local tribe, and on the first two days went off on archaeological excursions, returning to the boat at night. This qualified him to do something he loved – argue about the findings of his predecessors: 'Mr Niebuhr, the Danish traveller, agrees with Dr Pococke [about the location of Memphis]. I believe neither Shaw nor Niebuhr were ever at Metrahenny'.

Bruce was not a man to worry about libel or speaking ill of the dead so he carried on for another twenty pages. It is the one point in the *Travels* when he realizes he might be over egging the pudding: 'Our wind was fair and fresh, rather a little on our beam; when, in great spirits, we hoisted our main and fore-sails, leaving the point of Metrahenny, where our reader may think we have too long detained him'.

The journey had started in earnest. From Cairo onwards, every night Balugani would calculate the temperature and Bruce would take the longitude and latitude. They would record detailed notes of everything they did, things they saw and customs they observed. Until now they had been on an extremely well-organized painting tour but from the moment they left Cairo they were on a scientific expedition, measuring, weighing and recording everything they came across. The tables on which they measured the weather and distances they travelled are amazing documents in themselves, not merely for the information they contain. Even when they were sick from tiredness or seriously ill, Bruce would take the readings and Balugani would enter them. Bruce even charted every twist and turn of the Nile, inserting the names of the villages along the way, marking accurate longitude and latitude measurements that had never before been available. He was determined that his journey should not merely be a jaunt. This was not a sponsored expedition, but neither was it that of a rich young man going off to find himself: Bruce wanted it to be useful. It was to be a well-documented voyage of discovery, of value to people who followed in his footsteps. For he was quite sure of one thing: follow they would.

Every night they had to post guards, for the villages they passed through were teeming with robbers, notorious for swimming out to anchored boats and stealing anything they could lay their hands on. They encountered trouble only when Bruce broke his own rules and tried to visit some ruins in a place where he had no introduction to the locals.

> Abou Cuffi's son Mahomet went on shore, under pretence of buying some provision, and to see how the land lay, but after the character we had of the inhabitants, all our fire-arms were brought to the door of the cabin. In the meantime, partly with my naked eye and partly with my glass, I observed the ruins so attentively as to be perfectly in love with them.

Bruce was destined to venture no closer. Mahomet came racing back to the boat – his turban stolen – with the entire village chasing after him. A few shots were fired at the boat and they cast off hurriedly whilst Bruce ranted at the villagers.

> I cried out in Arabic, 'Infidels, thieves, and robbers! come on, or we shall presently attack you:' upon which I immediately fired a ship blunderbuss with pistol small bullets, but with little elevation, among the bushes, so as not to touch them. The three or four men that were nearest fell flat upon their faces, and slid away among the bushes on their bellies, like eels, and we saw no more of them.

Their progress was unhurried but they were covering a lot of ground and learning a great deal: 'I was then beginning my apprenticeship, which I fully completed,' remarked the explorer. One minute he would be drawing pictures of irrigation methods in his commonplace book and measuring the height of the wheat growing in the thin strip of land between the mountains that run parallel with the Nile, the next he would be exposing myths for future publication: 'I was very pleased to see here, for the first time, two shepherd dogs lapping up the water from the stream, then lying down in it with great seeming leisure and satisfaction. It refuted the old fable, that the dogs living on the banks of the Nile run as they drink, for fear of the crocodile'. He never entirely cured himself of these bizarre asides which, though irksome to the scholar, are a delight to the general reader (for whom, in the end, he wrote). The running dogs of the Nile, now unheard of, were evidently well-known to eighteenth-century audiences.

Each day they would stop at whichever ruin happened to be next and from studying them Bruce came to many conclusions, some of which were correct, others less so. He guessed the location of Memphis correctly, but when he visited Cleopatra's and Caesarian's temple at Dendera, he decided that the ancient Egyptians must all have lived in caves because he could only find the remains of temples and graves. He also came to some rather startling conclusions about the Egyptian language which he drew from his study of the hieroglyphics: that it grew out of Ethiopic. All these, though, must be taken in context for his was a rapid progress of the Nile and he had no time to do any detailed research. He does not claim to be an oracle on these points.

At Thebes, however, Bruce made an important discovery; important not only because he was the first person to describe an intriguing facet of Egyptian life, but also because it led to his being disbelieved when he returned to London. In the tomb of Rameses III he discovered a painting of a 'man playing upon a harp' thus dating anew the origins of music. The occupant of the tomb was not known at the time. Until this was verified, it became known, after his death – through the respectable medium of Murray's guide book of Egypt – as Bruce's Tomb.

> The whole principles on which this harp is constructed, are rational and ingenious, and the ornamented parts are executed in the very best manner.
>
> The bottom and sides of the frame seem to be fineered, and inlaid, probably with ivory, tortoise-shell, and mother of pearl, the ordinary produce of the neighbouring seas and deserts. It would be even now impossible, either to construct or to finish a harp with more taste or elegance.

Everything which Bruce wrote and said about this harp and its player is true. The fresco is still there, complete with Bruce's graffito upon it. It was, however, greeted with incredulity by many of his compatriots on his return to London. He described the harp to Doctor Burney, the musicologist, who then asked Bruce to write an article about it for his forthcoming *History of Music*. It was Bruce's first published writing and the reaction to it gave Bruce a chastening introduction to public criticism. Fanny Burney, Dr Burney's daughter, was quite wrong in her expectation of how Bruce's letter and paintings would be received when published. She wrote in her diary:

> Mr Bruce, that *Great Lyon*, has lately become very intimate with my father, and has favoured him with two delightful original drawings, done by himself, of instruments which he found at the Egyptian Thebes, in his long and difficult and enterprising travels, and also with a long letter concerning them, which is to be printed in the *History*. These will be great ornaments to the book; and I am happy to think that Mr Bruce, in having so highly obliged my father, will find by the estimation he is in as a writer, that his own name and assistance will not be disgraced, though it is the first time he has signed it for any publication, with which he has hitherto favoured the world.

Within days of the *History*'s publication, the cataloguer of the Theban lyre and the musical instruments of Ethiopia became known as the Theban *liar*. The ever acerbic Horace Walpole wrote to his friend, the Rev. William Mason,

> It is unlucky that Mr Bruce does not posses [sic] another secret reckoned very useful to intrepid travellers, a good memory. Last spring he dined at Mr Crauford's, George Selwyn was one of the company; after relating the story of the bramble [which we will hear later] and several other curious particulars, somebody asked Mr Bruce, if the Abyssinians had any musical instruments? 'Musical instruments,' said he, and paused – 'Yes I think I remember one lyre'; George Selwyn whispered his neighbour, 'I am sure there is one less since he came out of the country.' There are now six instruments there.

It is extraordinary that when Bruce was being scrupulously truthful he was disbelieved, for when he is genuinely glamorizing his account or being economic with the truth, he invariably gets away with it. It must have made him wildly angry in the early years after his return and could well have allowed him to justify to himself his embellishments, on the basis that no one was going to believe him anyway. Walpole's otherwise erroneous judgement on Bruce's character was, however, correct in one respect: he was not a man to be trifled with. He added a proviso in his letter to Mason: 'Remember this letter is for your own private eye, I do not desire to be engaged in a controversy or a duel.'

Bruce and Balugani had set up their easels to paint as many of the frescoes as they could but their guides were frightened of attack by the grave-robbers who lived in the surrounding hills and thus refused to stay. They extinguished all the torches and left Bruce and Balugani in the dark, forcing them to leave.

> Very much vexed, I mounted my horse to return to the boat. The road lay through a very narrow valley, the sides of which were covered with bare loose stones. I had no sooner got down to the bottom, than I heard a great deal of loud speaking on both sides of the valley; and, in an instant, a number of large stones were rolled down upon me, which, though I heard in motion, I could not see, on account of the darkness; this increased my terror . . . I accordingly levelled my gun as near as possible, by the ear, and fired one barrel among them. A moment's silence ensued, and then a loud howl, which seemed to have come from thirty or forty persons. I took my servant's blunderbuss and discharged it where I heard the howl, and a violent confusion of tongues followed, but no stones.

Bruce was learning quickly about how to deal with dangers on the road. 'When in doubt – shoot', was his policy, though he was careful about whom he shot at. When it seemed impolitic to harm an adversary he merely terrified them with bloodcurdling exhibitions of firepower. On this occasion Bruce and Balugani made it back to the boat with no casualties and believing 'it would be our fault if they found us in the morning', cast off and floated down to Luxor 'where there was a governor for whom I had letters'. He was impressed by the 'magnificent scenes of ruins' at Luxor and nearby Karnak although he did not purchase anything. Already, it seems, rapacious Westerners were buying up the best bits of ancient Egypt and taking them home. A row of sphinxes 'had been covered with earth till very recently, a Venetian physician and antiquary bought one of them at a very considerable price, as he said, for the king of Sardinia. This has accused several others to be uncovered, though no purchaser hath yet offered.'

The day before they arrived in Aswan, Bruce went to see the chief of a tribe of desert Arabs, Sheikh Nimmer. Bruce and the sheikh's son had met in Cairo where Bruce had dispensed some medicine for the old man. He had promised at the time that he would come and check on his patient later which, with an eye on the main chance, he was now doing. By prescribing some more drugs and teaching the servants how to make a special type of lime juice for the old sheikh, Bruce managed to extract a sincere oath of loyalty.

> The great people among them came, of about two minutes long, by which they declared themselves, and their children, accursed, if ever they lifted their hands against me in the Tell [the cultivated part of Egypt], or field, in the desert, or on the river; or in case that I or mine, should fly to them for refuge, if they did not protect us at the risque of their lives, their families, and their fortunes, or, as they emphatically expressed it, to the death of the last male child among them.

Bruce could not know how useful this would prove in the future. He sailed on down to Aswan with not a worry in his head. He had a letter of credit on a trader there and one of introduction to the head of the garrison and the ruler of the town He was sure of a good reception and a comfortable night's rest. Both of these he received before going to visit the first cataract, just above the town (no longer there due to the construction of the dam). After five days they began their return up the Nile towards Cus where they would strike out across the desert for the Red Sea and Abyssinia. It would be more than three years before Bruce saw Aswan again and it would be in markedly different circumstances. At Cus, he made his final preparations.

As I was now about to enter on that part of my expedition, in which I was to have no further intercourse with Europe I set myself to work to examine all my observations, and put my journal in such forwardness by explanations, where needful, that the labours and pains I had hitherto been at, might not be totally lost to the public, if I should perish in the journey I had undertaken, which, from all information I could procure, every day appeared to be more and more desperate. [This journal no longer exists. The Yale Center for British Art owns Bruce's letters, diaries and notebooks and a book which purports to be the journal of his travels. It is, however, transparently something which he transcribed on his return, for the writing is too uniform and it is in far too well-preserved a state to have been the journal that accompanied him on his travels.] Having finished these, at least so far as to make them intelligible to others, I conveyed them to my friends Messrs Julian and Rosa, at Cairo, to remain in their custody till I should return, or news come that I was otherwise disposed of.

On 16 February 1769, well aware of the dangers ahead, Bruce consigned himself to the desert. He had made friends with a group of Turkish pilgrims from Anatolia and an Arab to whom he had given transport up the Nile. The Turks had an odd claim on Bruce for they came from 'a district which they call Caz Dagli, corruptly Caz Dangli, and this the Turks believe was the country from which the English first drew their origin; and, on this account they never fail to claim kindred with the English wherever they meet, especially if they stand in need of their assistance'.

They were all part of a larger caravan but they distrusted their travelling companions, so they made plans with Bruce and his group to protect each other and fight as one if threatened by others in their caravan or by the local Atouni tribe. The Atounis made it their business to set upon and plunder such caravans as theirs. Bruce was to be in charge and all the valuables were put in his immediate baggage:

> I cannot conceal the secret pleasure I had in finding the character of my country so firmly established among nations so distant, enemies to our religion, and strangers to our government. Turks from Mount Taurus, and Arabs from the desert of Libya, thought

themselves unsafe among their own countrymen, but trusted their lives to and their little fortunes implicitly to the direction and word of an Englishman, whom they had never before seen.

Anticipating that he would see no more of his countrymen for some time, Bruce was suffering an attack of the kind of patriotism usually only inspired by the sight of a British consul from behind the bars of a foreign jail. The allies arranged passwords for use during the night, and set off into the desert 'full of terror about the Atouni'.

It was on this eight-day desert crossing that Bruce first succumbed to a temptation which his family would be unable to resist in generations to come: 'On each side of the plain, we found different sorts of marble, twelve kinds of which, I selected and took with me'.

The selection and removal of marbles when in foreign parts was to become something of a tradition among Bruce's descendants, reaching its apogee in his cousin twice removed, the 7th Earl of Elgin. His own interest in marble – though not on such an industrial scale: he only collected small stones – seems almost obsessive. The glowing mountains that punctuate the route to Cosseir are indeed impressive, eight miles of 'dead green, supposed serpentine marble' but Bruce describes them in intricate detail, even for him, from the *verde antico* – 'by far the most beautiful kind I had ever seen', to the 'red marble, in prodigious abundance, but of no great beauty'. It is almost as though he planned to return and start a quarrying enterprise to complement his coal mines.

It was not long before their fears of banditry were realized. An Arab was apprehended trying to steal from Bruce's tent and was beaten to death by his guards before the Scot could intervene. This was an unfortunate incident, the more so because the Arab worked for Sidi Hassan, the caravan leader. Relations only worsened from then on. After much negotiation, the two leaders had a cagey meeting in the desert at which their respective retinues squared off against each other but no blood was spilled: an uneasy truce was called. It was in this atmosphere that, after ten days, they arrived in Cosseir where Bruce wreaked his revenge. He reported Sidi Hassan to the Bey who promised to discipline him.

'Now Shekh,' said Bruce to the Bey, 'I have done everything you
have desired, without ever expecting fee, or reward; the only thing
I now ask you, and it is probably the last, is, that you revenge me
upon this Hassan.'

Before the Bey could take action, however, Hassan was set upon
by the Turks who had allied with Bruce in the desert crossing:

> The whole party drew their swords, and . . . they would have cut
> Sidi Hassan in pieces, but, fortunately for him, the Turks had great
> cloth trousers, like Dutchmen, and could not run, whilst he ran
> very nimbly in his. Several pistols, however, were fired, one of
> which shot him in the back part of the ear; on which he fled for
> refuge to the Bey and we never saw him again.

The fashionably hobbled Turks soon left on the boat that Bruce
was to charter for his journey to Jiddah (Jeddah).

This was not the only drama that occurred in the 'small mud-
walled village' that was their embarkation point on the Red Sea.
Abd-el-gin, one of Bruce's servants, was kidnapped and the
explorer unwisely charged off alone into the desert to negotiate
for his return. 'I had not got above a mile into the sands, when I
began to reflect on the folly of my undertaking. I was going into
the desert among a band of savages, whose only trade was robbery
and murder, where, in all probability, I should be as ill treated as
the man I was attempting to save.'

In a stroke of luck that showed the benefit of his medical training, the kidnappers turned out to be kinsmen of Sheikh Nimmer.
He was able to claim protection and rescue Abd-el-gin with the
noose, as yet untightened, around his neck.

The Bey soon left Cosseir to continue his tour and Bruce, as
the most important person remaining in the town, moved into
the fort. While waiting for the boat which would take him to
Jiddah, Bruce hired a smaller boat and sailed off to investigate the
emerald mountains which, according to Pliny, were supposed to
be in the vicinity. Unsurprisingly, they were not made of emeralds.
It was another unnecessary brush with death. As he described it
in his commonplace book: 'Nothing but a belief of pre-destination
should make a man embark in such vessels they are loaded till
within ten inches of the water's edge after which two planks are

added to the waist of the vessel and over these mats are fixed tarred at the joinings and this is all we have to rely upon to keep out the waves.'

They were on their way back to Cosseir after a peaceful voyage during which they had eaten shellfish and made maps of the rocks along the shore, when a storm blew up. It was soon discovered that the sail was nailed to the mast thus making it impossible to take down. The boat started to heave and was in imminent danger of sinking when the captain gave up and consigned their fate to Allah. Incensed, Bruce raged in fury.

'What I order you is, to keep steady at the helm,' shouted Bruce over the roar of the wind:

> mind the vane on the top of the mast, and steer straight before the wind, for I am resolved to cut that main-sail to pieces, and prevent the mast from going away, and your vessel from sinking to the bottom . . . D—n Sidi e Genowi, you beast, cannot you give me a rational answer? Stand to your helm, look at the vane; keep the vessel straight before the wind, or by the great G—d who sits in heaven . . . I will shoot you dead the first yaw the ship gives, or the first time that you leave the steerage.

With that, he lurched across the boat, having ripped off most of his clothes – in case it became necessary to swim – and tore the mainsail to pieces with a machete. When they eventually made it back to the tiny port at Cosseir, they discovered that three boats from that village alone had been lost that day.

On 5 April they were able to set sail for Jiddah in the boat which Bruce had previously chartered. This had canvas sails which could be furled and 'though small – was tight and well-rigged'. The ship's captain was experienced and trustworthy though he had an uncanny likeness to an ape, which Bruce found endlessly amusing. He was indeed known by everyone as Ali the Ape. Not one to go on a leisurely cruise when there was work to be done, Bruce decided that he must chart the Red Sea while he was there and hence spent much of his time taking measurements and hurling plummets over the side of the boat. Marine navigation was not some-thing he had studied, yet his chart of the Red Sea was used and valued for many years afterwards. Owing to the plethora of treacherous reefs in the narrow sea, it had previously been impossible for larger boats to travel its entire length. Combined with a treaty with the Bey of Cairo which he managed to forge on his way home, Bruce's soundings changed all that. He also made an exhaustive survey of where drinking water could be procured, where it was safe to land and which languages were spoken at which ports.

In his *Original Portraits*, first published forty years after Bruce's death, John Kay gave an example of how thoroughly Bruce had done the job: 'Sir David Baird,' he reported, 'while commanding the British troops in the Red Sea, publicly declared that the safety of the army was mainly owing to the striking accuracy of Mr Bruce's chart.'

Baird was a great popular hero who had been captured by Tipoo Sahib in India in 1780 and held captive for four years when he was in his early twenties. In 1801, by then promoted to general and knighted, he led a relief force from the Indian army to help in the removal of Napoleon from Egypt. He sailed up the Red Sea, using Bruce's chart, marched from Cosseir, using Bruce's map, and then sailed down the Nile – arriving in Alexandria with plenty of time left to assist in its capture.

The Red Sea inspired Bruce in many a way, yet though he succeeded in much that he set out to do there a few of his ambitions proved too challenging. He did chart the sea and open it up to British trade but failed in his desire to solve the riddles of the Bible and the classical writers. He had tracked down and rejected the emerald mountains; he now set himself the formidable task of discovering how Moses parted the sea when being pursued by the Egyptians: 'If the Etesian wind, blowing from the north-west in summer, could heap up the sea as a wall, on the right, or to the south, of fifty feet high, still the difficulty would remain, of building the wall on the left hand, or the north. Besides, water standing in that position for a day, must have lost the nature of fluid.'

After much time spent in these bizarre musings he eventually came to a conclusion he deemed satisfactory:

This passage is told us, by scripture, to be a miraculous one; and, if so, we have nothing to do with natural causes. If we do not

believe Moses, we need not believe the transaction at all, seeing
that it is from his authority alone we derive it. If we believe in
God that he made the sea, we must believe he could divide it
when he sees proper reason, and of that he must be the only judge.

The captain of the ship had various cargoes which needed collecting and depositing around the Red Sea so Bruce received a
guided tour on his way down to Jiddah. He stopped off in Yambo,
where the inhabitants were engaged in civil war and where he
watched a savage battle which halted only because of a lack of
ammunition, and he stretched his legs on islands whose wildlife
he decimated in order to vary the constant diet of fish. The voyage
gave him time to prepare his mind for Abyssinia and to ponder
which towns corresponded with the ones he had read about in
the works of the geographers Herodotus and Cosmas Indicoplustes.
It was 3 May before they 'anchored in the port of Jidda, close up
on the key, where the officers of the custom-house immediately
took possession of our baggage'.

When Bruce had set off to Cosseir across the desert he had been
excited by the fact that it was the last of civilization he would see
for some time. He had forgotten about Jiddah where British ships
from India came to trade with Arabia. They could go no further
thanks to insufficient treaties and the treachery of the waters but
they were firmly ensconced at the Red Sea port. There was a
factory and a small community of British working for the East
India Company who had to loiter there in between journeys,
waiting for the monsoon trade winds to turn to their advantage.
There were nine British merchantmen at anchor when Bruce
arrived and paid negotiators were busy making deals in a manner
which fascinated him:

> They sit down on the carpet, and take an Indian shawl, which
> they carry on their shoulder, like a napkin, and spread it over their
> hands. They talk, in the meantime, indifferent conversation, of the
> arrival of ships from India, or the news of the day, as if they were
> employed in no serious business whatever. After about twenty
> minutes spent in handling each other's fingers below the shawl,
> the bargain is concluded, say for nine ships, without one word ever
> having been spoken on the subject, or pen or ink used in any shape

whatever. There never was one instance of a dispute happening in these sales.

As a show of good manners as well as a way to ease his passage, Bruce always wore a native costume, usually that of a nobleman. When he went to the Bengal-house to meet his compatriots, however, he was dressed as a Turkish mariner.

> I desired to be carried to a Scotchman, a relation of my own, who was then accidentally leaning over the rail of the staircase, leading up to his apartment. I saluted him by his name; he fell into a violent rage, calling me villain, thief, cheat and renegade rascal; and declared, if I offered to proceed a step further, he would throw me over the stairs.

Bruce's disguise was obviously more effective, considering his size and manner, than one might otherwise have thought. The surly captain and relation was later claimed by James Boswell to be their mutual cousin, Bruce Boswell. He is not named in Bruce's *Travels* but, for some unfathomable reason, Boswell made this assertion in an article about his adventurous countryman that he wrote for the *London Magazine*. Bruce Boswell was indeed the kind of man to behave in such a manner. He was a famously appalling captain and was later cashiered before being accepted back as a trader after his influential cousin had interceded with the board in London. He was at this time only twenty – too young to be a captain – and according to well-kept East India Company records, employed in China. Whoever the man was, he did not give Bruce the reception he had hoped for. The insulted traveller decided to remain incognito and take the measure of the other captains at Jiddah. These captains were a glamorous lot, given to wearing tight, bright breeches, much gold braid and exotically coloured turbans. They adopted the manners of both East and West and were much respected by both. Bruce, however, did not initially warm to them: 'I thought within myself, if those are their Indian manners I shall keep my name and situation to myself while I am at Jidda'.

Still in disguise, he was taken to see another of the East India captains, William Thornhill, who very charitably arranged for his son to find Bruce a hot meal and a bed. Having eaten, Bruce then fell asleep under a tree whilst Thornhill's son went off in search of a room on his behalf. He awoke to find a very nervous Vizier of Jiddah looming over him. Bruce's luggage had been opened at the customs house revealing his collection of firmans and letters from the Sultan, the Sherif of Mecca and all the people who nominally ruled the Red Sea trading centre. This had put the local men into a panic. They realized that the man to whom the letters referred was extremely important, but they could not find him. The only person they could locate was this enormous and grubby servant – sleeping on a mat under a tree. Bruce eventually gave up his disguise and admitted who he was. The vizier asked him therefore, why he was so poorly dressed:

'You cannot ask that seriously' I said 'I believe no prudent man would dress better, considering the voyage I have made. But, besides, you did not leave it in my power, as every article, but what I have on me, has been these four hours at the custom-house, waiting your pleasure.'

'We then went all up to our kind landlord, Captain Thornhill, to whom I made my excuse, on account of the ill usage I had first met with from my own relation. He laughed very heartily at the narrative, and from that time we lived in the greatest friendship and confidence. All was made up and, even with Yousef Cabil [the Vizier]; and all heads were employed to get the strongest letters possible to the Naybe of Masuah, the king of Abyssinia, Michael Suhul the minister, and the king of Sennaar.'

Bruce spent three months at Jiddah, going on long night-time walks with his friends Captains Thornhill and Price. The merchant captains were both friendly and helpful towards him, exerting all their considerable influence upon the ruling Basha and Metical Aga – a former Ethiopian slave – who was the Basha's swordbearer and right-hand man. They eventually surpassed themselves by per-suading the Basha and Metical Aga to write extremely forceful letters to the Naybe of Massawa in which he was ordered, rather than asked, to show Bruce every courtesy. Metical Aga promised to send one of his servants with Bruce as well – 'and I do firmly believe, under Providence, it was to this last measure I owed my life'.

Mahomet Gibberti, the servant chosen to accompany the party, was on another mission for Metical Aga and would not be ready for some time, so Bruce decided to continue his investigation of the Red Sea.

It was on the 8th of July, 1779, I sailed from the harbour of Jidda . . . The wind was fair, and we sailed through the English fleet at their anchors. As they all honoured me with their regret at parting, and accompanied me to the shore, the Rais [the captain] was sur-prised to see the respect paid to his little vessel as it passed under their huge sterns, every one hoisting his colours, and saluting it with eleven guns, except the ship belonging to my Scottish friend, who showed his colours, indeed, but did not fire a gun, only standing upon deck, he cried with a trumpet, 'Captain – wishes Mr Bruce a good voyage.' I stood upon deck, took my trumpet, and answered 'Mr Bruce wishes Captain – a perfect return of his understanding;' a wish, poor man, that has not yet been accom-plished, and very much to my regret, it does not appear probable that ever it will.

This salute to Bruce as his tiny barque scudded across the harbour was a mixed blessing. It filled him with patriotic fervour and instilled him with confidence as he consigned himself to the unknown and it showed all observers that he had powerful friends; but it also gave the impression that he was a rich man and thus a worthy prize. The display of fire power had been seen by the governor of Dahalac island – a vassal of the Naybe of Massawa – who immediately raced across to Massawa and informed the divan of Bruce's imminent arrival: 'The consequence of all this was, the Naybe of Masuah expected that a man with immense treasures was coming to put himself into their hands'.

They spent the rest of July and August sailing up and down the Red Sea, charting everything and taking minute notes on the currents, sand banks and rocks. At the straits of Babelmandel, Bruce made everyone drink a toast to George III since the Indian Ocean was comprised of waves that Britannia ruled and he had not seen a British regulated wave for a long time. They were in constant fear of piracy on the high seas and also had to be very careful where they landed, for the inhabitants of the coast were famous for ambushing unwary sailors. A terrible incident had occurred a few years earlier when a British ship, the *Elgin*, had been destroyed and its company enslaved or killed. None the less, they took constant risks since they were forced to keep stopping for fresh water, and Bruce had an obsessive need to see a frankincense tree since one had never before been described or painted. Having succeeded in cataloguing an incense tree, Bruce returned to Loheia and met up with Mahomet Gibberti. A few days later they embarked on the 400 mile journey to Massawa and into the unknown.

Bruce had felt obliged to give about forty people transport in his boat and it was therefore a large company that made its slow progress across the sea, stopping at islands along the way to acquire drinking water and food. Bruce spent his days investigating the islands and harpooning sharks, impatient to be in Abyssinia. One of the passengers died of fever en route, which led to a great deal of fear and trepidation as the others decided that there was now a ghost on board. It was the physical world, however, that nearly brought the journey to an untimely end. On their twelfth day out, they hit a coral reef and were stuck solid, in danger of being smashed to pieces when the wind blew up. 'The Arab sailors were immediately for taking the boat [a small dinghy], and sailing to the islands the boy had seen. The Abyssinians were for cutting up the planks and wood of the inside of the vessel, and making her a raft.'

Bruce managed to assert his authority over the mutinous rabble and soon they were underway again, saved by the fact that the boat was sewn together with rope rather than nailed. The former method ensures that boats absorb shocks and spring repairable leaks when they hit sharp coral; those that are nailed quickly split apart and are hard to repair at sea. Yasine, a Moor to whom Bruce had given a berth, proved himself to the Scot by helping lever the boat off the coral when everyone else was panicking. It was the start of one of Bruce's firmest friendships in Abyssinia. On 19 September they caught their first glimpse of Massawa, a minaret on a small island that would be their home as well as their prison for some time to come.

CHAPTER 4

INTO THE UNKNOWN

Bruce dropped anchor at Massawa, the gateway to Abyssinia, a mere seven years and three months after setting off from England. He had grown in mind and body in the intervening years and by then had the strength and the necessary knowledge to reach his goal. Now all he needed was luck. The ramshackle island had once been an important port but, by the time Bruce arrived, it had long ago lost the bustle of its former days. The tatty mud-brick houses and shacks that lined the shore housed a people who lived off tax from the meagre passing trade and waited to prey on others' misfortunes rather than producing anything themselves. The arrival of a wealthy Westerner travelling with a large retinue of servants and many trunks filled with bizarre equipment soon shook them from their stupor.

Massawa was merely a toll Bruce had to pass on the way to his destination – Abyssinia – a country whose existence had been acknowledged for centuries yet was almost completely unknown. Ethiopia – as a civilization – has appeared in art and literature since the earliest of times. It is very difficult, however, to determine precisely when it emerged because of the wild diversity of names used to describe it. The Ethiopians themselves claim that theirs was a thriving kingdom when the Queen of Sheba set off from Axum, their early capital, to visit King Solomon in Jerusalem and that the product of this union was Menelik, the first Emperor of Ethiopia. Haile Selassie, say the Ethiopians, was a direct descendant of Sheba and Solomon. The Yemenis, however, disagree, claiming Sheba as their own. Suffice it to say that Ethiopia's is an extraordinarily old and sophisticated civilization.

A still-standing temple at Yeha and the monolothic obelisks at Axum in the highlands are thought by some to be as old as the fifth century BC. Both sites show many similarities with Yemeni structures of the period: this was no coincidence. Some theorists say that early Ethiopia was colonized by Yemenis, others vice versa. Certainly, the people of both countries have been related since pre-Christian times. In the five centuries before and after the birth of Christ, a powerful empire grew up around Axum which traded all over the Red Sea and Indian Ocean, built massive palaces and was then destroyed. In the fifth century AD Yemen was a colony of the Axumite empire and administered by the emperor's younger son. The two countries are also related by their early language – Sabaean – but despite its pre-Yemeni name, who gave the language to whom is a point of contention still.

The Axumite empire – which became Christian four years before the baptism of Constantine in the year 333 – gradually shrunk until the ninth century when the great queen of the Jewish Falashas rose up and all but destroyed it. (Falasha means 'exile'. Much of the previously Jewish and animist population became Christian after the emperor was converted by two boys from Tyre who were shipwrecked on the coast. The Falashas call themselves 'Beta Israel' – the House of Israel.) Judith ravaged the land, burning churches and harrying the Axumite emperors out of their own country. This departure led to a new dynasty being founded – the Zagwes. For a few hundred years they ruled the diminished empire from the inaccessible mountains of Lasta. In 1270, the last Zagwe, Naakuto Laab, abdicated and returned the throne to the Solomonid dynasty which had managed to survive in Shoa on the southern fringes of the empire. They were left undisturbed by all but themselves (there was near constant civil war) until the arrival of Ahmed al-Ghazi who finished off the work that Judith had started.

It is due to these two magnificent warriors that we know so little of Ethiopia for they wreaked such destruction upon the country that almost no records survived. Al-Ghazi, known as Mohammed Gragn (which means the left-handed) was a Somali from Harar who launched a jihad against the Christian highlands and waged it for well over a decade. In the dry season he would invade, in the rainy he would re-arm and regroup. He was eventually destroyed by the arrival of the Portuguese who stabilized the country and then proceeded to destabilize it by trying to convert the already Christian people to Catholicism. They in turn were thrown out and between 1632 and Bruce's arrival in 1769 the country had almost no contact with the outside world. Protected by its geographical inaccessibility and a violent distrust of foreigners, the country rejoiced in its religious freedom and its solitary independence: 'The monophysite churches resounded with a song of triumph', according to Gibbon, '"that the sheep of Aethiopia were now delivered from the hyaenas of the west" and the gates of that solitary realm were for ever shut against the arts, the science and the fanaticism of Europe.'

Thus when Bruce arrived at Massawa almost all that was known of Abyssinia was its coast line; the few vague maps that existed were zealously guarded by the Jesuits and the ones that were published were useless. When Joseph Conrad was drawn to Africa over a century later, the attraction was still the 'exciting spaces of white paper . . . The heart of Africa was white and big'. Bruce's first task was to get up from the coast and into the wondrous ancient land of Abyssinia, in itself a nigh on insurmountable task.

As soon as he stepped off the boat his life was in jeopardy and it was only a combination of careful planning and good fortune that was to save him. Throughout his travels he had constantly solicited firmans, passports and letters of introduction. For Massawa, he carried many letters to the ruling Naybe; in addition he spoke French, Italian, Portuguese, Greek (modern and ancient), Latin, Hebrew, Chaldean, Syriac, Geez, Amharic and Arabic. Sadly Arabic was the only one of any use in Massawa. He had learned Tigrinya – the current language of the Abyssinian court – as best he could but had not yet fully mastered it. Armed only with this astonishing array of linguistic skills, he was going to places that no European had visited for a very long time; the only thing that he knew for certain was that he would be unwelcome.

The situation of the country was barely known, no more; in parts surrounded by impenetrable forests, where from the beginning, the beasts had established a sovereignty uninterrupted by man; in part by vast deserts of moving sands, where nothing was to be found that had the breath of life; these terrible barriers enclosed men more bloody and ferocious than the beasts themselves, and more fatal to travellers than the sands that encompassed them; and, thus shut up, they had been growing every day more barbarous, and defied, by rendering it dangerous, the curiosity of travellers of every nation.

Massawa was a perfect example of the complications of travel in the eighteenth century; only a few hundred yards from the coast of Abyssinia, the tiny island came under the jurisdiction of the Turkish Sublime Porte (it is now connected to the mainland by a causeway built by the Swiss former governor of Eritrea, Werner Muntzinger). Bruce had a firman from the Grand Signor and from the Basha of Jiddah under whose administration the island fell. Metical Aga, the former Abyssinian slave, had interests in Massawa and from him Bruce had not only letters of recommendation but also the servant who had delayed their voyage – Mahomet Gibberti. None of these precautions did him any good. Instead, it was the kindness of strangers and Bruce's kindness *to* strangers that finally prevailed.

On the first night, before disembarking, Bruce managed to send messages to Janni, a Greek merchant who lived inland at Adowa, announcing his arrival and asking for assistance. So when, on 20 September, he was escorted ashore he was not overly worried. His main cause for anxiety would have been the imposing mountains that can be seen from the coast. The Naybe was at Arkeeko on the mainland, therefore Bruce was met by Achmet, his nephew, whom Bruce had been told was more trustworthy than most in the tiny principality.

Achmet was about twenty-five years of age, or perhaps younger; his stature near five feet four; he was feebly made, a little bent forwards or stooping, thin, long-faced, long-necked; small, but tolerably well-limbed, agile and active enough in his motions, though of a figure by no means athletic. He had a broad forehead, thick black eye-brows, black eyes, an aquiline nose, thin lips and fine teeth; and, what is very rare in this country, and much desired, a thick-curled beard.

Achmet passed all Bruce's baggage without searching it and installed him in a small house where he was given food and drink from Achmet's own table. Bruce – who had planned ahead – gave the young heir to the island a pair of English pistols (the same gift with which he had bribed Metical Aga – he travelled with a formidable arsenal) which he had been told in Jiddah were something Achmet particularly coveted but had been unable to buy. All looked promising, but later that evening Achmet arrived for a meeting and told Bruce of the consternation his arrival had caused. The normal practice, it seemed, with unannounced visitors to Massawa was to murder them and share the spoils. This was a policy fully supported by the Abyssinians; if Massawa was the gateway to their world, they wished to keep it firmly barred.

The Ethiopians had tired of visitors by the time they had thrown out the last of the Catholic Portuguese in 1632 and since then had paid successive Naybes to discourage visitors. Anyone who had succeeded in entering the empire by other routes had not been permitted to leave. Bruce was still alive only by a stroke of luck: the governor of Dahalac island had seen the grand salute which had been given to Bruce's small boat when it had left Jiddah and had sped back to Massawa to inform the divan with gushing hyperbole that a relation of the English king was on the way. Fearing an onslaught from the British ships at Jiddah, and encouraged in this by Achmet's kindly sentiments, the Naybe had therefore decided to mull matters over before doing anything rash.

Bruce saw his opportunity to influence the divan and once more traded on his lineage for his life: 'My ancestors were the kings of the country in which I was born,' he told Achmet on that first evening, 'and to be ranked among the greatest and most glorious that ever bore the crown and title of king.'

Regardless of his staunch Hanoverian tendencies, this boast was to become a favourite with Bruce though it was probably the implied but entirely unfounded threat of English retaliation that truly gave him authority. He blustered to his friend in the hopes that Achmet would pass on the dangers of meddling with the Englishman to the divan. 'This little sea would be too narrow for their [England's] ships; Your sun now so hot would be darkened by their sails; and when they fired their terrible wide-mouthed cannons, not an Arab would think himself safe on the distant mountains.'

After two days of confusion Bruce was at last allowed to meet the Naybe. Achmet seemed to have disappeared and Bruce was becoming worried. He was concerned that his only ally might have succumbed to smallpox.

> The inhabitants of Masuah were dying of the small-pox, so that there was fear the living would not be sufficient to bury the dead. The whole island was filled with shrieks and lamentations both night and day. They at last began to throw the bodies into the sea which deprived us of our great support, fish, of which we ate some kinds that were excellent. I had suppressed my character as physician fearing I should be detained by reason of the multitude of sick.

No one would tell him where Achmet was. His reception by the Naybe hardly helped since they disliked each other on sight. The Naybe was 'very tall and lean'. Bruce remarked,

> his colour black; had a large mouth and nose; in place of a beard, a very scanty tuft of grey hairs upon the point of his chin; large, dull, and heavy eyes; a kind of malicious, contemptuous, smile on his countenance; he was altogether of the most stupid and brutal appearance. His character perfectly corresponded with his figure, for he was a man of mean abilities, cruel to excess, avaricious, and a great drunkard.

The Naybe treated Bruce's letters and firmans with contempt and demanded gold which Bruce refused to give him; it was not long before their relationship descended into outright hostility. Soon after the meeting, Bruce's house was threatened but he marshalled his men and scared off the raiders with a display of fire power. They discharged their guns through gaps in the gate and won themselves a peaceful night. Having made no progress with the potentate, Bruce despaired that he would ever enter Ethiopia. The Naybe was furious not only because Bruce would not pay him but also because, when half the island was suffering from smallpox, he had disguised the fact that he was a physician. Moreover, the Sardar of the Janissaries, a man to whom Bruce was recommended by the Sardar of the Sublime Porte, had taken against him too. The whole divan, bar the mysteriously absent Achmet, wanted to see him killed, and all conspired to catch him off guard. 'These wretches,' Bruce bewailed, 'possess talents for tormenting and alarming, far beyond the power of belief.' Things were looking black, and on 15 October the Naybe brought the matter to a head. 'At last he peremptorily told me, that unless I had three hundred ounces of gold ready to pay him on Monday, upon his landing from Arkeeko, he would confine me in a dungeon, without light, air or meat, till the bones came through my skin for want.'

It was only because Achmet had publicly guaranteed Bruce protection that the Scot was saved from an untimely death. At one point he was nearly stabbed for defying the Naybe. A murderous henchman reached for a knife and threatened to kill him but was physically prevented from doing so by the head of the Janissaries. 'Achmet is the stranger's friend,' he said, 'and recommended me to-day to see no injury done him; he is ill, or would have been here himself.'

Dispirited and uncomfortable in the shattering heat of the Eritrean coast, Bruce whiled away the days fishing for and eating the local fish (a practice he had had to stop when the Massawans began to dump their mounting dead in the sea off the island), watching the stars (a comet was in transit at the time) and brushing up his Tigrinya. Most of all though he would have been hot, and heat was a subject on which he felt strongly:

> I call it *hot*, when a man sweats at rest, and excessively on moderate motion. I call it *very hot*, when a man, with thin or little clothing, sweats much, though at rest. I call it *excessively hot*, when a man, in his shirt, at rest, sweats excessively, when all motion is painful, and when the knees feel feeble as if after a fever. I call it *extreme hot*, when the strength fails, a disposition to faint comes on, a straitness is found in the temples, as if a small cord was drawn tight around the head, the voice impaired, the skin dry, and the head seems more than ordinarily large and light. This I apprehend denotes death at hand.

Massawa is 'excessive hot' most of the time and 'extreme hot' at others. The only relief to be found is by wallowing in the Red

Sea. The deep water in the port was awash with the corpses of smallpox victims so Bruce would have had to go to the beach to seek solace. The beach, however, is very flat, so having marched through the seaweed to some deep, cool water Bruce would then have been forced to wade back through the near boiling shallows in order to recover the shade.

During Achmet's sickness Bruce was stopped from seeing his only ally by the Naybe, who had ordered that no boatmen were allowed to take him to Achmet's home on the mainland; there was no news from Janni at Adowa, to whom Bruce had sent a letter, and every day the Naybe became more audacious in his insults. Achmet was powerful enough to protect Bruce from his sick-bed but most of this was done without Bruce being aware of it, thus leaving him with a sense of abandonment. Eventually, after weeks of inactivity, Bruce managed to visit Achmet and was promptly able to cure him of what was obviously not smallpox. After two apprehensive months being driven witless by the mind-numbing heat, relief came in the form of messengers from the emperor, Ras Michael (the governor of Tigre) and Janni of Adowa. Janni, having received the letters which Bruce had sent on his arrival at Massawa, had anticipated problems and solicited letters from the Emperor and Ras Michael in which it was demanded that the king's physician be allowed to pass into Abyssinia immediately. 'We left Masuah [Massawa] the 10th of November,' says Bruce, 'with the soldiers and boats belonging to Achmet. We had likewise three servants from Abyssinia, and no longer apprehended the Naybe, who seemed, on his part, to think no more of us.'

He spoke too soon. The Naybe had not yet finished with him. The tyrant still wanted money for allowing Bruce to pass but was put off by the Emperor's messenger who said that he should ask for all he wanted and present his bill to Ras Michael when next they met. This stymied the Naybe, who was terrified of Michael. He was left with only one course of action – to lie about the road ahead. A false messenger was produced who brought news of revolution in the region through which Bruce would have to pass. Bruce, however, was immediately able to demonstrate that this was not true, having received intelligence only that morning that the way was clear. Finally, after two months of anguish, the Naybe had run out of ways to detain his visitor. For the fifth time, on 15 November, Bruce struck his camp and attempted to set off for the imperial capital of Gondar. His one last problem was overcome when Achmet gave him a trustworthy guide to take them on a tortuous route to Tigre.

'You will be apt to curse me,' explained Achmet when, recovered as a result of Bruce's ministrations, he came to say goodbye,

> when you are toiling and sweating ascending Taranta, the highest mountain in Abyssinia, and on this account worthy your notice. You are then to consider if the fatigue of body you shall suffer in that passage is not overpaid by the absolute safety you will find yourselves in. Dobarwa belongs to the Naybe; and I cannot answer for the orders he may have given to his own servants; but Dixan is mine, although the people are much worse than those of Dobarwa. I have written to my officers there; they will behave the better to you for this; and as you are strong and robust, the best I can do for you is to send you by a rugged road, and a safe one.

'I look . . . upon the danger I escaped there as superior to all those put together that I have ever been exposed too,' claimed Bruce afterwards. This was an exaggeration since there were elements of this experience in almost every border crossing he made but it was with tremendous relief that he ventured inland.

He ultimately began his journey into the medieval, feudal world of Abyssinia on 17 November. After eight weeks on the coast he approached the task with gusto. Rather than instilling fear in him, the towering mountains of Eritrea had become a challenge. Bruce was heading into the unknown through country whose inhabitants had already shown themselves to be less than genial hosts. He was, however, quite aware of some of the potential difficulties. They were hard to miss. From Laberhey on the narrow coastal plain, he looked forward and upwards:

> The mountains of Abyssinia have a singular aspect from this, as they appear in three ridges. The first is of no considerable height, but full of gullies and broken ground, thinly covered with shrubs; the second, higher and steeper, still more rugged and bare; the third is a row of sharp, uneven edged mountains, which would be

counted high in any country in Europe. Far above the top of all, towers that stupendous mass, the mountain of Taranta, I suppose one of the highest in the world, the point of which is buried in the clouds, and very rarely seen but in the clearest weather; at other times abandoned to perpetual mist and darkness, the seat of lightning, thunder, and of storm.

Reading Bruce's *Travels*, one has the impression that he is striding through the unexplored interior of Africa with very little in the way of companionship. He is always attended by servants, guides and porters and does nothing to disguise the fact, but it is easy to forget that at least three of the party were European. Luigi Balugani – the artist he took along in much the same way as the modern explorer takes a film crew, or his nineteenth-century counterpart a taxidermist – hardly rates a mention in the book. Bruce was to claim many of Balugani's paintings as his own, so he presumably wanted to advertise his presence as little as possible. To Bruce, Balugani, genius though he was, was a servant, and Bruce felt free to disregard him. Bruce was Balugani's patron, not his friend. In the caravan there were also the two Irishmen given him as slaves by the Dey of Algiers. The Irish were not as sophisticated as the French and British but these two former soldiers would at least have afforded Bruce some conversation on the long marches across Ethiopia's mountain fastness. It is never said whether either survived the journey. On this stage of the march, he also had with him a party of Muslim traders and Yasine, the Moor.

It was therefore a substantial and extremely well-armed company that was ascending into the mountains. Bruce owned two ships' blunderbusses as well as rifles, shotguns and pistols which far outshone any of the primitive firearms then being used in Abyssinia. On the whole, this was a country where battles were fought with lances, swords and other such rudimentary weapons. Power was in the hands of the one man who had access to firearms – through Massawa – and they were of far inferior quality to Bruce's. The Moorish traders would not have been taking the risk of travelling with a Frank (the Ethiopian term for all Europeans since their first contact with the West) unless his was an extremely powerful fighting force. In a country where white men were hated, it would have been foolish to do so, no matter how many letters to emperors and firmans from sultans he was carrying.

Since on Achmet's advice they were travelling by a devious route, there were no paths to follow. Within a couple of days they were reduced to scrambling through dried-up river beds, a dangerous practice in Africa where flash floods can appear in seconds.

> The river scarcely ran at our passing it; when, all on a sudden, we heard a noise on the mountains above, louder than the loudest thunder. Our guides, upon this, flew to the baggage, and removed it to the top of the green hill; which was no sooner done, than we saw the river coming down in a stream about the height of a man, and the breadth of the whole bed it used to occupy.

They continued on, starting before dawn and resting during the heat of the day before battling on again in the afternoon. The going was rough wherever they happened to be: 'for some time our road lay through a plain, so thick set with acacia-trees, that our hands and faces were all torn and bloody with the strokes of their thorny branches'. But, there were some consolations. On the fourth day they drank their first fresh water since leaving Syria. Taranta was still ahead of them and, when at length they reached it, they immediately encountered problems. 'It was with great difficulty we could creep up, each man carrying his knapsack and arms; but it seemed beyond the possibility of human strength to carry our baggage and instruments.'

The quadrant, which required eight men in two shifts to carry, almost caused a revolt which Bruce promptly quashed in typical fashion.

> At last, as I was incomparably the strongest of the company, as well as the most interested, I, and a stranger Moor [Yasine], who had followed us, carried the head of it for about 400 yards over the most difficult and steepest part of the mountain, which before had been considered as impracticable by all . . . our hands and knees were all cut, mangled, and bleeding, with sliding down and clambering over the sharp points of rocks; our clothes torn to pieces.

This took so long that they had to spend the night halfway up the mountain, shivering with the sudden cold that comes with dusk. Mules were lost and recovered and Bruce kindly offered to pay for a mule belonging to one of the Arabs that had been injured during the night by a hyena, an act of charity that was to prove very advantageous. In the morning he was forced to increase everyone's wages and chivvy them with kind words before they would attempt the rest of Taranta. It was another difficult day.

> Our knees and hands, however, were cut to pieces by frequent falls, and our faces torn by the multitude of thorny bushes. I twenty times now thought of what Achmet had told me at parting, that I should curse him for the bad road shewn to me over Taranta; but bless him for the quiet and safety attending me in that passage.

At last they reached the summit, where Bruce discovered that the mountain was an amba – the Ethiopian name for their ubiquitous flat-topped mountains – and home to a tribe of shepherds. They passed another freezing night there and reached the town of Dixan in the afternoon of 22 November. Lying between the Naybe's territory and that of Abyssinia, it was a place whose only trade seemed to be in children:

> The Christians bring such as they have stolen in Abyssinia to Dixan, as to a sure deposit; and the Moors receive them there, and carry them to a certain market at Masuah, whence they are sent over to Arabia or India. The priests of the province of Tigre, especially those near the rock Damo, are openly concerned in this infamous practise.

(Nearby Debra Damo is a monastery and to this day one of Ethiopia's most revered places of pilgrimage. Accessible only by climbing a rope up a cliff at the top of a very steep mountain, it has survived intact since its founding in the fifth century. It has been stormed once through trickery but the buildings survive.)

By charging duty on the slave trade, Ras Michael had been able to supply himself with the firearms that insured his hold on power. After three days of argument with the Naybe's guides and customs officers over wages and duty, the party at last moved on and spent their first night on Ethiopian soil, under a daroo tree that provided the marker between the two administrations.

'We remained under this tree the night of the 25th; it will be to me a station ever memorable, as the first where I recovered a portion of that tranquillity of mind to which I had been a stranger ever since my arrival at Masuah.'

Having survived the attentions of the rapacious Naybe of Massawa, Bruce and his party now moved into really dangerous territory. For nigh on fifty years, a wily and brilliant general had been imposing his will upon his compatriots and Bruce was just about to enter his heartland: Tigre. Michael Suhul had first risen to national prominence in the reign of Bacuffa the Inexorable a quarter of a century earlier. As governor of Adowa, but not yet Ras of Tigre (a title in the gift of the king, similar to prime minister but which also held aristocratic connotations akin to a dukedom), Michael controlled all Abyssinia's access to the coast. He fomented rebellion against the king (by this time Yasous II), and by surrendering at the judicious moment, improved his position and thus gained his title. 'His course after that was stained with every pollution of treason and murder.'

For the next twenty-five years he had been the power behind the throne and never more so than at the present. But by achieving such influence for himself, he had considerably weakened the empire. Hannes II had been enthroned in the capital Gondar by Michael, who had arranged the assassination of his predecessor. By the time Bruce arrived, Michael had poisoned Hannes too and seen crowned a fifteen-year-old boy – Tecla Haimanout II.

There was always a choice of heirs to the throne of Abyssinia because of the old policy of imprisoning all princes of the royal blood in a mountain-top prison in order to prevent them rebelling against the king. A number of mountains were used throughout Abyssinian history and the present one was within Michael's domains. These were the mountains of Rasselas which provided the inspiration for Samuel Johnson's book of the same name. He portrayed them as happy, though dull, places laden with luxury. They were in fact no fun at all, although imprisonment was preferable to the fratricide favoured by the Ottomans and the Fung –

'In Abyssinia, the princes are confined for life on a mountain, and in Sennaar they are murdered in their father's sight, in the palace where they were born.'

The inadvertent result of these changes was a greater autonomy for the provinces. Tecla Haimanout was – in name – Emperor of Abyssinia and King of Kings, but the machinations of his prime minister Michael meant that the Kings of which he was King no longer looked to him for approval. The King of Shoa – ostensibly one of Tecla Haimanout's subjects governed an entirely indepen dent kingdom, if not in opposition to, then very much uncon- cerned with the goings-on at Gondar. Fasil, the hereditary governor of Damot further south, oversaw his own private fief- dom, supported by the pagan Galla, who though worse soldiers were equally as brave as Michael's Tigreans. It was Fasil who was now at war with Michael. Fasil's enemies both feared and admired him. One of Michael's generals described him to Bruce as, 'perfect a Galla as ever forded the Nile; he has neither word, nor oath, nor faith that can bind him; he does mischief for mischief's sake, and then laughs at it'. Both the leaders claimed allegiance to Tecla Haimanout but it was Michael who had the king in his thrall and was therefore able to fight with the legitimacy of the royal standard at his side.

It was into the midst of this war that Bruce was about to wander as he emerged from the shade of the daroo tree on the morning of 26 November. He 'set forward with great alacrity' into the territory of the Baharnagash, a vassal of Ras Michael's whose job it was to exact duty on Michael's behalf from all who passed through his province. The party was soon intercepted by the Baharnagash himself who had taken over the post when Michael had imprisoned the former incumbent, his brother. He was an unprepossessing figure but, as he accompanied Bruce through his region, the pair became friends. The Baharnagash decided that Bruce would not have to pay any duty on his baggage and Bruce rewarded him by buying from him a black horse.

We called the horse Mirza, a name of good fortune. Indeed, I might say, I acquired that day a companion that contributed always to my pleasure, and more than once to my safety; and was no slender means of acquiring me the first attention of the king. I had brought my Arab stirrups, saddle, and bridle, with me, so that I was now as well equipped as a horseman could be.

The Baharnagash provided pleasant food and companionship as Bruce travelled through the area, one of the few consistently flat lands that the explorer traversed. They walked through fields of teff (a grain from which Ethiopians make their staple injera bread), barley and wheat in the highly populated little region, unassailed by clawing acacias and threatening peaks. By night the two got drunk together on the local mead, an innocuous looking drink that resembles passion fruit juice but leaves you with a hangover that makes it almost impossible to function. It is used as a kind of disinfectant to this day: if you drink enough *tej*, together with chilli peppers, it kills the bugs in the raw meat of which the Ethiopians are so fond. 'I had gained the Baharnagash's heart so entirely, that it was not possible to get away the next day . . . For my part, the share I had taken yesterday of his hydromel had given me such a pain in my head that I scarce could raise it the whole day.'

When they entered Tigre itself, they were expected to pay tolls at many of the villages through which they passed and this became an increasingly difficult task. Like many European explorers, Bruce used beads to trade with the natives. He was confounded, however, when he discovered that his supplier had given him unfashionable colours. It was then that his (entirely selfish) policy of being kind to strangers saved the day. The trader whose baggage Bruce had ordered to be carried after the unfortunate demise of his mule on Taranta was the only one of the party to have suitable beads, brought from Murano in Venice. (They are less fashionable today; thus rapacious Westerners can buy them back to sell at vast profits in Europe.) He called Yasine over and his obligation to Bruce was paid – he 'gave him a large package, which he imprudently opened, in which was a treasure of all the beads in fashion'. The 'imprudent opening' nearly started a riot. Eventually they were able to move on, though not before Bruce had impudently opened the subject of paying for sex. He received his first education in Ethiopian sexual mores, to which he paid full attention and absorbed:

There were three of them [village girls] the most distinguished for beauty and for tongue, who, by their discourse, had entertained me greatly. I made each of them a present of a few beads, and asked them how many kisses they would give for each? They answered very readily, with one accord. 'Poh! we don't sell kisses in this country: Who would buy them? We will give you as many as you wish for nothing.' And there was no appearance but, in that bargain, they meant to be very fair and liberal dealers.

Sexual freedom was not so frowned upon in Bruce's times as it became in the Victorian era and is mentioned with only a little coyness. Two years earlier, Captain Wallis of the good ship *Dolphin* was discovering, and simultaneously introducing venereal disease to, the hapless Tahitians. His fellow sailors (Captain Cook was on the way) continued doing so, and mentioning it in their memoirs, for years. Wallis's ship nearly foundered since the Tahitians traded sex for nails, which in the ensuing shortage the sailors removed from the *Dolphin*'s decks. Reading between the lines of Bruce's *Travels*, it seems quite obvious that he took full advantage of the beauty and accessibility of the many women he encountered on his travels. Indeed he often appears to be at pains to tell the reader how promiscuous he is. Later in his journey Bruce relates being advised of the customs of the land by a Galla chieftain: ' "It is a custom that a stranger of distinction, like you when he is their guest, sleeps with the sister, daughter, or near relation of the principal men among them. I dare say you will not think," ' he adds archly ' "the customs of the Galla contain greater hardships than those of the Amhara." I bowed, but thought to myself, I shall not put them on trial.'

By repeating the advice he showed that he had not been entirely pure in Amhara whilst simultaneously saying that he would try and behave better. He did not.

Having taken his leave of the ladies, he walked on towards Gondar – presumably so lust-befuddled that he walked straight through Yeha, the oldest town in Ethiopia, without noticing that it is overlooked by an enormous temple of the fifth century BC. By now, Bruce was in sight of the mountains that soar above Adowa; truly bizarre in shape, they mirrored the violence of

Ethiopia's society – 'Their sides were all perpendicular rocks, high, like steeples, or obelisks, and broken into a thousand different forms.' For anyone to reach Gondar it was essential to cross these mountains and hence pass through Adowa, as it is today. Much of Ras Michael's strength derived from the fact that Adowa was his home. Though a small town of only 300 houses with none of the spiritual significance of nearby Axum, it was and is of overwhelming tactical significance. It is no coincidence that today it is the constituency of the Tigrean prime minister of Ethiopia.

Bruce found the town at once a joy and a shock. A joy, because it was home to Janni, Ras Michael's customs man, who had already proved himself a dependable friend of the traveller, and a shock because it was also where Ras Michael imprisoned his political enemies:

> His [Michael's] mansion-house is not distinguished from any of the others in the town unless by its size; it is situated upon the top of the hill. The person, who is Michael's deputy, in his absence lives in it. It resembles a prison rather than a palace; for there are, in and about it, above three hundred persons in irons, some of whom have been there for twenty years . . . most of them are kept in cages like wild beasts, and treated every way in the same manner.

Janni was horrified that Bruce had been so badly treated by the Naybe and straightaway started to make amends. Bruce – in paroxysms of embarrassment – had to hop about in the garden on his bleeding feet, which had been injured en route, in order to prevent the obsequious Greek (who chased him with a towel) from washing his feet. The letter which Bruce had sent from Massawa had a far better effect than the ones he had presented to the Naybe. This missive proved very useful whenever he came into contact with the Greeks (currently enslaved at home by the Turks), who were traders and administered all commerce in Ethiopia, for it was from their spiritual leader, the Patriarch of Alexandria, and it demanded that Bruce be given all possible help. In Gondar, its effect was to prove positively electrifying. In the meantime, Bruce was a little alarmed by Janni's behaviour, since he wanted him as a friend and felt under an obligation to him already:

'It was long before I cured my kind landlord of these respectful observances, which troubled me very much.'

Bruce spent more than a month in the environs of Adowa and claims to have occupied himself by visiting the ruined Jesuit monastery at Fremona, and in both his notebook and the *Travels* discusses the inaccuracies of Jesuitical writing about Ethiopia. There was, however, very little to see there and even less to do. He suggests that the road to Gondar was blocked by a rampant warlord but it must still have been so when he eventually left. He had no need to linger for so long, and the reason why he did is the second great mystery of the book and indeed of Bruce's life.

CHAPTER 5

ALL POINTS QUEST

Only a few miles from Adowa lies Axum, the ancient capital of Abyssinia, a town whose unique importance Bruce scarcely mentions to his readers. It is a baffling omission: Axum is integral to almost every part of Ethiopian life – its religion, its monarchy and its traditions. It has been since at least the fifth century BC, it still is and doubtless it always will be. There are two particularly significant things about the town. First and most obviously, it is dominated by a collection of timeworn stelae (obelisks) which mark its antiquity; one of them is the largest in the world. Second, it is believed by all Christian Ethiopians to be the home of the Ark of the Covenant, which contained the ten commandments and which the ancient Jews are reputed to have carried with them into battle.

Three of the obelisks are decorated in the most intricate manner and look rather like apartment blocks – complete with doors, handles and locks. (There were only two until recently since the Italians stole one during their brief occupation in the 1930s and erected it outside the office in Rome whence Ethiopia was administered. The Ethiopian government has successfully petitioned for its return.) The largest is 110 feet tall and though monolithic has thirteen storeys carved upon it. For Bruce it would have been a truly astonishing sight, even though he had recently visited the pyramids. The stelae throw up all the same questions: how were they moved from the quarry to their destination? What tools did the masons use? Did they live in thirteen-storey apartment blocks? Bruce studied them and came to the wrong conclusion: 'The lock and bolt are precisely the same as those used at this day in Egypt and Palestine, but were never seen, as far as I know, in Ethiopia, or at any time in use there. I apprehend this obelisk and the two larger that are fallen, to be the work of Ptolemy Evergetes.'

They were, in fact, erected by the Axumite empire at some time before the birth of Christ. It is hard to find fault with Bruce, though. No one has managed to date them conclusively 240 years later, but by studying the surrounding ruins – many of which at Bruce's time were covered and unexcavated   archaeologists have been able to make a best guess at a date somewhere near the beginning of the first millennium. In the outlying fields are the empty tombs of King Caleb and his son Guebra Muescal, who founded the monastery at Debra Damo and conquered the Yemen, a vast underground network of passages and an impressive palace said to be that of the Queen of Sheba.

The fact that Axum is claimed to be the repository of the Ark of the Covenant is raised and dismissed by the explorer in just one paragraph. Bruce was a keen academic Freemason and this surely had a bearing on his dismissal of Axum. He writes even less about it than he did about the mysteries of Egypt. In Egypt, he had an excuse: the pyramids had been written about many times before. In Axum he had none. Instead of his customary verbosity we are told scarcely anything about this the ancient capital and current religious centre. Bruce's involvement in Masonry is the only logical reason for his reticence. 'The Temple of Solomon is,' according to McCoy's *General History of Masonry*, 'one of the most sublime symbols in the Order of Freemasonry.' It was built to house the Ark and 'the use of this sacred symbol and the important moral lessons its discovery inculcates, are exceedingly interesting to Royal Arch Masons'. Bruce could not have helped but be exceedingly interested in the Ark, yet he hardly mentions it in his book or in any of his journals.

Ethiopia's religion is an ancient form of Orthodox Christianity with its own unique character; it has survived through centuries of isolation from the rest of the Christian world. Its unorthodoxy stems from the fact that it took on parts of other religions in order to remain at peace with its neighbours. Firstly, it is extremely Judaic. Ethiopian Christians take Saturdays just as seriously as

Sundays, they have special areas in their churches for menstruating women, their churches are surrounded by cedars (disease and encroachment by weed-like eucalyptus have caused most of these cedars to die but in Bruce's time they were everywhere), and they eat only kosher meat. All meat has to be specially slaughtered and, as Bruce discovered, anything that hasn't had its throat slit cannot be eaten unless it happens to have been killed by a lion.

The truly unusual aspect of Ethiopian orthodoxy, however, is the worship of the Tabot. Tabot is the Ethiopian word for the Ark, and a representation of the Ark – a Tabotat – is at the centre of every church in the land. The Ark is absolutely essential to their religion. In fact, Ethiopians do not consecrate the church, they consecrate the Tabotat. This is kept in a Judaic-style Holy of Holies at the centre of every church that can only be entered by priests. When explaining this in his strangely short chapter on 'State of Religion – Circumcision, Excision &c.' Bruce neglects to mention the Tabotats at all and absurdly puts down the fact that no one can enter the Holy of Holies to its physical properties: 'Within this is a square, and that square is divided by a veil or a curtain, in which is another very small division answering to the holy of holies. This is so narrow, that none but the priests can go into it'.

Once a year, from every church, on the feast of Epiphany, or Timkat, the Tabotat is brought out, covered by cloth, and paraded around the streets by the priests. An elaborate dance of David is performed in front of it and after a ceremony that lasts all night, it is taken down to the water's edge where a sort of baptism ceremony is celebrated. It is then taken back to the church where it remains unseen until the next year. Timkat is the most important feast in the Ethiopian religious calendar and Bruce was ten miles from Axum on the appropriate day in 1769. Rather than going there, where the object believed to be the real Ark would be on display, he has us believe that he saw the ceremony in Adowa. Then, rather than describing it properly – he does not even mention the Tabotat – he uses it as an excuse to denigrate the authentic description of an earlier traveller, Alvarez, without printing the parts of the Jesuit's report which refer to the Tabotat.

This entire episode is completely out of character for Bruce. He wastes thousands of words describing the most dull goings-on, yet Ethiopian Christianity is summed up in a third of a short chapter and its central pillar described and rejected in one paragraph. Whilst describing Saint Mary's Zion, the church at Axum and the Ethiopian equivalent of Saint Peter's in Rome, he mentions the Ark just once:

> The church is a mean, small building, very ill-kept, and full of pigeons' dung. In it are supposed to be preserved the ark of the covenant [sic], and copy of the law, which Menelik, son of Solomon, is said, in their fabulous legends, to have stolen from his father Solomon in his return to Ethiopia, and these were reckoned, as it were, the palladia of this country. Some ancient copy of the Old Testament, I do believe, probably that from which the first version was made. But whatever this might be, it was destroyed, with the church itself, by Mahomet Gragne, though pretended falsely to subsist there still. This I had from the king himself.

He even tries to disguise his one reference to the Ark by using lower case whilst at the same time glorifying the old testament with the then optional upper. Why? This is certainly a subject in which an eighteenth-century Freemason would have shown the keenest interest and Bruce was an extremely enquiring and dedicated one. When he was in Crete on the way to Alexandria he devoted two pages to discussing the Temple of Solomon merely because he had noticed that not many cedars grew on Crete any longer. His reticence at this much more valid point in his travels is extremely unusual.

I believe that Bruce deliberately concealed his knowledge of the Ark in the *Travels*; it is, however, a difficult case to prove for his sins are ones of omission. That he *should* have written more about it and that he *would* have taken more interest in Timkat (a ceremony he witnessed twice) are simply suppositions; yet why did he spend a month in the region and say almost nothing about it?

Ethiopian legend has it that the Axumite empire was founded by Menelik, the fruit of a union between the Queen of Sheba (an Axumite monarch) and King Solomon. It goes on to say that when Menelik came of age, he went to Jerusalem to learn at his father's knee. On his return, he is believed to have taken the Ark of the Covenant with him, accompanied by the son of Zadok the priest and eleven other sons of the nobility. According to the Bible, in one of its more easily proven historical moments, Solomon lived 1000 years BC. The Ark, however, does not disappear from the Temple until about 500 years later when it is suddenly reported missing. The Menelik legend is therefore just that. If he was the son of Solomon he could not have taken the Ark. Graham Hancock, who is the only other writer to have linked Bruce and the Ark, avers that the Ark must have disappeared during the reign of Mannaseh from 687 to 642 BC. By process of elimination, he showed that it was removed by the Jewish elders in order to protect it from the tree-worshipping tyrant who had become their king. It then vanishes with this wandering tribe of Jews for whom, under Mannaseh, Israel was no longer a safe place. After the reign of Mannaseh, it is only ever referred to as something that has been lost. While one needs to remain sceptical about many of Hancock's conclusions, my own researches show that in this he is most probably right.

The logical escape route for this wandering tribe of Israelites would have been directly up the Nile, one of the few routes not blocked by enemies. They would eventually have arrived at the small island of Elephantine off Aswan, an area that was separated from Ethiopia only by Nubia and Meroe (both of which were trading partners of the Ethiopians). At Elephantine archaeologists have discovered the remains of a Roman temple built in 410 BC and, underneath it, the remains of a Jewish temple which stood there between the seventh century and fifth century BC. Although destroyed before the erection of the Roman temple, the archaeologists ascertained that it was built to exactly the same proportions and with many of the same materials as the original Temple of Solomon. This confirms two things: there were Jews living in Elephantine at the time and they built a temple, something which, according to contemporary Judaic law, was done only to house the Ark of the Covenant. In all other circumstances a temple was never built, merely a meeting place.

In 410 BC the Aswan region, for a wandering Jew, was not a safe place to be for the Jews were resented by the neighbouring tribes. Once again, the most logical place to flee would have been further up the Nile. At Khartoum they could have gone left or right, up the Blue or White Niles: the White would have led them to unexplored territory, the Blue to Abyssinia which was obscure but at least known. If they took the obvious route and followed the Blue Nile, they would eventually have arrived at Lake Tana, its source.

Here we can no longer rely on facts or logic but have to resort to Ethiopian beliefs – a Gordian knot of history and legend. There is a collection of sacred islands on Lake Tana, one of which, Debra Kirkos, is traditionally believed to have been home to the Ark for 700 years until it was taken to Axum by Ezana, the king who converted Ethiopia to Christianity. Azarius, the son of Zadok the priest, is said to have founded the community there and many years later the Virgin Mary is commonly accepted to have sheltered there for three months in what must have been a very circuitous route between Egypt and Palestine. These traditions are believed by both the Jewish and Christian communities of Ethiopia.

There are Judaic sacrificial artefacts on Debra Kirkos which prove that it was an ancient Jewish religious site and that it must have been populated by Jews who had lost contact with Jerusalem prior to 628 BC. There is evidence of Judaic animal sacrifice there which was outlawed by King Josiah in 628. It is still one of the most sacred sites in Ethiopia, home of a cross said to belong to Frumentius. The first archbishop of Ethiopia, he is believed to have left it there as a symbol to show how Christianity had triumphed over Judaism. In a country where any twig is thought to be a fragment of the true cross, however, this is not wholly convincing evidence. All we can know for sure is that Jews who followed very unusual practices lived there in the early years of the first millennium AD and probably before. These Jews were Falashas (exiles) whose form of Judaism is so old that no modern Jew (however Orthodox), unless extremely learned, would realize they were Jewish at all. They have been practising an unchanging religion since the sixth century BC. (It was not until the 1980s that Israel acknowledged them as Jews and helped them return to Israel in Operation Moses. There are now only a very few left in Ethiopia.)

Bruce travelled extensively on Lake Tana, living on its shores for many months. Sailing in a small papyrus boat, similar to those used in Egypt and the Holy Land, he even mapped the islands.

Yet he mentions nothing of these deeply held traditions. A Mason would have been interested in them and, as an intimate of the king, Bruce would have been granted unique access despite the deeply distrustful nature of Ethiopian monasticism. Bruce was not simply a Freemason; he was by now a respected senior member of Canongate Kilwinning Lodge No. 2 (having been received in 1753). He was deeply interested in the history of 'the Craft'.

As the historian Andrew Sinclair has shown, Masonry grew out of the Knights Templar (whose full title is the Order of the Poor Knights of Christ and the Temple of Solomon, for they lived on the site of the temple in Jerusalem) many of whose traditions and secrets it inherited. Eighteenth-century Masons believed that they were the descendants of the military order that had protected the holy places of Jerusalem. Thus in 1769 Bruce was a member of a secret society that had shown enormous interest in Solomon's Temple – built only to house the Ark – since 1118.

In the twelfth century, Ethiopia was in frequent contact with Jerusalem: pilgrims went back and forth and news travelled with them. The Knights Templar by that time had modified Arabic banking for Western use and were an immensely powerful economic and fighting force, centred on Jerusalem but spread all over Europe and Latin Syria. It is not unlikely, indeed it is almost certain, that they had contact with the mysterious, devout Ethiopians who lurked about the holy places. They were after all next door neighbours: the Ethiopian church has been represented at the Holy Sepulchre since the fourth century. They had an altar there until, having lost their title deeds in a fire, they were relegated to the roof by their fellow Christians. If they had met, they are likely to have discussed the Ark and in this the Templars would have been supremely interested. Why then would not these brave Knights of Christ have travelled to Ethiopia to find out more of these strange tales? It was a relatively safe time to travel between the two places and the Templars – also known as the Red Friars – were scarcely lacking in courage and spirit of adventure, particularly when it involved a religious quest. This could also explain the mystery of how the Ethiopians managed to build the monolithic churches of Lalibela, for Templar confrères were at the same time intimately involved in the building of the great Gothic churches of France. Again, the evidence is almost entirely circumstantial, but does possess a certain symmetry.

Lalibela (named after the king of the same name) is an extraordinary village, high up in the mountains of Lasta which was the Abyssinian capital under the Zagwe dynasty. Bruce never travelled there but he was aware of its existence, since it had been visited by the Portuguese. In it are a collection of churches whose construction defies belief. There are so many of such beauty that the village has been called 'the Venice of Abyssinia'. They are carved out of solid rock like Petra in Jordan, but unlike those in Petra which are dug out of the side of cliffs, Lalibela's are underground and surrounded by trenches. They were built from the roof downwards by armies of masons chipping away until, years later, they were left with their church in the middle.

Incredibly ornate, they are wondrous to look at. Ethiopian legend holds that they were built with the help of tall, white angels with red hair. (This could also help to explain how Bruce survived his trip to Ethiopia. The Ethiopians are very superstitious and although he certainly was no angel, he was tall, white and had red hair.)

The only early, independent report of the churches is by the Armenian traveller Abu Salih who visited Ethiopia during Lalibela's reign and said that he saw the Ark being carried by men who were 'white and red in complexion with red hair'. Lalibela – prior to becoming king – had spent twenty-five years living in Jerusalem. Alvarez, too, claimed that the churches were built by white men, although in his case this was hearsay reported 300 years later. Many have noted that the churches are covered in Templar crosses, but then Templar crosses are also found in the recently excavated King Caleb's tomb at Axum (and are known as Caleb crosses) and he died 500 years before the order was created. Also, the churches at Lalibela, however splendid, are no great technical feat. Anyone with enough determination and a good supply of chisels could have built them. It would merely have required extraordinary vision and a steady supply of highly efficient slaves and slave drivers.

The cosmopolitan Zagwes became emperors of Ethiopia when the country had been overrun by the Falasha Queen Judith: the legitimate but insular Solomonid dynasty fled to Shoa. In 1270, the Zagwe Naakuto Laab abdicated in favour of the Solomonids who had survived in exile. On their restoration, they would not have liked the fact that foreigners were being allowed access to their Ark. This was after all a powerful and deeply significant relic which they believed had been passed down their dynasty from King Solomon himself. A few reigns later in 1307, Wedem Araad, the current king, sent an embassy to the Pope who was then under the sway of the French king in Avignon. Wedem Araad, in Bruce's otherwise exhaustive annals of Abyssinia is written off in one sentence: 'To these princes succeeded Wedem Araad, their youngest brother, who reigned fifteen years, probably in peace'.

It is known that this, Ethiopia's first papal embassy, was received by Clement V – who was just beginning the Babylonian captivity in Avignon – but not what was said. Had the embassy demanded the removal of the Knights Templar from Ethiopia it would have added ammunition to the campaign for their destruction. At this time, the bankrupt Philip IV was desperate to purloin the immense Templar riches and to curb their power. Only a few months later, Clement V, under pressure from Philip, sent a bull from the pontiff d'Avignon in which he excommunicated all Templars and ordered their immediate arrest. Many later confessed under torture to a catalogue of bizarre crimes and were executed, but some did escape.

Thus began one of the great mysteries of modern history. On the night of Friday 13 October 1307 the world's mightiest fleet – that of the Templars – sailed from La Rochelle in France and was never seen again – nor was the vast majority of Templar wealth. Most European countries reluctantly (for the Templars were powerful in their own countries) followed the Pope's orders. Scotland and Portugal were notable exceptions. Surprisingly few Templars outside France were actually caught and put to death but their years in power were over.

In Scotland they were given sanctuary by Robert the Bruce, James's illustrious ancestor, who was then at war with the English and needed all the help he could get. Seven years later at the Battle of Bannockburn the Templars saved the day with a decisive intervention. By way of thanks Robert gave them Kilwinning where they founded the first Freemasons' Lodge. Members of the lodge still swear fealty to his descendants at their initiation ceremonies. James Bruce's membership of the same lodge has already been established.

In Portugal, the king was a Templar, so overnight the name of the Knights Templar was changed to the Order of Christ and no one was arrested. They kept their lives, their property and their riches and went on to be great explorers in the Age of Discoveries. All but two of the known early travellers to Ethiopia were Portuguese and all of them sailed under the banner of the Order of Christ. For centuries, the Portuguese tried to discover the lands of Prester John, a Christian king who was believed to live in Africa or India and could, they thought, be a great ally against the Muslim world.

With the destruction of their order elsewhere, the Order of Christ had been overtaken by events. Muslim uprisings, vicious wars in the Sudan and Arab control of the Red Sea meant that Ethiopia once more became cut off from the outside world and Portugal could not make contact with the ally they sought. Yet, every ship that left Lagos and Lisbon did so with a great red cross on its sail and a devout zealot at the tiller. These men – all generals were members of the Order – searched the seas, seeking riches and the destruction of Islam in equal measure. This combination of zeal and greed made them a formidable force. Sworn to secrecy when they joined the Order, it is not clear how much it influenced their lives but it is known that the first question that a Portuguese general asked at any port was for news of Prester John. (There is almost no recorded information about the furtive Order of Christ despite its having been such an integral part of Portuguese life for centuries.) Theirs was not simply a religious quest. The Portuguese wanted to be able to use the Red Sea with impunity and a Christian ally on its shores would have been an invaluable asset. This remains a Western obsession; witness the current diplomatic flirtation with Eritrea.

Prince Henry the Navigator, who was Grand Master of the Order of Christ and commanded the Portuguese fleet, devoted his entire life to the quest for Prester John. The son of an English-woman, he held court at Sagres in the south. It thronged with cartographers, shipwrights and linguists to the exclusion of all

others, having none of the social attributes normally associated
with courts and, since Henry was never king, it was also closed
to foreign ambassadors and thus inaccessible to spies. The court
was secretive beyond reason, but we do know that all Henry's
generals took letters to the elusive Christian king. Eight years
before he died in 1460, Henry was rewarded for his persistence
when envoys from the Ethiopian court arrived in Lisbon. As a
result, in 1488 Pero de Covilham, a contemporary of future Grand
Master Vasco da Gama, was sent to Ethiopia where he was detained
until his death. Before he died firm links between the two countries
had at last been established. Missions were sent back and forth and
Jesuits (the Society of Jesus was and is much more than a monastic
order. They took over as the soldiers of Jesus from the Templars
and were the greatest diplomats of their day) flitted hither and
thither. Contact was maintained until the mid-sixteenth century
by which time the Jesuits had built an infrastructure of monasteries
and Catholic churches and converted the king to Catholicism.
This last was too much for the Ethiopians who threw them out
in 1632 and ordered that all future visitors be detained at Massawa.
Ethiopia once more became a closed country.

Prior to Bruce's arrival 150 years later, the only European to
return from a journey to Ethiopia had been Charles-Jacques
Poncet, a French doctor who had been sent for in 1698 to cure
Emperor Iyasu I of a particularly virulent skin disease. In 1704 du
Roule, the French ambassador, was killed in Sennaar on the way
to Ethiopia and in 1735 some European silversmiths were allowed
in but never allowed to leave. Bruce was risking death by going
there and one must presume he had a good reason: he had read
the books of all the Portuguese missionaries who had blighted the
country two centuries earlier. One can see that he ordered them
by a list in his notebook of a few years earlier and that they arrived
by the fact that he was holding a copy of one when he eventually
reached the source of the Blue Nile: 'This relation of Paez's was
in my hand the 5th of November, when I surveyed these fountains,
and all the places adjacent'.

He knew, therefore, from the outset, that at least two Portuguese
Jesuits claimed to have visited the source before him. He seeks to
disprove them in the *Travels* but the travels of the Jesuits in Ethiopia

had been published in 1710 and in 1735 Samuel Johnson had translated Lobo from the French with the following introduction, quoted by Bruce in a different context:

> The Portuguese traveller has amused his reader with no romantic absurdities, or incredible fictions. He seems to have described things as he saw them; to have copied nature from the life; and to have consulted his senses, not his imagination. He meets with no basilisks that destroy with their eyes; and his cataracts fall from the rock without deafening the neighbouring inhabitants.

Bruce, on the other hand, described Lobo as 'the greatest liar of the Jesuits'. This Portuguese discovery of the Nile's source was utterly ignored by the West; perhaps because it was kept a secret for so long, perhaps because they had been unable to fix its coordinates, maybe because the Jesuits were thought to be untrustworthy. It was known that the source of the Nile was in Abyssinia and it appeared vaguely on maps but it was still considered an 'opprobrium of geography' when Bruce set off on his quest. Less than ten years after Harrison had solved the longitude measurement problem and before his methods had yet been accepted by the Board of Longitude, Bruce would be the first person to plot the source accurately, but was this sufficient reason for him to be risking life and limb in pursuit of being the second white man at the source of the Nile, indeed the third?

It is hard not to speculate upon other reasons for his being there, important enough to make him set off on a quest from which he was unlikely to return. Why in a book as verbose and detailed as the *Travels* does he scarcely mention the Ark? Its very absence is conspicuous. Why did he come back to England and wait eighteen years before writing the book of his travels if he was not satisfied that he had already completed his mission? Why, in quitting Ethiopia, did he follow the presumed route of the Ark from Jerusalem, thousands of miles through uncharted and utterly lethal country, when he was only 200 miles from the Red Sea and safety? Why did he spend so long in Latin Syria – Templar country – prior to his arrival in Ethiopia and never mention its exciting history after the Greeks and Romans? Why did he spend over a month in dreary Adowa and by his own admission only spend a day in

Axum ten miles away, the ancient capital and most interesting archaeological site in the country? I believe that Bruce ascertained that the Ark – or something the Ethiopians claim to be the Ark – was in Axum and that the entire nation would sacrifice itself before yielding it to another. Assured of its safety, his search for the Ark was complete, and thus he could continue with his journey.

Whatever happened in the missing month, Bruce had not finished his journey. We rejoin him in Axum on 20 January when he set off along the road to the court. Leaving one capital behind him, he made for the next – Gondar. Even through today's over-populated Ethiopia this is one of the world's most magnificent journeys. For Bruce it must have been wonderful to walk through the wild, empty and for once unthreatening countryside after the travails of the past few months. Perhaps he had just discovered where the Ark was reputed to be but, even if he had not, he had just survived a hair-raising journey. He passed through beautiful flower-filled meadows, drinking in the fresh highland air, intoxicated by the whole experience.

> For our road, on every side, was perfumed with a variety of flowering shrubs, chiefly different species of jessamine; one, in particular, of these, called Agam (a small four-leafed flower), impregnated the whole air with the most delicious odour, and covered the small hills through which we passed, in such profusion, that we were, at times, almost overcome with its fragrance.

Soon though, he bumped into three men who were going to cause him a great deal of trouble.

> Not long after our losing sight of the ruins of this ancient capital of Abyssinia, we overtook three travellers driving a cow before them. The drivers suddenly tript up the cow . . . One of them sat across her neck, holding down her head by the horns, the other twisted the halter about her forefeet, while the third, to my very great surprise, in place of taking her by the throat, got astride upon her belly before her hindlegs, and gave her a very deep wound in the upper part of her buttock . . . let my people go forward, and staid myself, till I saw, with the utmost astonishment, two pieces,

thicker, and longer than our ordinary beef-steaks, cut out of the higher part of the buttock of the beast . . .

One of them still continued holding the head, while the other two were busy in curing the wound. This too was not done in the ordinary manner; the skin which had covered the flesh that was taken away was left entire, and flapped over the wound, and was fastened to the corresponding part by two or more skewers, or pins. Whether they had put anything under the skin, between that and the wounded flesh, I know not; but at the river side where they were, they had prepared a cataplasm of clay, with which they covered the wound; they then forced the animal to rise, and drove it on before them, to furnish them with a fuller meal when they should meet their companions in the evening.

It is impossible to tell from Bruce's notebooks when this happened. Bruce was well aware of the fact that this story was universally disbelieved because, when he started telling it to people at dinner parties on his return to London, it immediately became the talk of the town. Horace Walpole instantly pounced upon the story in correspondence with his friends: 'There is just returned a Mr Bruce, who has lived three years in the court of Abyssinia, and breakfasted every morning with the maids of honour on live oxen.'

Walpole was only one of many who did not believe the Scot, who as a result stormed off to Scotland in high dudgeon. Bruce knew his story would be doubted and he defends himself on the next page:

When first I mentioned this in England, as one of the singularities which prevailed in this barbarous country, I was told by my friends it was not believed . . . My friends counselled me further, that as these men were infallible, and had each the leading of a circle, I should by all means obliterate this from my journal, and not attempt to inculcate in the minds of my readers a thing, that men who had travelled pronounced to be impossible . . .

Far from being a convert to such prudential reasons, I must forever profess openly, that I think them unworthy of me. To represent as truth a thing I know to be a falsehood, not to avow a truth I ought to declare; the one is a fraud, the other cowardice;

I hope I am equally distant from them both; and I pledge myself
never to retract the fact here advanced, that the Abyssinians do
feed in common upon live flesh, and that I myself have, for several
years, been partaker of that disagreeable and beastly diet.

Bruce had been looking forward to meat for lunch but, since
the butchers had only cut off two steaks, he was disappointed and
had to continue his journey. The ennui was soon interrupted,
however, by an afternoon of pig-sticking sat astride Mirza, his new
horse. This too was ultimately to prove a goad to his appetite.
Despite having killed five boars he was unable to eat their meat
because he was travelling in the company of halal restricted
Muslims. It must have been more than a little dispiriting but the
view made up for it: 'the country here has an air of gaiety and
cheerfulness superior to anything we had ever yet seen'.

He agreed with Poncet, the last European to survive an Abyssinian tour in 1698, who had compared that part of the country
'to the most beautiful part of Provence'. But sadly for Bruce,
Poncet's Ethiopia had been rather more peaceful. The banditry
which Bruce claimed had detained him in Adowa was unresolved
and no one in the countryside was at all sure who was in charge
anymore. Ras Michael and the king had last been heard of in the
field, pursuing Fasil, the rebellious governor of Damot. Since the
result of this altercation was unknown, local shums were chancing
their arms and trying to exact extortionate duties from anyone
passing their way. (A shum was roughly the equivalent of a mayor
but in those turbulent times this also involved doubling up as a
warlord.) Just before Bruce's party arrived in Sire, they had their
first experience of this. What little law and order there was had
broken down and the population of a village soon threatened them
and their baggage. 'We saw a number of armed men, from sixty
to eighty; and we were told that they were resolved to oppose
our passage.'

Bruce made off for the nearby governor's house with some of
the governor's servants in the hopes that it would be a defendable
position but in the end their detour proved unnecessary. Yasine
fired a blunderbuss over the villagers' heads and they scattered
like frightened rabbits. It had been an easy introduction to the

lawlessness then prevailing in Ethiopia. Over the next months Bruce would suffer much more of the same.

In Sire itself they expected and received a similar reaction but were saved by the fact that unconfirmed news of Michael's victory came through. This quietened the terrified populace who had thought they had rid themselves of the tyrant who had been plaguing their lives for the last fifty years. Bruce was anxious to hurry on.

> Although Sire is situated in one of the finest countries in the world, like other places it has inconveniences. Putrid fevers, of the very worst kind, are almost constant here; and there did then actually rage a species of these, that swept away a number of people daily. I did not think the behaviour of the inhabitants of this province to me was such, as required my exposing myself to the infection for the sake of relieving them; I therefore left the fever and them to settle accounts together, without anywise interfering.

They soon came in sight of the Simien mountains, the last barrier between them and Gondar. Massive and flat-topped, they stretched ahead of the travellers for many miles. These mountains look rather like claw and ball feet, amputated from a vast table and laid one behind the other on the earth, every ridge a little higher than the last. The deep grooves between the talons, which in the rainy season course with floodwaters, are emphasized by the clear air and the harsh sunlight. The party had now been climbing up mountains and walking across plateaux for two months. Not even Taranta behind them on the coast had prepared them for Lammalmon, the pass they had to negotiate before arriving in Gondar. But first, they had to cross the mighty Tacazze, the second largest river in Abyssinia and a major tributary of the Nile. Similar to the Blue Nile, it can be seen from miles away; this is caused by the clouds that form along its course. It was not in flood at the time so Bruce was lucky. At almost any other time of the year it would have been impassable.

> But three fathoms it had certainly rolled in its bed; and this prodigious body of water, passing furiously from a high ground in a very deep descent, tearing up rocks and large trees in its course,

and forcing down their broken fragments scattered on its stream, with a noise like thunder echoed from a hundred hills; these very naturally suggest an idea, that, from these circumstance, it is very rightly called the *terrible*.

The next day they crossed the river and headed into bandit country. The local governor, Ayto Tesfos, had objected to the fact that Michael had murdered his friend, King Joas. Slightly behind the times and unaware that Michael had by now killed the next king too, he was living on the top of Amba Geshen, the tallest mountain in Ethiopia, known as the Jews Rock because it is to where the royal family used to flee when the Jewish Falasha tribes were in revolt. He was known for making occasional brutal forays into the countryside to attack traders; Bruce was understandably wary: 'For these reasons, as well as that it was the most agreeable spot we had ever yet seen, we left our station on the Tacazze with great regret'.

As they trudged towards Lammalmon they began to see why Michael was so feared. All around them lay the remains of ravaged villages which Michael, in his wrath against Ayto Tesfos, combined with a genuine enjoyment of destruction, had laid waste. They soon stopped at Tabulaque for a little rest and recreation.

> None but the young women appeared. They were of a lighter colour, taller, and in general, more beautiful, than those of Kella . . . They seemed to be very hard in all bargains but those of one kind, in which they were most reasonable and liberal. They all agreed, that these favours ought to be given, and not sold; and that all coyness and courtship was but loss of time, which always might be employed better to the satisfaction of both.

They moved on in the afternoon into mountain country. Bizarre rock formations – volcanic plugs and flukes, eroded cliffs and massive boulders – dominate the landscape and make it look strangely otherworldly: 'a variety of mountains, all of different and extraordinary shapes; some are straight like columns, and some sharp in the point, and broad in the base, like pyramids and obelisks, and some like cones'.

Blind to their immediate surroundings, they walked nervously through tall bamboo groves (bamboo was used for making spears) whilst the ominous mountains looked down upon them. Addergey, their next destination, means place of bamboo. Sadly, this has become a misnomer: all the bamboo has now died, probably killed by disease. At Addergey its shum

> bade us a seeming hearty welcome, but had malice in his heart against us, and only waited to know for certainty if it was a proper time to gratify his avarice. A report was spread about with great confidence, that Ras Michael had been defeated by Fasil; that Gondar had rebelled, and Woggorra was all in arms; so that it was certain loss of life to attempt the passage of Lammalmon.

The shum was not their only problem. Simultaneously they were being besieged by ants that reputedly had a worse sting than a scorpion. Hyenas and lions dogged their steps and they were running out of food. The wasteland through which they were travelling meant that they had been unable to restock, but in Addergey, where they could reasonably expect to buy food, the shum had forbidden people to sell it to them and would give them none himself. He wanted them to pay a hefty toll before continuing, but obstinate as usual, Bruce refused, insisting that he was 'the King's stranger' and should be fed and watered before being allowed to leave without paying duty. The shum was uncertain what to do. If he killed the king's doctor and it turned out that Michael had not been defeated, he would have a very short life expectancy. Michael was famous for three things – soldiering, ruthless cruelty and never forgetting a slight. Hence, the shum played for time.

Bruce resolved to brazen it out and leave in the morning whether the shum liked it or not. He had the arrogance to pull it off and, if needs be he had an arsenal in his baggage. That next morning though the expedition descended into farce.

> While employed in making ready for our departure, which was just at the dawn of day, a hyaena, unseen by any of us, fastened upon one of Yasine's asses, and had almost pulled his tail away. I was busied at gathering the tent-pins into a sack, and had placed my musket and bayonet ready against a tree, as it is at that hour,

and at the close of the evening, you are always to be on guard against banditti. A boy, who was servant to Yasine, saw the hyaena first, and flew to my musket. Yasine was disjoining the poles of the tent, and, having one half of the largest in his hand, he ran to the assistance of his ass, and in that moment the musket went off, luckily charged with only one ball, which gave Yasine a flesh wound between the thumb and forefinger of his left hand. The boy instantly threw down the musket, which had terrified the hyaena and made him let go the ass; but he stood ready to fight Yasine, who, not amusing himself with the choice of weapons, gave him so rude a blow with the tent-pole upon his head, that it felled him to the ground; others with pikes put an end to his life.

Affairs became more serious when they eventually set off. Just as, unimpeded, they reached the river that formed the boundary of the shum's territory, a party of horsemen appeared to bar their way. Bruce's men rushed across the river as Bruce kept an eye on the riders, one of whom galloped towards him. 'When the horseman was within twenty yards distance of me, I called upon him to stop, and, as he valued his life, not approach nearer.' This brought the horseman up abruptly but soon the shum arrived and negotiations commenced. They took place in and on the other side of the river so Bruce was in a commanding position, though he feared that the shum had a rearguard ready to attack them. Janni's servants and the imperial messengers, however, took courage from the fact that they had left his jurisdiction and, strangely, the shum seemed to concur with them. After a tense standoff, the shum was bought off with some trade goods. 'I gave him a piece of red Surat cotton-cloth, and added some cohol, incense and beads for his wives. I gave to the young man that carried the gun, two strings of bugles [beads] to adorn his legs, for which he seemed most wonderfully grateful.'

Bruce's party moved on, leaving the sun and his followers – save the happy boy with the gun – glowering on the other side of the river. These negotiations were an essential part of travel in Ethiopia and were often protracted because Bruce hated paying tolls. Wherever he went, he was willing to risk death rather than part with a scrap of material or dent his pride. It is astonishing

that he survived at all, but it is worth remembering though that
he was a man of enormous size. He scared people in England,
never mind anywhere else, so it is not hard to imagine his effect
in a country where white men were seen but once a century and
where well-fed Europeans still tower over most of the population.
Fanny Burney, who called Bruce 'His Abyssinian Majesty', said
that his 'grand air, gigantic height, and forbidding brow awed
everybody into silence. He is the tallest man you ever saw gratis'.
She reported a joke made by a Mr Twining who had come to
visit them much later in London. As Twining waited for the arrival
of the man 'who looks as if born to command the world', he 'said
he felt in fear of his life; "for, if he [Bruce] should come in hastily,"
cried he "and overlook me, taking this chair to be empty, it will
be all over with me! I shall be crushed!"'

Bruce was big, and he thought big. His descendant, the present
Lord Elgin told me, 'Bruce considered himself twice royal of
course, so he made the Bruce of Kinnaird tartan with fourteen
colours – twice the royal seven'. Needless to say, it is gaudy in
the extreme.

This regal behaviour, though it frequently got him into trouble,
was often highly effective. Having been inspired by Bruce's travels,
Joseph Banks and the board of the African Association eventually
sent Mungo Park out to the Dark Continent to track the course
of the Niger. Park favoured humility over aggression as a means
of survival, and, although it worked for a good few years (but
ultimately failed), he had a horrible time and seems to have spent
half his days in the nude:

> Their intentions were now obvious; and I thought that the easier
> they were permitted to rob me of everything, the less I had to
> fear. I therefore allowed them to search my pockets without resist-
> ance, and examine every part of my apparel, which they did with
> the most scrupulous exactness. But observing that I had one waist-
> coat under another, they insisted that I should cast them both off;
> and, at last, to make sure work, stripped me quite naked.

After dealing (fully clothed) with the shum, Bruce and his party
climbed upwards towards Lammalmon, passing Dobarke market
which even today is a great crossroads on the road to Gondar. Icy

winds compete with the blazing sunshine and people with eyes
asquint, ruined by sunlight at high altitude, walk for miles to barter
on the eroding mountainside. The country about was riddled with
hermits and exiles pretending to be hermits, who lived in caves
outside the bounds of normal society. The road grew progressively
worse as they made their way up the mountain.

> Torrents of water, which in winter carry prodigious stones down
> the side of this mountain, had divided this path into several places,
> and opened to us a view of that dreadful abyss below, which few
> heads can (mine at least could not) bear to look upon. We were
> here obliged to unload our baggage, and, by slow degrees, crawl
> up the hill, carrying them little by little upon our shoulders round
> these chasms where the road was intersected. The mountains grew
> steeper, the paths narrower, and the breaches more frequent as we
> ascend. Scarce were our mules, though unloaded, able to scramble
> up, but were perpetually falling; and, to increase our difficulties,
> which, in such cases, seldom come single, a large number of cattle
> was descending, and seemed to threaten to push us all into the gulf
> below.

They had to be constantly on their guard for 'the people are much
addicted to robbery, and rebellion, in which they were engaged
at the time'. Added to this, Bruce carried letters to Ras Michael,
and whereas this had been a useful alliance in the past, in a province
where he was universally hated (that was a norm) but no longer
feared, it had become a problem. Near the top of the pass, they
came to the last customs post before Gondar and once more were
faced with opposition. Bruce managed to bluff his way through
with the help of Janni's servants, the imperial messengers and his
own audacity but his Mahometan friends were not so fortuitous.
Bruce felt creditably guilty about this and endeavoured to get them
passed as members of his party. The shum and his son, meanwhile,
were violently anti-Muslim and tried to delay the group until news
came of the king and Ras Michael. Depending on the news, the
officials would let them through or steal everything they had spent
the last two months dragging up from the coast.

Bruce showed off some of his riding and shooting skills in an
attempt to befriend the customs officer's son. At his size, Bruce

was unlikely to have been the world's best rider, but he had a huge advantage over the Ethiopians in that he had Arabian tack. Having ridden all his life, he had learnt some special tricks from the desert Arabs earlier in his travels; combined with the fact that Ethiopians still used pieces of rope, wooden saddles and iron toe-hoops instead of stirrups (and indeed still do), this meant that he could ride rings around them (Ethiopians remove their boots before riding, rather than put them on). Bruce paraded up and down showing off his double-barrelled shotgun – one-shot muskets were all that Ethiopia had ever seen – and shooting quail and pigeon at the gallop. He invited the shum's son to Gondar where he promised to teach him more tricks and it was agreed that Yasine and his friends could pass customs without having to pay too steep a levy.

As soon as this agreement was finalized, the entire episode became academic. A messenger arrived – cleft stick in hand – from Janni's brother in Gondar, who ordered the customs man to allow everyone to pass and delivered the news that Ras Michael had indeed defeated Fasil. (To this day, a cleft stick is the symbol of the Ethiopian post office and postmen, even in the roughest of times, have the same sort of immunity from persecution that they enjoyed in Bruce's and Boot's times.) Moreover, Bruce was even more cheered by the news that Fasil had retreated to the other side of the Nile where he would have to stay until the end of the rainy season. The path to the source of the Nile was open.

The next morning they reached the plateau at the top of Lammalmon where they passed through fields which were still being cultivated, despite the fact that the villages of the farmers had been destroyed by Michael's armies the previous year. They were in Falasha country. Even then the Jewish Falashas were an anachronism. Generally they lived as far away as possible from roads, for two reasons. Firstly, they wanted to avoid people like Michael but secondly, and probably more importantly, they had so many rules commanding their behaviour that it was very difficult for them to interact with people of different religions. Even today, merely shaking hands with a gentile can ruin their day for they have ritually to purify themselves before going home. If the hand-shaker is a menstruating woman the whole day is given over to ritual ablutions. Menstruating Falashas have to spend a week in isolation and then an entire day bathing before returning to their families.

Bruce was fascinated by the Falashas but so close to Gondar he did not stop to study them. He had not been invited to do so by his host, the emperor. (He later made an exhaustive study of all facets of them except for their central tradition of having brought the Ark from Jerusalem, which once again is glossed over.) The party sped on across the ravaged plain, fully aware that they were approaching their destination for the cost of provisions was steadily rising. All along the road, they met Tigreans heading home with great herds of cows, hordes of slaves and other booty looted during the campaign against Fasil.

> After having suffered with infinite patience and perseverance, the hardships and danger of this long and painful journey, at forty minutes past ten, we were gratified, at last, with the sight of Gondar, according to my computation about ten miles distant. The king's palace (at least the tower of it) is distinctly seen, but none of the other houses, which are covered by the multitude of wanzey-trees growing in the town, so that it appears one thick, black wood. Behind it is Azazo, likewise covered with trees. On the hill is the large church of Tecla Haimanout, and the river below it makes it distinguishable; still further on is the great lake Tzana, which terminates our horizon.

On 15 February 1770 the triumphant party arrived on the outskirts of Gondar. They had been in Africa for five months of almost constant peril, besieged by wild animals, disease, hunger and, most dangerously, the local population. Bruce may even have discovered the whereabouts of the Ark of the Covenant but whether he did so or not, surviving the journey intact was an extraordinary achievement.

CHAPTER 6

COURTING DISASTER

In Gondar, Bruce was not granted the reception he had anticipated. He had learned all that he could about his destination and had equipped himself with letters of introduction to the king, Ras Michael, Negade Ras Mahomet and the Greek community. All his preparations were in vain, however, for the entire élite of Gondar was rejoicing with the victorious army, now on the long march home from their campaign against Fasil. There was no one to whom he could present himself. He was fortunate that he had looked after Yasine and his friends on the journey from the coast, for his kindness was rewarded when the remaining traders in the Muslim town decided to give him the house which had been prepared for Metical Aga. At last Bruce was able to relax and spend a day or two at rest.

Gondar had been the capital of Abyssinia since the reign of Fasilidas in the mid-seventeenth century and it was Fasilidas who had created a permanent capital after centuries of a movable court. The earliest capital of Abyssinia was Axum; following the overthrow of the Solomonid dynasty by Queen Judith, Lalibela became the centre of the empire. In the period after the abdication of the Zagwes there had been terrible civil wars, Muslim invaders and cyclical famines. With Ethiopia constantly at war, the capital had become wherever the king pitched his tent. Fasilidas was the first emperor strong enough to lay down roots and all his descendants had followed suit, 'as the kings of this country have a fixed aversio [sic] to houses built by their predecessors'. Later kings had added wonderfully romantic looking but none the less practically impregnable castles and palaces to the by now crowded imperial compound at Gondar: 'The palace, and all its contiguous buildings, are surrounded by a substantial stone-wall thirty feet high, with battlements upon the outer wall, and a parapet roof between the outer and inner, forming a gallery'.

A thriving town had grown up around the seat of government. Birhan Selassie, a church and place of pilgrimage, had been built on the hill overlooking the compound to house religious treasures important to the court. Ras Michael had built a stronghold on the very edge of the royal enclosure as a symbol of his power. Just a few miles away was another of Fasilidas's castles and Koscam, a monastery and palace where the queen mother, the Iteghe Mentuab, lived. Thousands now lived in the city: the minority Muslim quarter had 3000 houses alone. The price of food was extortionate and firewood was unobtainable for miles around: the trees in the city itself were protected by royal decree. (The problem of firewood was not solved until Menelik II introduced the now ubiquitous eucalyptus in the early twentieth century.)

Not withstanding all this seeming permanence, with the court on the march the town was merely an ornate veneer with little below the surface. All the civil servants, the great officers of state, the soldiers, the bakers, the butchers, the Falasha weapon makers, the porters, the mule drivers, the cooks, the thieves, their wives and their lovers were away with the army. To have stayed in Gondar when there was fighting to be done would have been tantamount to treason. It would also have meant a lost opportunity for looting. In an utterly feudal country, in the absence of the king the capital simply did not function. The only people remaining in Gondar were the young, the sick, the old and the inconsequential.

Bruce was nervous that, without the expected protection, his plans would be hindered by the zealously insular priests of the Ethiopian church. The Ethiopians had never met any Europeans who were *not* Catholic and all had been murdered, or thrown out of the country with the strict admonition never to return. Ironically, given Bruce's loathing of Catholicism, they believed Bruce to be a Catholic and thus a great threat to the established church. The clergy was still smarting from having been challenged by the Catholics in the sixteenth and seventeenth centuries. Bruce had to make it clear to the people that mattered that he was not a Frank and that he hated Catholics just as much as the Ethiopians. In the absence of anyone of substance, however, he had to avoid the priests whilst at the same time trying not to antagonize them. He lived in the Muslim town, dressed as a Muslim and ate as a Muslim, though as he was a Christian he could not eat halal meat. Whilst all his companions feasted on meat and lived the high life, he had to make do with vegetarian fare: 'As for flesh, although there was an abundance of it, I could not touch a bit of it, being killed by Mahometans, as that communion would have been looked upon as equal to a renunciation of Christianity'.

Though Ethiopian vegetarian food is quite delicious, the enforced diet pained Bruce. On the first evening, he sat in his friend's house reading a copy of the Book of Enoch, his stomach rumbling after an unsatisfactory dinner. Lost to the world for centuries, and still surviving complete only in the Ethiopic version which Bruce brought back from his travels, the Book of Enoch, whilst not exactly a gripping read, would none the less have been exciting and pleasurable. Masons are fascinated by apocryphal books so Bruce must have felt that he had at last achieved something concrete in his ghastly and as yet (*pace* Axum) unsuccessful tour of Ethiopia. His reading was interrupted by a ruckus in the street outside.

Ayto Aylo, the Iteghe's chamberlain, had come to visit him. For decades Aylo had been a friend to the foreign merchants in Gondar, but this was thought to be the first time that he had ever entered the Muslim town. His greatest ambition was to retire from court life and to make a pilgrimage to Jerusalem. With his ability to speak Tigrinya, Bruce made a good first impression and he and Aylo soon became friends: 'Come, come he'll do,' said the chamberlain at the end of the evening, 'if he can speak; there is no fear of him, he'll make his way'. Bruce's reputation had pre-ceded him and the queen mother had sent Aylo to demand Bruce's attendance on her in the persona of Hakim Yagoube – Dr James. It was arranged that he would attend her in the morning.

The two men took breakfast together and rode down the hill and across the plain to Koscam, the smallpox-infested home of the queen mother. Bruce showed off his horsemanship and Aylo – once a famous rider himself – was duly impressed: 'He cried out with fear when he saw him (Mirza) stand upright upon his legs, and jump forward, or aside, with all four feet off the ground'.

When they arrived at the spectacular palace, crowned by a circular church with a mirrored roof, Bruce discovered that his talents were no longer needed. The royal patient, Welled Hawaryat, was to be treated by a holy hermit who had eaten nothing for twenty years. Aylo and Bruce saw ink and a sacred portrait – the medicine – being carried into the sickroom by a procession of monks. Aylo remained with the queen mother and Bruce returned to Gondar to discover that Janni's brother, Petros, had returned to the city. Sadly, however, Petros was a gibbering wreck and not the useful ally Bruce had hoped for.

On Janni's orders Petros had hurried to meet the army on its return to Gondar and had visited Ras Michael's tent to discuss Bruce's arrival. He had not achieved a great deal:

> for going to the Ras's tent, he had seen the stuffed skin of the unfortunate Woosheka, with whom he was well acquainted, swinging upon a tree and drying in the wind. He was so terrified, and struck with such horror at the sight, that he was in a kind of hysteric fit, cried, started, laughed hideously, and seemed if he had in part lost his senses.

Petros had at least sent a message to Ras Michael via Negade Ras Mahomet, the leader of the foreigners in Ethiopia. Michael, busy with other things, had replied, 'Let Yagoube stay where he is in the Moor's town; Saleh [Hagi Saleh, Bruce's host in the Muslim town] will let no priests bother him there'. Aylo too was appalled by the news of Woosheka, so Bruce sent them both to bed with a dose of laudanum and entertained himself for the evening. It was an increasingly bizarre and not a little unnerving introduction to Gondar society.

> In the morning Petros was really taken ill and feverish, from a cold and fatigue and fright. Aylo and I went to Koscam, and, for a fresh amusement to him, I shewed him the manner in which the Arabs use their firelocks on horseback; but with this advantage of a double-barrelled gun, which had never before been seen. I shot also several birds from the horse; all which things he would have

pronounced impossible if they had been only told him. He arrived at Koscam full of wonder, and ready to believe I was capable of doing everything I undertook.

This was a lucky break for Bruce. The royal family were dropping like flies; the miracle cures had failed and the Iteghe was becoming desperate. Bruce was particularly knowledgeable about smallpox as a result of his medical studies in Arabia, for it was the Arabs who had discovered that inoculation with the smallpox virus gave immunity from the disease, information that had been picked up and passed on to Europe by Lady Mary Wortley Montagu fifty years earlier. (This was still though before Jenner made his cowpox discoveries.) With Aylo's praise ringing in his ears thanks to reports on his extraordinary shooting and riding talents, Bruce was given a free rein to do whatever he liked in order to cure the princes and princesses: 'I set the servants to work. There were apartments enough. I opened all the doors and windows, fumigating them with incense and myrrh, in abundance, washed them with warm water and vinegar, and adhered strictly to the rules which my worthy and skilful friend, Doctor Russel, had given me at Aleppo'.

Bruce set about curing the entire court of smallpox and in fact moved into Koscam in order to give the sick his constant attention. He was fortunate in the people he cured and that no one especially popular succumbed to the disease. He met Ozoro Esther and managed to save her favourite child from near death. This was the beginning of a relationship that, whilst it certainly had its dangers, also had a great many rewards. Princess Esther was the beautiful wife of Ras Michael and hence had immense power in the fragile times in which Bruce found himself. In addition she was the Iteghe's daughter and thus twice powerful. Bruce made sure that he did not let her down:

I removed my bed to the outer door of Confu's chamber, to be ready whenever he should call; but his mother's anxiety kept her awake in his room all night, and propriety did not permit me to go to bed. From this frequent communication began a friendship between Ozoro Esther and me, which ever after subsisted without any interruption.

Esther was not, however, a woman to cross. After Bruce had already reached Koscam, letters came from Ras Michael ordering him there to attend and cure the royal family, something which Bruce, a man not accustomed to receiving orders, found galling. Michael's command it emerged was the result of Esther's manipulation of the old Ras. Bruce had also discovered that the stuffing of Woosheka had been Esther's work. As soon as Aylo heard about it, his first words were: 'This is Esther, this is Esther; nobody knows her but I'.

Driven to distraction by the high mortality rate amongst her husbands and relations (Michael was her third spouse) Esther could be highly irrational. Her second husband had been killed by Woosheka on the late king's orders and since then she had devoted her life to the utter eradication of the southern Galla race. Notwithstanding her brutality, Bruce adored her. He soon had a 'sincere attachment . . . to her, as one of the most lovely and amiable women in the world'.

He was also highly regarded by the Iteghe. He had already complied with Ethiopian customs by donning a new outfit, having previously been dressed as a Mahometan. That was not all: 'My hair was cut round, curled, and perfumed, in the Amharic fashion, and I was thenceforward, in all outward appearance, a perfect Abyssinian'.

Whilst this might be stretching the reader's imagination somewhat – how much like an Ethiopian can a red-headed, sun-burnt giant really look – he had at least made an effort and it was appreciated by the elderly queen mother. He had long conversations with the sprightly dowager about Jerusalem and the holy places that he claimed to have visited. It is strange that, as far as we can tell, Bruce failed to see the city for he was often very close to it when he was recording the ruins of the ancient world. The ease with which one could visit the Holy City at that time was probably his motive for avoiding it; he did not like doing what others had done, wishing only to make new discoveries. More important than this assumed knowledge of Jerusalem was that Bruce managed to convince the Iteghe early in their relationship that, like her, he was a Christian but not a Catholic. 'I declare to you,' said Bruce, his hand upon a Bible:

by all those truths contained in this book, that my religion is more different from the Catholic than yours is: that there has been more blood shed between the Catholics and us, on account of the difference of religion, than ever was between you and the Catholics in this country; even at this day, when men are become wiser and cooler in many parts of the world, it would be full as safe for a jesuit to preach in the market-place of Gondar, as for any priest of my religion to present himself as a teacher in the most civilised of Frank, or Catholic countries.

Bruce also managed temporarily to calm the fears of Abba Salama, the head priest then at Koscam, who was outraged that the queen should be talking to a Frank. By deferring to him, he managed also to silence him.

The Iteghe, however, was his most important conquest. She was a woman of extraordinary resolve. Born royal, she had first risen to prominence forty-eight years earlier when still a beautiful young girl. Bacuffa the Inexorable, then emperor, was in need of a wife and had simply sent off his men to find one. Alipius, one of his courtiers, returned to Bacuffa's Moorish castle in Gondar with the news that he had found a woman whose foot, so to speak, fitted the glass slipper: 'Mentuab, said Alipius, is "a daughter of kings; her eyes are as stars; joyful as the clusters of the vine. Her face is bright as the olive oil; her hair soft as the silk. Her stature is like the palm; her lips drop modesty and honour. In truth she is lovely."'

Half a century and four reigns later, she was still one of the most important power brokers in the country, with her own court, her own palace and her own loyalties. After the death of the late emperor, her son, she had left Gondar, ostensibly to become a nun and to devote her life to prayer. She had built a church and a palace five miles away on the opposite side of the Keha valley and since then had been plotting and planning and wielding her influence over the new king's court. To have converted her to his cause was a great achievement for Bruce and would stand him in good stead. Soon she had even given him a house within the grounds of her palace.

On 9 March, the royal children cured, image changed and allies made, Bruce rode out from Gondar to meet the incoming army.

He was not initially impressed by the Ras, nor by the audience he was granted. 'He was dressed in a coarse dirty cloth, wrapt about him like a blanket and another like a table-cloth folded about his head: He was lean, old, and apparently much fatigued; sat stooping upon an excellent mule, that carried him speedily without shaking him; he had also sore eyes.' When they were introduced he took 'no notice of me' but was assailed by thousands of queries from his men. 'We returned to Koscam, very little pleased with the reception we had met with.'

Ras Michael and the king had arrived with 30,000 hungry men and had thrown the town into disarray. It was soon awash with blood and a particularly vile sort of jelly: 'The first horrid scene Michael exhibited there, was causing the eyes of twelve of the chiefs of the Galla, whom he had taken prisoners, to be pulled out, and the unfortunate sufferers to be turned out to the fields, to be devoured at night by the hyaena.' With typical foresight, Bruce took advantage of their blindness. 'Two of these I took under my care, who both recovered, and from them I learned many particulars of their country and manners.' The blinded men never left Bruce's house for, had they returned to their own country, their master would have killed them for fear of his troops seeing the fate of anyone captured.

> The next day, which was the 10th, the army marched into the town in triumph, and the Ras at the head of the troops of Tigre. He was bareheaded; over his shoulders, and down to his back, hung a pallium, or cloak, of black velvet, with a silver fringe. A boy, by his right stirrup, held a silver wand of about five and a half feet long, much like the staves of our great officers at court.

He was followed by the king and the forty-five kettledrummers who always preceded him, the cavalry, the lord high executioner and the great officers of state who wore silver horns on their foreheads like unicorns, all followed by their victorious troops and hordes of prisoners. For every enemy killed on the battlefield there was a scrap of red material attached to the clothing of his despatcher and a forlorn pair of testicles secreted somewhere about his person which would later be thrown at the feet of the king. Last of all came a man carrying a long stick from which hung the straw-stuffed body of Petros's and Ayto Aylo's friend, Woosheka. All in all it was a fearful procession.

The king and the Ras were immediately caught up in affairs of state and the visitor to their country was left with time on his hands. There were plans, prisoners and past allies to be executed. Bruce was unable to approach them until summoned but in the meantime his friends were working on his behalf behind the scenes. Mahomet Gibberti had returned to the city having delivered a letter to Michael in which Metical Aga asserted that Bruce came from an immensely powerful country, that he had vouched for the traveller's safety and that he was relying on Michael to look after him. Not very reassuringly, Michael was amused by this. The old man took one look at it and cried:

> Metical Aga does not know the situation of this country. Safety! where is that to be found? I am obliged to fight for my own life every day. Will Metical call this safety? Who knows, at this moment, if the king is in safety, or how long I shall be so? All I can do is to keep him with me. If I lose my own life, and the king's, Metical Aga can never think it was in my power to preserve that of his stranger.

Bruce's letter to the Greeks was somewhat more effective. Father Christopher, Bruce's former chaplain in Algiers and companion on the Nile, had excelled himself. The letter he had persuaded the Greek Patriarch Mark to write to the Greeks at Gondar had the full authority of the Greek Orthodox Church. It commanded them to demean themselves on Bruce's behalf and give him all the assistance they could:

> He ordered them in a body to go to the king, in the manner and time they knew best, and to inform him that I was not to be confounded with the rest of white men, such as Greeks, who were all subject to the Turks, and slaves; but that I was a free man, of a free nation; and the best of them would be happy in being my servant, as one of their brethren, Michael, then actually was.

The Greek delegation's contribution was successful and at last Bruce was summoned before Ras Michael in his palace, adjoining the royal compound, where he prostrated himself before the tyrant.

Michael said that he had spoken to Ayto Aylo about Bruce and that he had thought at length about what to do with him. He had absorbed the fact that Bruce was a private traveller and a man of science but still anticipated interference from robbers and priests. 'Therefore the King,' he said, 'has appointed you Baalomaal [lord of the bedchamber], and to command the Koccob horse . . . Go then to the king, and kiss the ground upon your appointment. I see you have already learned this ceremony of ours.'

Bruce was then dismissed and the room emptied, but, as he was leaving, Michael took him to one side to discuss his son Confu's health. He acknowledged Bruce's help in curing him: 'Yagoube,' he said, 'it will take a long time to settle that account with you'. The interview had been a success.

He soon received his comeuppance when he went to visit the king. The king was 'not so dark in complexion as a Neapolitan or a Portugueze, had a remarkably fine forehead, large black eyes, but which had something very stern in them, a straight nose, rather of the largest, thin lips, and small mouth, very white teeth and long hair.'

He had spent his entire life in exile on Mount Wechne, with all the other princes of the royal line and had only just been crowned. Completely under the Ras's power – he always called Michael father – he was none the less quite aware of who he was and could play the king as well as any of his forebears.

That night, he kept Bruce and the delegation of Greeks standing before him for hours without offering them food or seats. He quizzed Bruce minutely about life in England and, as did everyone else, about Jerusalem and the church of the Holy Sepulchre. At last a message was brought to the king, 'he laughed, said he thought we had supped, and dismissed us'. Bruce and the Greeks made off for a by now extremely late supper in a 'violent rage, such anger as is usual with hungry men'. Rather than raging about hunger pangs, Bruce should have been well satisfied. He dined that night a lord of the bed chamber to the king, commander of the emperor's Black Horse and, what is more, with the king amused by him and the Ras indebted to him. He had every reason to be pleased with himself rather than be petulant because his legs ached and his stomach was empty. He had also avoided being made Palumbras

– an idea that had been mooted and put to Ras Michael by Princess Esther – which would have involved him being constantly at court, attending the king.

The party was joined by Bruce's fellow Baalomaals and Guebra Mascal, one of the most feared generals in Michael's army, who was as accomplished a soldier as he was proud. They drank a great deal and Bruce and Guebra Mascal had an argument in which Bruce claimed he was a better shot than the general and could fire a tallow candle with his gun more effectively than Guebra Mascal could an iron ball. Bruce's argument did him little credit. Equipped with the eighteenth-century equivalent of cruise missiles against Guebra Mascal's barrels of gunpowder, it was nearly his undoing at the end of what should have been a triumphant day.

His pride stung, Guebra Mascal kicked the Scotsman, calling him a Frank and a liar. As Bruce recounts it:

> I was quite blind with passion, seized him by the throat, and threw him on the ground, stout as he was. The Abyssinians know nothing of either wrestling or boxing. He drew his knife as he was falling, attempting to cut me in the face; but his arm not being at freedom, all he could do was to give me a very trifling stab, or wound, near the crown of the head, so that the blood trickled down over my face. I had tript him up, but till then had never struck him. I now wrested the knife from him with a full intention to kill him; but providence directed better.

Instead, he struck Guebra Mascal on the head with the butt of the knife and quickly sobered up. The room was in uproar: Bruce's new friends, fearing for their lives and wondering what to do about the situation, the insensible Guebra Mascal recumbent on the floor. Both men had committed an act of high treason, for to raise a hand in the king's palace was one of the very worst crimes imaginable. Bruce walked home alone and slept despite having made a blood enemy of one of Ras Michael's most favoured generals (Michael had even overlooked the fact that Guebra Mascal, who was also his nephew, had conceived a child with one of his wives) and committed treason within an hour of meeting the king for the first time. The Greeks sought out Ayto Aylo for his advice for Bruce had endangered their lives as well as his own. The host and company would be held culpable for the offence. Guebra Mascal fled to the house of his friend and cousin, Kefla Yasous, where he spent the night.

Bruce awoke the next morning to find Ayto Aylo hovering over him with the news that Guebra Mascal had already been seized by the Ras and was in chains in the governor's dungeons. It had been an eventful twenty-four hours. Gondar was overflowing with 20,000 of Guebra Mascal's fellow Tigrean soldiers – all drunk – and 2000 of the best of them were under the general's direct command. In Bruce's absence he had been pardoned and blame for the fracas had been heaped on Guebra Mascal. The Ras was furious with his nephew, but Bruce realized that this would do him no good. If he wanted to stay alive for much longer he had to ensure that the general too was forgiven. Accordingly he went straight to his ally Princess Esther who was deeply angry about what had happened to her new friend. When Bruce, in order to calm her worries, showed her the trifling cut on his forehead and said that he thought Guebra Mascal was in more pain than he, she riposted 'is he wounded too? I hope it is in his heart'. Clearly she would be little help in trying to acquire forgiveness for Guebra Mascal.

Ras Michael heard of Bruce's arrival at his palace and immediately sent for him. Bruce and Aylo found him in his audience chamber: 'He was naked, sitting on a stool, and a slave swathing up his lame leg with a broad belt or bandage.' Bruce immediately set to healing the rift. 'He looked at me with a grin, the most ghastly I ever saw, as half displeased.' Aylo pleaded for mercy on Guebra Mascal's behalf by saying that, if anything happened to Michael's general, Bruce would be held responsible. Meanwhile Bruce went back to Esther where he found Welletta Selassie, a friend of Guebra Mascal's, who had come to beg for his life. They eventually returned together to Michael who had made his decision.

'You are a wise man' said the prime minister, 'It is a man like you that goes far in safety, which is the end we all aim at. I feel the affront offered you more than you do, but will not have the punishment attributed to you; this affair shall turn to your honour and security, and in that light only I can pass over his insolence – Welletta Selassie' says he falling into a violent passion in an instant,

'What sort of behaviour is this my men have adopted with strangers; and my stranger too, and in the king's palace, and the king's servant. What! Am I dead? or become incapable of governing longer? . . . Go, Welletta Selassie, and free that dog from his collar, and direct him to go to Welletta Michael, who will give him his orders to levy the meery [collect taxes] in Woggorra; let him not see my face till he returns.'

Once again Bruce had turned defeat into victory. All Gondar now respected him for his mercy. He had even won round the Tigreans by securing the life of their beloved Guebra Mascal. Michael showered him with gifts, the king invited him to dine with him and Esther loved him all the more. Gondar was in a ferment. The king had just put down a rebellion and Ozoro Ayabdar, a granddaughter of the Iteghe, was to be married to Powussen, the governor of Begemdir. Weddings are extremely important in Ethiopia; the greater the expenditure, the more prestigious the event. The king and his extended family, therefore, put on a great show.

The Ras, Ozoro Esther and Ozoro Altash, entertained all Gondar. A vast number of cattle was slaughtered every day, and the whole town looked like one great market; the common people, in every street, appearing loaded with pieces of raw beef, while drink circulated in the same proportion. The Ras insisted upon my dining with him every day, when he was sure to give me a headache with the quantity of mead, or hydromel, he forced me to swallow, a liquor that never agreed with me from the first day to the last.

After dinner we slipt away to parties of ladies, where anarchy prevailed as completely as at the house of the Ras. All the married women, ate, drank, and smoked, like the men; and it is impossible to convey to the reader any idea of this bacchanalian scene in terms of common decency.

Later on in the *Travels*, Bruce overcame his scruples and regaled his readers with a description of a typical Gondar banquet. It is worth reciting at length. First you procure a cow, whose throat is nicked to comply with kosher laws, and is butchered whilst being kept alive for as long as possible. This is all part of the spectacle. Then:

The company are so ranged that one man sits between two women; the man with his long knife cuts a thin piece, which would be thought a good beef-steak in England, while you see the motions of the fibres yet perfectly distinct, and alive in the flesh. No man in Abyssinia of any fashion whatever, feeds himself, or touches his own meat. The women take the steak and cut it length-ways like strings, about the thickness of your little finger, then cross-ways into square pieces, something smaller than dice. This they lay upon a piece of the teff bread, strongly powdered with black pepper, or Cayenne pepper, and fossile salt; they then wrap it up in the teff bread like a cartridge.

In the mean time, the man having put up his knife, with each hand resting upon his neighbour's knee, his body stooping, his head low and forward, and mouth open, very like an idiot, turns to the one whose cartridge is first ready, who stuffs the whole of it into his mouth, which is full that he is in constant danger of being choked. This is a mark of grandeur. The greater the man would seem to be, the larger piece he takes in his mouth; and the more noise he makes in chewing it, the more polite he is thought to be. They have, indeed, a proverb that says, 'Beggars and thieves only eat small pieces, or without making a noise.' Having dispatched this morsel, which he does very expeditiously, his next female neighbour holds forth another cartridge, which goes the same way, and so on until he is satisfied. He never drinks until he has finished eating; and, before he begins, in gratitude to the fair ones that fed him, he makes up two small rolls of the same kind and form; each of his neighbours open their mouths at the same time, while with each hand he puts their portion into their mouths. He then falls to drinking out of a large handsome horn; the ladies eat till they are satisfied, and then all drink together, 'Vive la joye et la jeunesse!' A great deal of mirth and joke goes round, very seldom with any mixture of acrimony or ill-humour.

All this time the unfortunate victim at the door is bleeding indeed, but bleeding little. As long as they can cut off the flesh from his bones, they do not meddle with the thighs, or the parts where the great arteries are. At last they fall upon the thighs likewise; and soon after the animal, bleeding to death, becomes so tough that the cannibals, who have the rest of it to eat, find very hard work to separate the flesh from their bones with their teeth like dogs.

In the mean time, those within are very much elevated; love lights all its fires, and everything is permitted with absolute freedom There is no coyness, no delays, no need of appointments or retirement to gratify their wishes; there are no rooms but one, in which they sacrifice both to Bacchus and Venus. The two men nearest the vacuum a pair have made on the bench by leaving their seats, hold their upper garment like a screen before the two that have left the bench; and, if we may judge by sound, they seem to think it as great a shame to make love in silence as to eat. Replaced in their seats again, the company drink the happy couple's health; and their example is followed at different ends of the table, as each couple is disposed. All this passes without remark or scandal, not a licentious word is uttered, nor the most distant joke upon the transaction.

It is quite possible that at one of these parties Bruce and Esther first consummated their relationship. We rely almost entirely on Bruce's reportage to find out what happened to him during his journey, and though he often got things wrong – he made himself look more important, he left out bits that he did not want the reader to know – in the principal things which he claimed he was generally truthful. Sir Robert Playfair interviewed Antoine and Arnaud d'Abbadie who spent ten years exploring Ethiopia. They said that 'they had occasion to consult his work as a daily text book, [and] they had never discovered a mis-statement, and hardly even an error of any considerable importance'.

Whilst Bruce was willing to be fairly lewd when discussing village girls, he was a great deal more discreet about Esther. She is generally considered, however, to have been the love of his life (Lord Elgin describes her thus) and Bruce himself was fairly frank: 'It was impossible to see Ozoro Esther, and hear her speak, without being attached to her for ever after'. When last at Koscam, I discovered that to this day there is no doubt about the love that blossomed between Bruce and the beautiful Esther.

The Guardian of Koscam, where Bruce and Esther lived, is a grand old man called Mergeta Sehat Worquene. He is always delighted to have guests. Being so close to the beautiful Fasilidas's bath and the wondrous fairy-tale castles of the imperial compound, Koscam, hidden from the road, does not get very many visitors. In the centre of the compound is the church built by the Empress Mentuab. It has been very badly restored by the occupying Italians in the late thirties, who simply slapped on some concrete to stop it from falling down. The palace, however, has now been allowed to dilapidate gracefully. The whole is surrounded by ornate but practical battlements and some very tall, beautiful cedar trees. Near the centre is the ruined house of Basha Eusebius, which the Empress Mentuab gave to Bruce. The keeper describes it as the house where James Bruce and Princess Esther lived together, and he told me this before he was aware that I even knew who Bruce was. He continued that Bruce was an English traveller who came to Ethiopia to look for the Ark and lived at Koscam. 'They had a daughter,' he told me, 'but she died before she was christened.' My interest aroused, I told the monk that I was writing a book about Bruce and would like to know anything that I could about him. He said he would talk to his friends and meet me the next day before mass.

I returned at dawn. Koscam was shimmering in the intensely powerful highland sunshine. Mist lurked in the darker recesses before being burnt off by the sun. On the steps of the circular church sat five old monks, so bowed by antiquity that I felt nervous when they insisted on standing up to greet me. They had all spent their entire lives at Koscam, going back to their monasteries every year or so to keep in touch with their communities. All their knowledge had been passed down to them by their novice masters but, since all their books had been burnt or stolen at Magdala, they could give me no written proof of this knowledge.

In the late 1860s there had been a strange altercation between Emperor Theodros and Queen Victoria which eventually led to the suicide of Theodros at Magdala after his defeat at the hands of a British expeditionary force led by Lord Napier. The entire affair was caused by a clerk in the Foreign Office forgetting to reply to a letter. Theodros, who was somewhat unhinged and also drank a great deal, was furious that Victoria had not replied to his letter and reacted by holding the British ambassador hostage. He was made to suffer the consequences. Before retreating to the supposedly impregnable fortress at Magdala, he collected together as much of the wealth of Ethiopia as he could. This included the entire library at Koscam which with the rest was later burnt and looted by the English. The fire was a mistake, but the looting was intentional. All the priceless manuscripts which had survived Queen Judith's wars in the tenth century, Mohammed Gragn's invasions in the fifteenth century and countless other dangers were either lost to the fire or taken back to England.

This 'collecting' of Ethiopian souvenirs was started by Bruce and has continued since then to such an extent that Britain now has a far greater collection of Ethiopian historical documents and manuscripts than Ethiopia itself has. A few libraries have survived – notably Debra Damo's – but Britain still has the vast majority of early Ethiopian historical sources.

The most important book to be taken was the Kebra Negast (the annals of the kings of Ethiopia), first copied and shown to the West by Bruce. It was returned a few years later when Theodros's successor, the mighty Menelik II, said that he could not rule without it. Unfortunately there is no mention of Bruce or his child in the documents which Napier brought back. The one-time existence of written records of the child's birth, however, is still asserted by the venerable monks at Koscam, and they still recall what was written in them. If they did indeed exist, they must have been burned at the siege.

The monks said that they had been told that Esther and Bruce lived in the house they had shown me and that his study was on the second floor, from where he used to look at the stars. They knew that Esther and Bruce had had a child because they had been told as much and, 'everyone knows that they were lovers'. When I asked them again why Bruce had been in Ethiopia, they all agreed that it was to look for the Ark of the Covenant. Not to look for the source of the Nile? I asked. No, no, they replied, the Portuguese had done that already. By comparing the monks' testimony with Bruce's it appears that in the spring of 1770 Bruce had already made friends with the king, been adopted by the Ras, and was even conducting a love affair. He still was not entirely at ease, however.

Although the King's favour, the protection of the Ras, and my obliging, attentive, and lowly behaviour to everybody, had made me as popular as I could wish at Gondar, and among the Tigrans fully as much as those of Amhara, yet it was as easy to perceive, that the cause of my quarrel with Guebra Mascal was not yet forgot.

Every now and then people would ask Bruce whether he too had been drunk on the night of the fight with Guebra Mascal. Bruce assured them that he was not until at last even the king's curiosity was piqued: 'Did you then soberly say to Guebra Mascal, that an end of a tallow candle, in a gun in your hand, would do more execution than a ball in his?' asked the king.

Bruce assured him that he had and the king demanded proof. Bruce claimed he could pierce a table at the other end of the great banqueting hall in Fasilidas's castle at Gondar. The king, who valued his tables, suggested a servant or a horse instead but they eventually settled on three strong shields placed on top of each other: 'The candle went through the three shields with such violence, that it dashed itself to a thousand pieces against a stone-wall behind it . . . A great shout of applause followed from about a thousand people that were gathered together'.

All Gondar was astounded by this trick that for Bruce was perfectly easy – he had the latest and best guns – but for an Ethiopian, armed with more primitive muskets, was quite impossible. He later repeated the feat, using a cheap table instead of good war shields, for Ras Michael and others who had not witnessed the first exhibition. Bruce was thereafter the king's favourite:

> It made the most favourable and lasting impression upon his mind; nor did I ever after see, in his countenance, any marks either of doubt or diffidence, but always, on the contrary, the most decisive proofs of friendship, confidence, and attention, and the most implicit belief of every thing I advanced upon any subject from my own knowledge.

Soon after this Bruce's position was made even more secure when he was made governor of Ras el Feel, the buffer province between the Fung kingdom of Sennaar and the Abyssinian empire. This was an excellent trading province but was by no means comparable with Tigre or Gojam and hence was always governed by a Moslem deputy. To Bruce though it was vitally important for it provided him with an alternative route out of the country (which happened also to be the presumed route of the Ark from Jerusalem) and enabled him to reward his friend Yasine. Bruce claimed he was determined 'to return by Sennaar, and never trust myself more in the hands of that bloody assassin the Naybe of Masuah, who I understood had, at several times, manifested his bad intentions towards me when I should return by that island'.

He installed Yasine as his representative and the trader whose donkey had been eaten by a hyena on their journey to Gondar as Yasine's second-in-command.

> The having thus provided for those two men, and secured, as I thought, a retreat to Sennaar for myself, gave me the first real pleasure that I had received since landing at Masuah; and that day, in company with Heikel, Tecla Mariam, Engedan, Aylo, and Guebra Denghel, all my great friends, and the hopes of this country, I, for the first time since my arrival in Abyssinia, abandoned myself to joy.

Bruce had risked all to reach Gondar, risked it again to be accepted by society there and had succeeded admirably. He had conquered the court and made useful friends but he was still a long way from the Nile.

CHAPTER 7

THE COY SOURCES

It would have infuriated Bruce to know that, whilst he was showing off his firearms in Gondar, he could in fact have marched to
the source of the Nile, discovered it and been on his way back to
Europe before anything untoward happened to him. His quest for
the Ark, however, would not have allowed him to quit Ethiopia
so soon. As it was, he stayed in the capital teaching the young
princes to ride and canoodling with Princess Esther, while there
was still relative peace in the country. He did not think of travelling
until it was too late.

Whilst in Gondar, he spent much of his time trying to stay out
of the religious debates that were sweeping the city. Ethiopians
like nothing more than a good schism: the country is constantly
rent by obscure theological points of contention. These are made
especially complicated by the religious language, Geez, which –
like Latin – was at this point already defunct. Many of the priests
did not even understand it. Furthermore, the monastic system
was itself developed by the early Syrian exiles who so influenced
Ethiopia's religion and there was another part of the church that
did not believe in monasteries at all. Such confusions were exacerbated by the great power of the church, which at this time was
embroiled in a prolonged argument on the subject of Nebuchadnezzar's status. Was he, the question was asked, the avenging hand
of God and indeed a saint?

This seems such a bizarre argument that one suspects it was
some sort of masonic code: Nebuchadnezzar, the Babylonian king
who destroyed the Temple of Solomon, does not seem a very likely

candidate for sainthood. He appears in no Ethiopian Synaxaire and in none of the standard Christian dictionaries of saints, scarcely surprising since he predates Christianity.

Bruce found himself drawn into the controversy. Was Nebuchadnezzar a saint or not, he was asked by the young king. 'Your majesty knows I am no judge of these matters, and it makes me enemies to speak of them,' replied Bruce.

For once an evasive answer was not good enough. Usually this kind of response served Bruce well but, with the city full of marauding monks and pernicious priests, more directness was required. Prompted by the king, he eventually came down on the side of sainthood but, after a risky few days when Bruce dared not go out in public for fear of being branded a Frank, the matter was dealt with by Michael in his inimitable way. Having been lured into the debate, Ras Michael soon tired of it and solved it by decreeing that all monks should leave Gondar: 'if any such people, after twelve o'clock tomorrow, be found in the city, or in the roads adjoining thereto, they shall be punished like rebels and robbers, and their fault not prescribed for seven years'. He may not have been fair but one has to admire his style.

While Bruce lurked in his house, the Nile continued to beckon. Later geographers believed that the source of the Blue Nile was the heart-shaped Lake Tana but Ethiopians today, Bruce and the Jesuits who preceded him, believed it to be at a place called Gishe Abbay about seventy miles on the other side of Tana. Gishe means 'source' and Abbay means 'Nile', and the little river that runs into Tana is called the Little Abbay. This makes travelling there extremely difficult as I discovered when asking the residents of Gishe Abbay (the village) where the source of the Nile (gishe Abbay) was. Due to our shaky grasp of Amharic it took a good fifteen minutes to get my point across. Until recently the river was thought to flow straight across Tana and into the real Blue Nile that emerges at the other side. For Bruce's quest to be successful, much depended on the weather for it was only possible to travel when rivers were fordable and the roads passable, but the main obstacle was the war.

Fasil's provinces of Gojam and Damot are almost completely encircled by the world's most impressive moat – the Blue Nile –

and in the centre lies its source. Bruce desperately needed Michael
to defeat Fasil or at least for a peace treaty to be made. If neither
was achieved he would never reach Gishe Abbay. Meanwhile he
was unable to leave Gondar for news had come of a new conquest
by Fasil, who had set up his headquarters at Bure, then the nearest
town of any note to the source of the Nile. With Abyssinia in a
state of almost perpetual civil war and peace seemingly out of the
question, Bruce now had to rely on Michael's success on the
battlefield to gain access to the 'coy fountains'.

Fasil had also succeeded in crushing the Agows, a tribe who
provided almost all of Gondar's food. Not difficult in itself, this
was none the less a tactical triumph. Incensed and worried about
future shortages of food, Michael decided to attack as soon as
possible despite the fact that the rainy season had begun. Gusho
of Amhara and the recently married Powussen of Begemdir were
sent to marshall their troops. Bruce, who until then had been
simultaneously avoiding priests and celebrating Powussen's nup-
tials, took the opportunity to travel to nearby Emfras to have some
tents made for the approaching safari. He took his leave of the
king at court and went to Koscam to say goodbye to Esther and
the Iteghe. The queen mother tried to persuade him to stay:

See! See! says she 'How every day of our life furnishes us with
proof of the perverseness and contradiction of human nature; you
are come from Jerusalem, through vile Turkish governments, and
hot unwholesome climates, to see a river and a bog, no part of
which you can carry away were it ever so valuable, and of which
you have in your own country a thousand larger, better and cleaner;
and you will take it ill when I discourage you from the pursuit of
this fancy, in which you are likely to perish, without your friends
at home ever hearing when or where the accident happened. While
I, on the other hand, the mother of kings, who have sat upon the
throne of this country more than thirty years, have for my only
wish, night and day, that, after giving up everything in the world,
I could be conveyed to the church of the Holy Sepulchre in
Jerusalem and beg alms for my subsistence all my life after, if I
could only be buried at last in the street within sight of the gate
of that temple where our blessed Saviour once lay.'

Even this effusive exhortation could not dissuade Bruce from leaving Emfras and preparing to follow the king and Ras Michael into the field. His friends were willing to try and persuade him not to go but they would not let him in on their secret. The Iteghe knew that if things went according to her plan, this would be Michael's last campaign. Gusho and Powussen were returning home to prepare armies to fight *against* Michael, not for him, and even Michael's mother-in-law, the Iteghe, was banking on the rebellion being a success.

Blind to the machinations going on around him, Bruce set off for Emfras and prepared for war. He intended to explore the Nile with the army, as Ptolemy's scholars had done before him and as Napoleon's would after him. He was convinced that 'safe in the middle of a victorious army, [he] should see, at [his] leisure, that famous spot'. Once he had arrived at Tana's lakeside town he made his customary calculations, catalogued the local flora and fauna, set the Muslim tent-makers to work and settled down to await the army. He still had to rely on Michael's prowess and on the strength of his word. He was thus not at his happiest when he wrote to a friend from Emfras which he sited at the 'utmost verge of safety': 'I shall only say that I never yet saw a nation so barbarous and I think I have seen many Barbarians.'

Meanwhile, Gusho and Powussen were frantically sending messages to Michael advising him not to wait for reinforcements lest the rivers be too high for his troops to cross and that he should hasten to Bure as soon as possible. Secure in the knowledge that he had recently wed a relation to Powussen, Michael agreed and set off: 'Hitherto not a word had transpired that could raise the smallest suspicion of treachery'. A few days after Bruce's arrival, Michael's Fit-Auraris (a highly trusted officer whose task it was to scout the route ahead of the army and decide where to make camp every night) sped past Emfras and the town emptied. Clutching their most valuable possessions and gathering their wives and daughters, the residents of Emfras fled for the hills, for 'Ras Michael, advancing at the head of an army, spread as much terror as would the approach of the day of judgment'.

Bruce, confident that he was in favour, remained and next morning mounted Mirza and made his way towards the army.

Seeing that the king and Ras Michael were busy plotting, he went to visit Esther who immediately demanded that he give her a thorough medical examination.

> She then began to enumerate several complaints, which she thought, before the end of the campaign, would carry her to her grave. It was easy to see they were of the slightest kind, though it would not have been agreeable to have told her so, for she loved to be thought ill, to be attended, condoled with, and flattered; she was, however, in these circumstances, so perfectly good, so conversable, so elegant in all her manners; that her physician would have been tempted to wish never to see her well.

They settled down to breakfast, which was followed by a long drinking session; by the time Bruce went to see the king, he was half drunk and was almost coerced into a job that, although a great honour, he did not want in the slightest. So high did he now sit in the king's estimation that the boy wanted him to become his Fit-Auraris. In having to act as the king's route surveyor he would have been prevented from performing the one kind of sally that he was interested in – that which led him towards the source. He managed to weasel his way out of the honour without causing offence and was allowed to proceed onwards to Gishe. Strates – a Greek buffoon who became Bruce's constant companion and servant – was sent on ahead of the group with the baggage. 'It was, I suppose about noon, when we saw our servants coming back, and Strates also among the rest, stript of everything that he had, except a cotton night-cap which he wore on his head.'

Humorous though this sight was, it was accompanied by news of the worst possible kind. Gusho and Powussen had openly rebelled against the king and were racing around behind the army in the hopes of cutting off Michael's retreat to Gondar. This came as a surprise to almost no one except Bruce, the king and Ras Michael. The country ahead was in turmoil and the baggage had been looted by two acquaintances of Bruce's – dissolute nephews of the Iteghe called Guebra Mehedin and Confu – whom he had previously trusted. Before he had even absorbed this news, the miscreants themselves appeared on the other side of the small river which Bruce's caravan was about to ford. Bruce fired two shots at them, one of which wounded Guebra Mehedin. Surprised by this retaliation, the attackers galloped off and Bruce and his party followed at a more leisurely pace. They met up again with Strates that evening; the Greek was by now wrapped in a blanket and waving a gun around his head in an alarming manner:

> 'I have been stripped naked' squealed Strates 'and within an inch of having my throat cut, besides being gelded; and well may you laugh now at the figure I make. If you had seen those damned crooked knives, with their black hands, all begging, as if it had been for charity, to be allowed to do my business, you would have been glad for my making no worse figure than I do with this carpet on my head.'

Strates no longer wished to accompany Bruce to the source and was desperately anxious to get out of his contract: 'Do you think, it is not tempting Providence to come so far from your own country to seek these d—n'd weeds and flowers, at the risk of having your throat cut every hour of the day, and, what is worse, my throat cut, too, and of being gelded into the bargain?'

Before the argument could be settled, however, a shot was fired at them and the entire party dismounted and prepared for an attack. Although typical of the air of unrest, it turned out to be a false alarm and the party arrived at the small village of Dara with no casualties. There Negade Ras Mahomet awaited them and great preparations were made for both Muslim and Christian dinners. Bruce, though, 'had no stomach for either of their suppers, but ordered some coffee and went to bed'.

Only fifty miles from the source and fifteen from the great waterfall at the first cataract, Bruce was tantalizingly close to his goal yet it seemed suicidal to attempt such a visit. The situation in the country had changed irrevocably in the course of the day and there was more trouble to come. On top of the rebellion of Begemdir and Amhara, there was yet another obstacle. A psychopath was on the loose. 'In his character, he was avaricious, treacherous, inexorable, and cruel to a proverb; in short, he was allowed to be the most merciless robber and murderer that age had produced in all Abyssinia.'

The much-feared rebel, a man named Woodage Asahel, was

thought to be in the area and this spelled trouble for anyone who was a friend of Michael's. He would customarily travel with about 200 men and pounce on any stragglers from Michael's army whenever the chance arose, before disappearing into the mountains again. The presence of this marauding criminal did not deter Bruce, however. Despite all the grim news, which had been confirmed by Negade Ras Mahomet, he decided to forge ahead to the cataract. His Muslim friend, seeing that Bruce was resolute, decided to help him regardless of personal risk. He was not worried for his immediate safety but knew that, if he led Bruce to an early death, the Iteghe, Esther, the king and Ras Michael would all quarrel over the privilege of cutting his throat. In a relatively short time, Bruce had become extremely popular and thus required protection.

> 'When day-light is fairly come' said Negade Ras Mahomet that evening 'for we do not know the changes a night may produce in this country, take half a dozen of your servants; I will send with you my son, and four of my servants; you will call at Alata, go down and see the cataract, but do not stay, return immediately, and, Ullah Kerim – God is merciful.'

Bruce and his well-armed posse set off early the next morning on horseback and headed for Alata where Mahomet's son knew the shum. A steep road led up to the shum's house and a servant was sent out to lead Bruce's horse: 'Good Lord! to see you here! Good God! to see you here!' cried the Arabic servant in English.

Bruce was both astonished and confused for he did not recognize the Arab chattering away at his stirrups. It turned out that he was a man whom Bruce had met in Jiddah on his way in to Abyssinia and who had delivered Bruce's invaluable letter of introduction from Metical Aga to Ras Michael. By the time that the reunited pair had reached the top of the hill, the Arab was shouting the only other English he knew and waving a drinking horn in the air: 'Drink! no force! Englishman, very good! G–d damn drink!' The shum believed that his servant had gone insane but Bruce was able to put him right. So seductively close to the falls – Bruce could hear the dull roar – he had to stop to eat the proffered food and water their horses. It would have been insulting not to have done so.

They did not linger for long, however. It would have been dangerous but regardless of that, Bruce was desperate to see the famous cataract and was unable to rest so close to his goal. They marched across the Portuguese-built bridge and walked towards the noise of the falls. It is not called 'the smoke that thunders' for nothing, although the name is not as romantic as it sounds. Virtually every other waterfall of note on the continent – from Murchison to Victoria – has a similar name in the local language.

At last it came into view. 'The cataract was the most magnificent sight that I ever beheld,' declared the explorer. Bruce was seeing the Blue Nile in full flood but at any time of the year it is a most impressive sight. Victoria Falls, though bigger in almost every respect, pales by comparison. One becomes gradually deafened when approaching but the surrounding hillocks keep it out of sight until the very last moment and the first view that greets one is usually a rainbow or two scything through the vast plume of spray above the pool. Although they are not the tallest or the widest in the world, the waters of the Tissisat Falls are forced to perform the most intricate contortions. Having plummeted off the cliff face they drop 150 feet into a deep pool and immediately make a 90° turn, gouging away at the surrounding banks. This means that one can walk very close to the face of the waterfall whilst still standing on land. There is a permanent mist which soaks onlookers within a second of stepping too close.

Jeronimo Lobo, one of the Jesuits whose description of the falls Bruce had read prior to his arrival, had been there in the dry season and sat on a rock under the curtain of the waterfall. Bruce was outraged by Lobo's claim to have braved the stream – an impossible feat when Bruce was there – but he was at the falls in the rainy season, Lobo in the dry. Major R. E. Cheesman, an intrepid British consul in the twenties and thirties who mapped much of the then unknown Blue Nile canyon, performed the same feat, although he nearly lost a companion who 'caught hold of a half-grown python, thinking it was part of the exposed tree root in which it was sleeping'. Bruce's only excuse for his blatant denial of the fact that Europeans had been there before him is that there is an enormous difference in the falls between the wet and the dry seasons. He was also in a foul temper for, although he had been

able to see the falls, he discovered that he would be unable to continue to the source. Fasil's army now barred the only route forwards.

Bruce returned disappointed to Dara and the news that Guebra
Mehedin was no longer attacking travellers in the vicinity: he was
dead, and it was known that his first wound had been inflicted by
Bruce. Strates was overjoyed – no doubt thinking that his testicles
were once again safe – but Bruce felt otherwise, 'for, I had much
rather, considering whose nephew he was, that he should have
lived, than to have it said that he received his first wound, not a
mortal one, indeed, but intended as such, from my hand'.

The rainy season was gathering momentum and the Nile was
by now more than usually full. It was a great struggle to ford – 'a
fall there would have been irrecoverable' – but there was a bright
side to the icy crossing. They were 'much comforted by the assur-
ance that no crocodile passed the cataract'.

Well-armed though they were, Bruce and his party were in an
extremely dangerous position: they were caught between two
opposing armies, and open to the threat of the electrical storms that
rent the air. The countryside seemed utterly deserted but they had
to keep a constant watch for fear of attack by either army as they
ploughed through the driving rain or camped in burnt-out houses:

> From the passage to Tsoomwa, all the country was forsaken; the
> houses uninhabited, the grass trodden down, and the fields without
> cattle. Every thing that had life and strength fled before that terrible
> leader, and his no less terrible army . . . everything bore the marks
> that Ras Michael was gone before, whilst not a living creature
> appeared in those extensive, fruitful, and once well-inhabited plains.
> An awful silence reigned everywhere around, interrupted only at
> times by thunder, now become daily, and the rolling of torrents,
> produced by local showers in the hills, which ceased with the rain,
> and were but the children of an hour.

Faced with this appalling landscape and the inherent danger of
travelling through it, Bruce sank into gloom:

> Since passing the Nile, I found myself more than ordinarily de-
> pressed; my spirits were sunk almost to a degree of despondency,
> and yet nothing had happened since that period, more than what

was expected before. This disagreeable situation of mind continued
at night while I was in bed. The rashness and imprudence with
which I had engaged myself in so many dangers, without any
necessity for so doing; the little prospect of my ever being able to
extricate myself out of them, or, even if I lost my life, of the
account being conveyed to my friends at home; the great and
unreasonable presumption which had led me to think that, after
every one that had attempted this voyage had miscarried in it, I
was the only person that was to succeed; all these reflections upon
my mind, when relaxed, dozing, and half oppressed with sleep,
filled my imagination with what I have heard other people call the
horrors, the most disagreeable sensation I ever was conscious of,
and which I then felt for the first time.

Astonishingly, this was the first time that Bruce had given in to
despair. His extraordinary cheerfulness in the face of adversity was
always an important factor in his ability to stay alive. The Naybe
of Massawa had irritated him but he hadn't allowed the constant
threat of death either to oppress him or change his plans. The
priests at Gondar had conspired to have him hanged as a Frank
but he had held his course. The carnage that Ras Michael left in
his wake had horrified him but it was only when combined with
extreme danger, failure to reach his goal and hideous discomfort
that he gave into depression. Having been in Abyssinia for nine
tense months and just returned from within sixty miles of the
source without seeing it, he was entitled to feel downcast.

None the less, he squared his shoulders and forged on towards
Michael's army. Both Fasil's and Michael's armies were in chaos.
Neither knew what Gusho and Powussen (who held the balance
of power) intended to do and both wheeled and turned their
unruly troops so as to avoid being surprised by the other. Spies
were everywhere and rumour mixed with counter-rumour so that
neither commander-in-chief knew who to trust. Constant vigil-
ance was made more difficult by the heavy rain and lack of food,
which conspired to keep the soldiers preoccupied with their own
comforts rather than the serious business of fighting. When Bruce
eventually caught up with the Ras and the king, he found that the
army was indeed in utter disarray. A herd of antelope and other

wild animals had been caught between Lake Tana, the Nile and the army and had stampeded, driving its way through the army; on seeing so much fresh meat passing by, many soldiers had started shooting wildly. This led to a wholesale onslaught which convinced non-participants that they were being attacked by Woodage Asahel. On Bruce's arrival, Michael was still trying to regain control: 'The firing, however, continued, the balls flew about in every direction, some few were killed, and many people and horses were hurt; still they fired, and Ras Michael, at the door of his tent, crying, threatening, and tearing his grey locks, found, for a few minutes, the army was not at his command'.

To a man whose life depended on Michael's success this must have been a discouraging sight. Worse was to come. Having discovered that Strates had been injured in a mule accident, Bruce went to the tent of Kefla Yasous to be told yet more disheartening news – the campaign was over. The rains had come unseasonably early and overturned both Michael's and Fasil's plans. The two generals had hoped to be able to meet each other before the roads became impassable and the rivers too deep to cross. Instead they had strutted round Lake Tana, killing a great many men in the process, whilst resolving nothing. Bruce's plans for reaching the source had been doubly thwarted, first by the weather, then by the fact that it was now firmly controlled by the Galla commander, Fasil. It was with a sense of despair that Bruce mustered his men and prepared to return with the army to Gondar. The sodden and hungry army had no guarantee of safety even then, for somewhere in the region was the army of Gusho and Powussen and no one knew whether they would force a fight or even whose side they would support.

On 26 May 1770, after the trials and tribulations of the last few weeks, with Bruce tagging along the army started the arduous march back to Gondar. The Ras immediately took his anger out on a community of monks who had arrogantly failed to flee in the face of the army. Suspected of having sided with Fasil, some were immediately put to the sword while others were thrown in irons for future execution. Luckily for the survivors and, in the fullness of time, for Michael, the imprisoned monks were given over to Kefla Yasous for the return journey to Gondar. Bruce was put in charge of the Sire and Serawe horse – a great honour – and commanded to hold the ford which the king would use later in the day. The exact crossing point had already been decided upon by the Fit-Auraris who had in turn been guided by a locally hired scout. Bruce sallied forth and took command of the crossing but the sight of the river filled him with dismay whilst simultaneously reminding him of his homeland.

> From the time we decamped from Coga it poured incessantly, the most continued rain we ever had yet seen; violent claps of thunder followed close upon one another, almost without interval, accompanied with sheets of lightning, which ran on the ground like water; the day was more than commonly dark, as in an eclipse; and every hollow, or foot-path, collected a quantity of rain, which fell into the Nile in torrents. It would have brought into the dullest mind Mr Home's striking lines on my native Carron –

> Red ran the river down, and loud and oft
> The angry spirit of the water shriek'd.

The climate was also having a detrimental effect on the army: 'It was plain, in the face of every one, that they gave themselves over for lost; an universal dejection had taken place, and it was but too visible that the army was defeated by the weather, without having seen an enemy.'

In the late afternoon the skies brightened and the army arrived at the river bank. Netcho, the Fit-Auraris who had crossed with difficulty that morning, had sent back word that the king must try and cross immediately or risk being trapped on the wrong side of the Nile by more rain. In the course of the night the entire army, save for Kefla Yasous and his men who were covering the rear, managed to cross the river without too much loss of life. Michael had insisted that Esther cross as well despite it being more dangerous to do so at night:

> She was with child, and had fainted several times; but yet nothing could prevail with the Ras to trust her on the other bank till morning. She crossed, however, safely, though almost dead with fright. It was said, he had determined to put her to death if she did not pass, from jealousy of her falling into the hands of Fasil.

They had succeeded only through luck, for when day broke it soon became apparent that they had used the wrong ford, and should by rights have been lost to the river. The captured monks – who, if they had been left with Michael would have been dead already – had been bargaining for their lives with Kefla Yasous. The monks claimed that the army was marching into a cleverly set trap. Kefla Yasous had discovered that their guides were working for Fasil. His last minute interrogation saved the army from falling into Fasil's ambush; by the time the two armies met, Kefla Yasous had reinforced Michael, the Ras's troops were dry and rested and they were on home ground. Fasil took one look at them and withdrew. The Battle of Limjour had been fought and won with scarcely a shot being fired.

The king and his army retreated to Dingleber in good order and were able to rejoice if not at their victory, at least at their escape. It had been a strange campaign. At times the king's army had given up all for lost yet they were able to commemorate their victory with almost all those who had first set out from Gondar, for there had been no fighting. Their success was compounded when messengers arrived from Fasil's camp, suing for peace.

Through his messengers, Fasil declared:

> never again to appear in arms against the king, but that he would hold his government under him, and pay the accustomed taxes punctually; he promised also, that he would renounce all manner of connection with Gusho and Powussen, as he had already done, and he would take the field against them next season with his whole force, whenever the king ordered him.

The dry season over, the final battle having been washed out and indefinitely postponed, the two armies retreated to their former positions to await the end of the rains. It seemed, however, that Fasil had won the civil war for Ras Michael gave him one of his grand-daughters in marriage, and the king immediately proclaimed him governor of Agow, Maitsha, Gojam and Damot. Fasil conceded nothing at all:

> It was scarce 43 hours since Fasil had laid a scheme for drowning the greater part of the army in the Nile, and cutting the throats of

the residue on both sides of it; it was not twenty-four hours, since
he had met us to fight in open field, and now he was become the
king's lieutenant-general in four of the most opulent provinces of
Abyssinia.

In Dingleber Bruce was able to see more of his friend, Ozoro
Esther, but not as much as he would have liked, for there was
competition for her attentions at the incestuous court.

> Late in the evening Ozoro Esther came to the king's tent. She had
> been ill, and alarmed, as she well might, at the passage of the Nile,
> which had given her a more delicate look than ordinary; she was
> dressed all in white, and I thought I seldom had seen so handsome
> a woman ... After this the room was cleared, and she had an
> audience alone for half an hour. I doubt very much whether Ras
> Michael had any share in this conversation; the king was in the
> very gayest of humour, and went to rest about twelve. The Ras
> loved Ozoro Esther, but was not jealous.

This lack of jealousy was fortuitous since Esther was rather free
with her favours. Ras Michael was her third husband yet here she
was spending time alone with her stepcousin, the king. She had
already captured Bruce's heart by now and she was, as we know,
pregnant. Whose child it was was open to conjectures. At a recent
gathering in Gondar Bruce had noticed a number of men, any
one of whom might have been the father. 'Ozoro Esther sat late;
there was no occasion of the compliment of seeing her home, as
she had above three hundred men with her.'

Bruce and the army made their way back to Gondar, the more
foolish amongst them believing that the empire was safe again,
the more intelligent realizing that absolutely nothing had been
resolved.

> I, in particular, had very little reason to be pleased; for, after having
> undergone a series of fatigues, dangers, and expenses, I was returned
> to Gondar disappointed of my views in arriving at the source of
> the Nile, without any other acquisition than a violent ague. The
> place where that river rises remained still as great a secret as it had
> been ever since the catastrophe of Phaeton.

It had not been the most successful of journeys.

Although they had never directly engaged in the campaign, Gusho and Powussen still held the balance of power and it was widely suspected that they would attack Ras Michael in Gondar as soon as the flooding Tacazze had cut off Michael's retreat. Accordingly, the Ras decided that he must immediately fall back with the army and the king to Tigre. Michael believed that he could afford to leave the capital unguarded since he had the king with him and he planned to raze Gondar and stop off at Wechne (the mountain prison) to kill all the princes on his way home. Such an atrocity would have left no heirs to the throne.

The campaign had eroded Michael's power to an extent that only six months earlier would have been unimaginable. Formerly a tyrannical leader whose every word was law, he had failed to crush Fasil again and now he found himself explaining his decisions. The order to kill the princes and burn the capital, he claimed, had been passed down to him by the Archangel Michael who had appeared to him in a dream. He allowed the king to overrule him and eventually set off to Tigre, leaving both the city and princes intact.

Before they left, however, Bruce managed to coax two important concessions from the king. He had not given up his quest to see the source of the Nile and was willing to risk the predicted anarchy in Gondar against the wishes of the king. First though he had to insure access to the source if it ever became possible to go there. He had made friends with the Galla messengers who had been sent from Fasil by giving them and their masters presents. He had also sent medicine to one of Fasil's favourite generals, and thus had gone some way to insuring his safety in the Galla commander's territory. He still needed the king's sanction, however. Thus, when asked by the young emperor what he wanted as a reward for commanding the king's bodyguard, he replied:

'You shall give me, and oblige Fasil to ratify it, the village Geesh' . . . They all laughed at the easiness of this request; all declared that this was nothing, and wished to do ten times as much. The king said, 'Tell Fasil I do give the village of Geesh, and those fountains he is so fond of, to Yagoube and his posterity for ever, never to appear under another name in the deftar [a sort of regal accounts book], and never to be taken from him, or exchanged, either in peace or war.'

Trying to persuade the king to allow him to stay in Gondar, instead of leaving with the court, was another matter entirely. The king had grown fond of Bruce and wanted to keep him. The sentiment was reciprocated but Bruce had a higher mission. It was only after Tecla Haimanout had granted his request to be allowed to stay at Gondar that Bruce mused upon the king's virtues: 'He was a king worthy to reign over a better people; my heart was deeply penetrated with those marks of favour and condescension which I had uniformly received from him ever since I entered his palace'.

The army left the next day with the king begging Bruce not to stray from the Iteghe's palace where he would be safe. The city was destined for a period of extreme instability and the king was worried that he would be unable to protect Bruce. Within days of Michael's and the king's departure, Gusho and Powussen arrived in the capital and took over Ras Michael's fortress. Despite having conspired with them before, the Iteghe refused to give them legitimacy by declining to act as regent. After ten days Bruce decided that he must visit them or risk their becoming his enemies. It was a difficult interview. He had left matters a little too late:

> I saw them in the same room where Ras Michael used to sit. They were both lying on the floor playing at draughts, with the figure of a draught-table drawn with chalk upon the carpet; they offered no other civility or salutation, but, shaking me each by the hand, they played on, without lifting their heads, or looking me in the face.

This was a tense time for Bruce for with the departure of the king had gone his status at court. He was at the whim of his enemies for he no longer had powerful patrons. He was still in favour with the Iteghe but, whilst she continued to oppose Gusho and Powussen, her position was also far from sure. This did not last for long, however, since having proved that they could take Gondar the two young governors set off for home with their as yet untested armies. Gondar at once became a power vacuum and the Iteghe, wily old campaigner that she was, rushed to fill it. 'In the beginning of August the queen came to Gondar, and sat on the throne all day. She had not been there these three years, and I sincerely wished she had not gone then.'

Within two days, a new king had been found and Socinios, a twenty-four-year-old illegitimate princeling, began his brief reign by begging the Iteghe, who had favoured a closer relation for the throne, to act as regent. For the rest of August, Gondar was in a state of nerves. No one knew whether or not Michael was finished, for even the greatest of generals could not ford the Tacazze during the rainy season. What would happen when the rivers subsided, allowing both Fasil and Michael to return to Gondar? Who would reach the capital first and who would prevail?

Meanwhile there occurred a gruesome little episode that Bruce managed, as usual, to turn to his advantage. Fasil had obtained new information about the murder of King Joas and with the aid of this intelligence – sent by messenger to Gondar – the body of the king was soon exhumed from an unknown pauper's grave. Michael's murder of King Joas had sparked the war between Fasil and the old Ras, so this was a sensitive issue even with the two protagonists so far away, Michael in Tigre, Fasil in Bure. Digging up the body of the old king was quite daring enough for the residents of Gondar and so the putrid cadaver was left in a church until someone could decide what to do with it. Bruce was horrified by the fact that the decomposing body of the king should be allowed to rot with no shroud, so he bought a carpet, gave it to a priest and told him to cover the body properly. The matter remained unresolved until permission came from King Tecla Haimanout, at that time in Tigre with Ras Michael, for the body to be reburied. Sent to the Iteghe, it was not the most friendly of messages: 'Bury your boy, now you have got him,' wrote the king, 'or, when I come, I will bury him, and some of his relations with him'.

(An almost identical saga is currently preoccupying Ethiopia. Twenty-five years after his death Haile Selassie's body lies unburied in a mausoleum within the grounds of the imperial palace in Addis Ababa, having been exhumed after the rebel takeover from Mengistu. The new regime gave the royal family permission to bury the bones but withdrew it when the now late crown prince's advisers tried to arrange a grandiose state funeral, complete with foreign dignitaries and processions. There is now a stalemate, with both sides refusing to give ground.)

Bruce's actions, risky though they were, served him well with everyone – the church, Fasil, both kings, the common man, the Iteghe and Esther. The Iteghe told him: '"God has exalted you above all in this country, when he has put it in your power, though but a stranger, to confer charity upon the king of it." All was now acclamation, especially from the ladies; and, I believe, I may safely say, I had never in my life been a favourite of so many at one time.'

This last comment leaves a great deal unsaid. With whom was he a favourite and what was he doing for the entire rainy season, from the beginning of May to the end of October 1770? Throughout this period of near anarchy Ozoro Esther was also in residence at Gondar (although he only mentions her once in his narrative), separated from her husband by an impassable torrent. We must presume that at this point their romance was at its zenith and that it was the period in which their child, if indeed they had one, was born.

Towards the end of October, Bruce decided that he must try to discover the source again or forever lose the opportunity. It was an even more dangerous time than it had been earlier in the year.

[The Iteghe] was exceedingly averse to the attempt; she bade me remember what the last trial had cost me; and begged me to defer any further thoughts of it till Fasil arrived in Gondar; that she would then deliver me into his hands, and procure from him sure guides, together with a safe conduct. She bade me beware also of troops of Pagan Galla, which were passing and repassing to and from his army, who, if they fell in with me, would murder me without mercy. She added, that the priests of Gojam and Damot were mortal enemies to all men of my colour, and, with a word, would raise the peasants against me. This was all true; but then many reasons, which I had weighed well, concurred to shew that this opportunity, dangerous as it was, might be the only time in which my enterprise could be practicable; for I was confident a speedy rupture between Fasil and Michael would follow upon the king's return to Gondar. I determined, therefore, to set out immediately without further loss of time.

CHAPTER 8

THE SIREN SOURCES

Bruce's departure was delayed by favourable news from Tigre: Ras Michael had succeeded in reasserting his authority over his home province. He had spent the rainy season besieging a rebellious army occupying a Tigrean mountain-top. The siege had been successful thanks to a cunning night raid and most of the defenders had joined Michael's army. He would be returning to Gondar with his prestige restored and his army reinforced. In the joy of the moment, Bruce had not been forgotten. The king, it was reported, was bringing a gift for Bruce, an ancient inscribed stone from Axum. Now lying at the foot of the king's bed, it would be brought to Gondar as soon as the Tacazze could be crossed. 'I looked upon these news as a good omen, and experienced a degree of confidence and composure of mind, to which I, for a long time, had been a stranger. I slept sound that night, and it was not until half after nine in the morning that I was ready for my journey.'

This recent intelligence was much to Bruce's advantage – his most powerful allies were back in the ascendancy – but for the old Iteghe it augured ill. She had been somewhat duplicitous in the king's absence and had connived at the enthronement (if not the coronation, which had to take place in Axum to be legitimate) of the usurper Socinios. Ignoring the plight of his friend the Iteghe, Bruce set off once more for the source, this time without Strates.

In the evening before, I had endeavoured to engage my old companion, Strates, to accompany me on this attempt, as he had done

on the former; but the recollection of past dangers and sufferings
was not yet banished from his mind; and, upon my asking him to
go and see the head of this famous river, he coarsely, according to
his stile, answered, 'Might the devil fetch him if ever he sought
either his head or his tail again.'

Bruce did, though, have his usual team of servants, porters and
guards who transformed the trip from a cross-country jaunt into
a slow-moving, scientific expedition: 'The reason of this slowness
was the weight of my quadrant, which, though divided into two,
required four men to carry it, tied upon bamboo, as upon two chair
poles. The timekeeper and two telescopes employed two men
more'.

Luigi Balugani, of whom little has been heard, was in charge
of these instruments and as always would take minute recordings
of distances travelled, temperature and rainfall while at the same
time recording Bruce's more complicated astronomical observations and painting the local plants and animals. They set off on 28
October 1770 for what should not have been a particularly arduous
journey. They had no great distance to travel and the level of the
rivers was falling, even if there were quite a number of them to
cross: 'Our road was constantly intersected by rivers, which
abound, in the same space, more than in any other country in the
world'.

The main problem, as before, was that Fasil's formidable and
unruly army stood in their way. On their second day they passed
the abandoned sixteenth-century monastery at Gorgora which
Bruce, in a rare flash of charity for anything remotely Catholic,
described as 'one of the first and most magnificent churches and
monasteries of the Portuguese Jesuits'. Since they had only recently
left Gondar, they were still able to eat from their own supplies
and had no need for the local fish from Lake Tana. 'I never could
make them agree with me, which I attribute to the drug with
which they are taken; it is of the nature of nux vomica, pounded
in a mortar, and thrown into streams, where they run into the
lake; the fish, feeding there, are thus intoxicated and taken.'

On only their fourth day out of Gondar, they were alarmed to
encounter Fasil. The rains continue for longer in the highlands

hence Michael was still in Tigre when Fasil was already mobile. This made it all the more important to reach the source and return to Gondar before the entire country fell once more into anarchy. For the next few days there was still ostensibly a truce between the two generals but this would not last for long. They were only halfway around Lake Tana when they climbed the amba Mescala Christos, only to discover that the residents had bolted at the news of Fasil's approach. Later in the day they 'met multitudes of peasants flying before the army of Fasil, many of whom, seeing us, turned out of the way'.

They were in an exceedingly dangerous position. Although they could be fairly certain that Fasil would not kill them if they presented themselves to him, his army could not be trusted. They managed to find Woldo, Fasil's Fit-Auraris, before they were set upon by the pagan Galla who would have killed any white men without compunction. Woldo 'gave us a man, who, he said, would take care of us, and desired us not to dismiss until we had seen Fasil, and not to pitch our tent, but rather to go into one of the empty houses of Bamba, as all the people had fled'.

Bruce thought that once he was in Fasil's camp his troubles would be over. He could not have been more wrong. When he was eventually received, the great warlord was 'sitting upon a cushion, with a lion's skin upon it, and another, stretched like a carpet, before his feet, and had a cotton cloth, something like a dirty towel, wrapped about his head'.

Lions are of great significance in Ethiopia. Ethiopian emperors were called the conquering lions of Judah and always kept lions about them, whether on the march or at court. The royalist party is called 'Moa Anbesa' (lion) to this day; lions signify not only royalty but also power. The tyrannical Mengistu Haile Mariam, who overthrew Haile Selassie, used to keep lions at the imperial palace despite the fact that he – like a good Communist – lived in a bungalow in the grounds rather than in the palace itself. The two remaining lions very nearly starved during Mengistu's downfall but were saved by the foreign press corps, which at the time included myself, who were well aware that they provided a good story. We fed them beef stroganoff and croissants from the Addis Hilton.

Bruce paid his respects to the general and asked Fasil to help him reach the source at Geesh. Fasil demanded of Bruce if he knew where this was.

Bruce replied, 'All Abyssinia knows the head of the Nile.'

'Ay,' says he, imitating my voice and manner, 'but all Abyssinia won't carry you there, that I promise you.'

Bruce claimed that he was relying on Fasil to help him to the source and would never have come if Fasil's envoys had not already promised to show him there. The warlord countered that he had been told by the Abba Salama (one of the priests who hated Bruce) that it was illegal to allow Franks to rove around the country and that, if he did, he would suffer the consequences.

> I was as much irritated as I thought it possible for me to be. 'So so' said I, 'the time of priests, prophets and dreamers is coming on again.' – 'I understand you,' says he, laughing, for the first time; 'I care as little for priests as Michael does, and for prophets too, but I would have to consider the men of this country are not like yours; a boy of these Galla would think nothing of killing a man of your country. You white people are all effeminate; you are like so many women; you are not fit for going into a province where all is war, and inhabited by men, warriors from the cradle.'

As Fasil had intended, this drove Bruce to lose his cool. Incensed by the denigration of his beloved country, he reacted by demanding satisfaction. He would take on any two of Fasil's soldiers, he ranted at the governor, before sustaining an explosive and unexpected nosebleed. 'That instant, Aylo's servant took hold of me by the shoulder, to hurry me out of the tent. Fasil seemed to be a good deal concerned, for the blood streamed out upon my clothes.' This bizarre scene seemed to do the trick. Before Bruce had much time to regret his absurd loss of temper, he was assured by a messenger that Fasil would help him to see the source. The next morning a groom arrived with a horse which Fasil intended to give him. This, however, seemed at first to be something of a practical joke. 'For the first two minutes after I mounted, I do not know whether I was most on the earth or in the air; he kicked behind, reared before, leaped like a deer, all four off the ground . . . I then, between the two hills, half up the one and half up the other, wrought him so that he had no longer either breath or strength.'

Bruce's description perhaps shares too many similarities with Alexander the Great's account of his first experience with Bucephalus to be entirely believable; none the less, his display impressed the camp. By the time they returned, the horse could scarcely walk and its flanks were torn where Bruce's spurs had taught the unfortunate animal who was in charge. 'Carry that horse to your master,' he told the groom, 'he may venture to ride him now, which is more than either he or you dared to have done in the morning.'

Bruce stormed off on his own horse and went kite shooting in sight of the army, something that he found always impressed an Abyssinian audience. Fasıl sent for him immediately:

> Fasil, who heard I was hurt, and saw the quantity of blood on my trowsers, held up his hands with a shew of horror and concern, which plainly was not counterfeited; he protested, by every oath he could devise, that he knew nothing about the matter, and was asleep at the time; that he had no horses with him worth my acceptance, except the one that he rode, but that any horse known to be his, driven before me, would be a passport, and procure me respect among all the wild people whom I might meet, and for that reason only he had thought of giving me a horse.

Fasil's regret seemed to be heartfelt and he immediately had the luckless groom beaten and put in irons. Astonished that he again appeared to be in favour, Bruce appealed for clemency and the man was released. His humanity once more gained him admiration and new friends. Fasil turned to a courtier and whispered, 'A man that behaves as he does may go through any country.' Bruce then wreaked his revenge by supplying news of Michael which was so unlikely that Fasil had not dreamed it possible:

> 'Pardon me' says I 'if I have unawares told you unwelcome news; but the mountain is taken, the garrison put to the sword, and Za Menfus, after surrendering, slain, in cold blood by Guebra Mascal, in revenge for the death of his father.' Upon hearing what I said, he threw it [a glass] violently upon the ground, and broke it into a thousands pieces. 'Take care what you say, Yagoube,' says

he; 'take care this be not a lie' . . . I cannot say but I enjoyed heartily the fright I had visibly given him,' mused Bruce.

He enjoyed his vengeance but was clever enough to also make capital out of it. By telling Fasil this, he was in fact spying against his friends and performing a great service for the chieftain. Fasil could now speed up his advance to Gondar and, whilst the news of the taking of the mountain did not please him, he at least knew what lay ahead. They exchanged presents. Bruce gave Fasil a hookah and some expensive sashes. Fasil's presents were more practical – a new suit of clothes (a symbolic present which signified hospitality), the Lordship of Geesh – already given to Bruce by the king but now confirmed by its previous owner – a horse which would prove to be a useful passport, and a bodyguard of extremely rough looking bandits.

> 'Hear me what I say' said Fasil 'you see those seven people (I never saw more thieflike fellows in my life) – these are all leaders and chiefs of the Galla – savages, if you please; they are all your brethren.' I bowed. 'You may go through their country as if it were your own, without a man hurting you; you will soon be related to them all; for it is their custom that a stranger of distinction, like you, when he is their guest, sleeps with the sister, daughter, or near relation of the principal men among them. I dare say' adds he archly 'you will not think the customs of the Galla contain greater hardships than those of Amhara.'

Evidently, news of Bruce's relationship with Esther had travelled. Although he shrugged off the comment, it seemed as though he was destined to be well entertained on his way to the source. He took leave of Fasil – who was now desperate to get on to Gondar – and galloped off to catch up with his servants, most of whom he had sent on ahead that morning. Shalaka Woldo, a fifty-five year-old who had been a trusted companion of Fasil's father, accompanied him as a guide. The source of the Nile was at last within Bruce's grasp.

They marched all day and through the night until they met up with the Jumper, the man who was to command their bodyguard. Bruce had first met this bandit by the River Kelti, anointing his body with tallow and wrapping the small intestine of an ox around his neck, in the fashion of the Galla. Bruce had to disguise his disgust, despite being 'overcome with the disagreeable smell of blood and carrion'. This was not a man whom it was wise to insult.

> This Jumper was tall and lean, very sharp faced, with a long nose, small eyes, and prodigious large ears; he never looked you in the face, but was rolling his eyes constantly round and round, and never fixing them upon anything; he resembled very much a lean keen greyhound; there was no sternness nor command to his countenance, but a certain look that seemed to express a vacancy of mind, like that of an idiot. With this, he was allowed, on all hands, to be the most cruel, merciless murderer and spoiler, of all the Galla.

At Kelti, he encountered not only the Jumper but also a more welcome intrusion. Strates had come to join them with a messenger from Ozoro Esther. All was not well, however, in Gondar; Ras Michael had been sending bloodcurdling messages to Esther's mother, the Iteghe, saying that he would hang her and Socinios on his arrival in the capital city. 'It was well known, besides, to his wife Ozoro Esther, and to the whole kingdom, that his performance on these occasions never fell short of his threatenings.'

Esther was unwell and wanted Bruce to come back and look after her. In love with Esther and chivalrous to a fault, Bruce was in a difficult position. Which came first, the damsel in distress or the quest? He was less than thirty miles from the source of the Nile – the search for which had occupied his every waking hour for the last few years – yet here was one of his most loyal patrons and beloved mistresses beseeching him to return. Bruce took into account Esther's renowned hypochondria and made his decision.

> I therefore resolved to run the risk of continuing for a time under the imputation of the foulest and basest of all sins, that of ingratitude to my benefactors; and I am confident, had it been the will of heaven that I had died in that journey, the consideration of my lying with apparent reason under that imputation would have been one of the most bitter reflections of my last moments.

He gave instructions for Esther to be attended by a Greek priest, who doubled as a doctor, and said that he would be back as soon as he could. The next morning they set off for the final assault on the headwaters of the Nile.

It was a leisurely walk through rolling country, dotted with market towns where Shangalla gold was exchanged for honey and hides:

> In the dry bed of a river, at the foot of a small wood, before you ascend the market place at Roo, we found the Lamb, our friend the Jumper's brother, concealed very much like a thief in a hole . . . Woldo was very much in praise of this officer, the Lamb. He said he had a great deal more humanity than his brother, and when he made an inroad into Gojam, or any part of Abyssinia, he never murdered any women, not even those that were with child; a contrary custom, it seems, prevailing among all the Galla.

Ras Michael's brutal behaviour, when he had forced Esther to cross the Nile at night during the last campaign, must have been in the back of Bruce's mind. Everywhere they travelled, they drove Fasil's horse before them. It proved an excellent laissez-passer, often outshining its keeper: 'Although the Lamb, and the other Galla, his soldiers, paid very little attention, as I have said, to us, it was remarkable to see the respect they shewed Fasil's horse. The greatest part of them, one by one, gave him handfuls of barley, and the Lamb himself had a long and serious conversation with him'.

No longer on the main road to Bure, Bruce's party marched through open country whilst their leader stopped occasionally to pick and sketch flowers. Strates wandered about in the woods with a shotgun and, soon after their meeting with the Lamb, shot a very beautiful bird so that Bruce could paint it. 'This was scarcely done, and we again moving forward on our journey, when we heard a confusion of shrill, barbarous cries, and presently saw a number of horsemen pouring down upon us, with their lances lifted up, in a posture ready to attack us immediately.'

Everyone rushed for the guns and blunderbusses but all was well. The Lamb believed Bruce was being attacked and had raced to protect him. The bandit leader claimed that 'he was very much grieved that it had been a false alarm, for he heartily desired that some robbers really had attacked us, that he might have shown us how quickly and dexterously he would have cut them to pieces'. Strates put away his gun, the Lamb and his men peeled off to their parallel route and the expedition continued, confident that they could not be better protected. They wandered in the gentle shade of acacia trees through meadows full of wild oats, which induced in Bruce an attack of homesickness. He picked some of the oats and baked them into oatcakes to remind him of Scotland.

In the afternoon of 2 November they came to a point where the Little Abbay, at 260 feet wide but only four feet deep, was fordable. Their difficulties, however, were spiritual rather than physical. The surrounding population insisted that no one was allowed to cross the river wearing shoes or riding on horseback. Theirs must have been a very deeply held belief for Bruce and his escort were scarcely people who took kindly to being told what to do: 'My servants were by this provoked to return rudeness for rudeness, and Woldo gave them two or three significant threats, while I sat by exceedingly happy at having so unexpectedly found the remnants of veneration for that ancient deity still subsisting in such vigour'.

Woldo took his revenge by forcing the animists to carry all the baggage across for no payment and then falsely accusing them of stealing his money, which he then forced them to reimburse. Bruce did not countermand the order but the episode determined him to be a benevolent landlord when they eventually arrived at Gishe. After their humiliation at the ford, the local population ran away, taking their livestock and supplies of food with them. But they had not bargained on Woldo who, whilst Bruce was off inspecting a less than spectacular cataract, had wandered around the surrounding area, amorously mooing in imitation of a cow. His calls were answered and by the time Bruce returned and went to bed, there was freshly slaughtered beef on the table. In the all-night revelry that followed, the house they occupied was almost burnt down.

In crossing the river, they had moved into bee-keeping country and spent the next day being stung frequently. The river, too, was making their march more difficult: 'In this plain, the Nile winds more in the space of four miles than, I believe, any river in the world; it makes above a hundred turns in that distance.'

The hardships were increasingly easier to bear as the size of the river diminished as they approached the source. By the evening it was no more than twenty feet across and only one foot deep. Woldo, however, was becoming a problem and Bruce could not discern why.

> Woldo declared himself so ill, that he doubted if he could go any farther, but believed he should die at the next village. Though I knew too much of the matter to think him in any danger from real disease, I saw easily that he was infected with a counterfeit one, which I did not doubt was to give me as much trouble as a real one would have done.

Woldo was vexing, but he was also essential to the mission. None of Bruce's servants spoke the local language nor had they ever been to Gishe before. Woldo was also the conduit between the expedition and its bodyguard of murderers who occasionally appeared on the horizon but otherwise had little contact with them. Bruce cajoled Woldo into continuing and was rewarded for his perseverance with his first sight of the Mountains of the Moon. He claims them as such, but judging by his description, he was not entirely convinced.

> This triple ridge of mountains, disposed one range behind the other, nearly in form of portions of three concentric circles, seems to suggest an idea, that they are the Mountains of the Moon, or the Montes Lunae of antiquity, at the foot of which the Nile is said to rise; in fact there are no others. Amid-amid [a mountain] may perhaps exceed half a mile in height; they certainly do not arrive at three-quarters, and are greatly short of that fabulous height given them by Kircher. [Athanasius Kircher published one of the Jesuit accounts.]

Bruce does at least have the grace to qualify his comments but the hills around Gishe Abbay are far too small to be said to resemble mountains, let alone the fabled Mountains of the Moon.

In the evening they arrived at a small village which had been abandoned when the inhabitants had first sighted the expedition approaching. Fasil's horse was proving useful in ensuring that no one hindered their progress but it also instilled instant fear in villagers. Everywhere they went the people ran away, so that Bruce and his men had to forage for food rather than have it provided for them, as was the usual custom. That day, however, they were fortunate for the people whose village they entered had, in their haste to flee, left their cooking pot bubbling away: 'We appropriated to ourselves, without scruple, this ensete [a fine tasting vegetable]; and, by way of reparation, I insisted upon leaving, at parting, a brick, or wedge of salt, which is used as small money in Gondar, and all over Abyssinia.'

On 4 November they made their final crossing of the Little Abbay.

> Nothing can be more beautiful than this spot; the small rising hills about us were all thick-covered with verdure, especially with clover, the largest and finest I ever saw; the tops of the heights crowned with trees of a prodigious size; the stream, at the banks of which we were sitting, was limpid and pure as the finest crystal; the ford, covered thick with a bushy kind of tree, that seemed to affect to grow to no height, but thick with foliage and young branches, rather to court the surface of the water, whilst it bore, in prodigious quantities, a beautiful yellow flower, not unlike a single wild rose of that colour.

At the top of the 'small rising hills' they came at last, in sight of their goal:

> At three quarters after one we arrived at the top of the mountain, whence we had a distinct view of all the remaining territory of Sacala, the mountain of Geesh, and church of St Michael Geesh, about a mile and a half distant from St Michael Sacala, where we then were. We saw immediately below us, the Nile itself, strangely diminished in size, and now only a brook that had scarcely water to turn a mill. I could not satiate myself with the sight, revolving in my mind all those classical prophecies that had given the Nile up to perpetual obscurity and concealment.

Bruce's musings were disturbed by the news that Woldo had disappeared. No one could remember where he had last been seen,

which in itself gives us an idea of the size of Bruce's party. Had
Woldo succumbed to the mysterious illness? Had he been eaten
by the enormous apes that Strates claimed to have seen? Bruce
sent out a search party which soon found the limping guide who
claimed 'he could go no farther than the church'. Frustrated at
encountering so close to his goal the eternal problem with servants
that Europeans seemed always to meet in Africa, Bruce resolved
to sort out the matter.

At first Woldo claimed that he dared go no further because he
had killed so many people in the region that their relations might
exact revenge. Bruce did not doubt that Woldo had indeed killed
many people but was not convinced that his guide had a conscience
about it or, for that matter, any degree of fear. There had to be
another reason. Absurdly, it transpired that Woldo's reluctance
stemmed from an item of clothing. He coveted Bruce's sash and
was convinced that the explorer would be so disappointed by the
source that he would punish his guide and not give him a present.
Bruce further explained:

> This rational discourse had pacified me a little; the sash was a
> handsome one; but it must have been fine indeed to have stood
> for a minute between me and the accomplishment of my wishes.
> I laid my hand then upon the pistols that stuck in my girdle, and
> drew them out to one of my suite, when Woldo, who apprehended
> it was for another purpose, ran some paces back, and hid himself
> behind Aylo's servant.

The matter was finally resolved when Bruce gave the guide his
sash: Woldo took Bruce to the other side of the church before
pointing at the swamp that lay below them: 'it is in that the two
fountains of the Nile are to be found,' he said.

> Half undressed as I was by loss of my sash, and throwing my shoes
> off, I ran down the hill, towards the little island of green sods,
> which was about two hundred yards distant; the whole side of the
> hill was thick grown over with flowers, the large bulbous roots of
> which appearing above the surface of the ground, and their skins
> coming off on treading upon them, occasioned me two very severe
> falls before I reached the brink of the marsh; I after this came to

the island of green turf, which was in the form of an altar, apparently the work of art, and I stood in rapture over the principal fountain which rises in the middle of it.

It is easier to guess than to describe the situation of my mind at that moment – standing in that spot which had baffled the genius, industry, and inquiry, of both ancients and moderns, for the course of near three thousand years. Kings had attempted this discovery at the head of armies, and each expedition was distinguished from the last, only by the difference of the numbers which had perished, and agreed alone in the disappointment which had uniformly, and without exception, followed them all. Fame, riches, and honour, had been held out for a series of ages to every individual of those myriads these princes commanded, without having produced one man capable of gratifying the curiosity of his sovereign, or wiping off this stain upon the enterprise and abilities of mankind, or adding this desideratum for the encouragement of geography. Though a mere private Briton, I triumphed here, in my own mind, over kings and their armies; and every comparison was leading nearer and nearer to presumption, when the place itself where I stood, the object of my vain-glory, suggested what depressed my short-lived triumph. I was but a few minutes arrived at the source of the Nile, through numberless dangers and sufferings, the least of which would have overwhelmed me, but for the continual goodness and protection of Providence; I was, however, but then half-through my journey, and all those dangers which I had already passed, awaited me again on my return. I found a despondency gaining ground fast upon me, and blasting the crown of laurels I had too rashly woven for myself.

(The source of the Blue Nile had a similar effect on me and my companion when we arrived there in 1995. After a slightly less harrowing but none the less gruelling journey, we arrived at Gishe where – after paying an extortionate sum – we were led by the hand of the Guardian to the source. We discovered a metal pipe emerging from a lump of concrete. They had paved paradise and put up a tourist spot.)

Could Bruce's disappointment have had something to do with the fact that he knew full well that he was not the first European to see the source; or was it merely the anticlimax of the whole affair?

He had found a swamp from which the greatest known river in the world was born but, in the words of the Iteghe, 'no part of which you can carry away were it ever so valuable'. He was also well aware that he was unlikely to be able to tell anyone about his discovery before something went disastrously wrong and brought an end to his spectacular run of good luck.

Not a man to brood for long, he pulled himself together: 'Strates' said, I, 'faithful squire! come and triumph with your Don Quixote, at the island of Barataria, where we have most wisely and fortunately brought ourselves! Come and triumph with me over all the kings of the earth, all their armies, all their philosophers and all their heroes!'

The pair drank toasts, from a coconut cup, to George III, Maria (this may have been Maria, the Italian from Tunis on Margaret Murray as his more respectful biographers suggest) and Catherine the Great (who was currently fighting the Turks, to the benefit of the Greeks): 'The water from these fountains is very light and good, and perfectly tasteless; it was at this time most intensely cold.'

Strates agreed that the water was icy and refused to drink to Maria but the ceremony was finished amicably, if not related entirely truthfully. For Bruce had with him his Irish servants, who might have been expected to join in the hilarity, and Luigi Balugani, who as Bruce's longest standing companion, servant or otherwise, would undoubtedly have shared in the pleasure of finding the source. We know that Balugani was with Bruce at the source because it was he who meticulously wrote up the journal every night. The original documents still exist and they are all in Balugani's hand. There are also two letters which Balugani wrote in which he gives his own impressions of *el fontano del Nilo*. In his book, however, Bruce claims that Balugani died long before this point, in fact before anything had really happened to them. He claims that on the day that he fought Guebra Mascal in the precincts of the king's palace, which was also the day on which he first met the king, he was busy trying to bury his companion:

I more than twenty times resolved to return by Tigre, to which I was more inclined by the loss of a young man who accompanied me through Barbary, and assisted me in the drawings of architecture which I made for the king there, part of which he was still advancing here, when a dysentery, which had attacked him in Arabia Felix, put an end to his life at Gondar. A considerable disturbance was apprehended upon burying him in a church-yard. Abba Salama used his utmost endeavours to raise the populace and take him out of his grave; but some exertions of the Ras quieted both Abba Salama and the tumults.

It is one of the stranger mysteries of Bruce's ultimately mysterious life. The writer intentionally excludes Balugani but to what purpose? Because he wanted to trade off Balugani's paintings as his own, if so, why not say that the artist died even earlier? Was it because he wanted to be the only European to have been at the source of the Blue Nile? It is unlikely; as expedition leader he need never have shared such laurels with a servant. Balugani's testimony about being at the source (not published until after Bruce's death) both in the following letter and in the notebooks, would indeed have given greater legitimacy to Bruce's claims when people were later inclined not to believe him. In fact, Balugani seems to have been an ardent, loyal and constant supporter of Bruce despite the fact that in an earlier letter, he had complained of not having had a day off for eight months. Balugani, indeed, defers to Bruce and gives him the credit when he writes of their triumph:

> The journey to the fountains of the Nile, our principal object, is accomplished, and we can say, in the face of many sovereigns of antiquity, that we have seen what they had so long desired to see, but always, for want of information, took those roads which led them far from their purpose. Now, that this is done, if it please God, we shall not delay long to return home; and the world shall have a true account of Ethiopia, with a map of those places which we have visited, and their positions ascertained by most accurate observation with large instruments; shewing that errors have been committed by those who have given maps of Ethiopia, and what nonsense and false assertions have been uttered concerning the

manners, religion, government, and, in short, all that relates to the history of the country – to the most part of which, I, who am on the spot, can bear witness, that it has either been absolutely falsified, or stated very far from the truth, whether through ignorance, or other causes, I know not; but the fact is so clear as to be indisputable.

I shall not enter into a detail of our journey, as that might displease my master who intends to give a complete account of it.

So Bruce spoils his moment of glory by lying about the company he was keeping and then compounds his offence by trying to debunk the accounts of the Jesuits, Lobo and Paez. His next chapter is entitled: 'Attempts of the Ancients to discover the Source of the Nile – No Discovery made in latter Times – No Evidence of the Jesuits having arrived there – Kircher's Account fabulous – Discovery completely made by the Author.' Bruce's gracelessness is frustrating for there is so much about him to be admired. Visiting and giving the coordinates of the source of the Nile, be it the Blue or the White, for the first time was a noble achievement, yet he unintentionally demeans his own success in the manner in which he relates the story.

Bruce's first complaint about Pero Paez's description (which he read in Kircher) is that he spells Sacala with a B. His thesis is therefore based on what is probably no more than a typographical error. He continues by complaining of Lobo's and Paez's geographical descriptions, the distances measured and the fact that they did not mention the worship of the Nile indulged in by the locals (this last accusation is plainly incorrect). When read in full, rather than as selectively quoted by Bruce, it becomes perfectly clear that Bruce must have known that he was 150 years too late. Surely this is why he devoted so much time to sullying the name of the Jesuits and disguising the fact that Balugani was with him at the discovery of the source. It did him no credit in the eyes of those who followed in his footsteps, although to a greater or lesser extent all the Victorian explorers denigrated their rivals and inflated their own achievements. Richard Burton – whose *First Footsteps in East Africa*, although brilliant, contrives to overlook many early footsteps – despised Bruce for calling Lobo an 'ignorant peasant and a liar'. He wrote:

His [Bruce's] pompous and inflated style, his uncommon arrogance, and over-weening vanity, his affectation of pedantry, his many errors and misrepresentations, aroused against him a spirit which embittered the last years of his life. It is now the fashion to laud Bruce, and to pity his misfortunes. I cannot but think he deserved them.

Like Burton, Bruce was not a man with the same sense of fair play as, for instance, Scott of the Antarctic. His keen sense of honour was shaken when it came up against Portuguese Jesuits and his lies became confused after he made the decision to discredit their achievements. After years of searching for the source of the Nile, Bruce was damned if he was going to admit that an Amundsen had been there before him when there was no one alive to contradict him: 'I hope that what I have now said will be thought sufficient to convince all impartial readers, that these celebrated sources have, as it were, by a fatality, remained to our days as unknown as they were to antiquity'. He begins his detailed description of the source, sure of his subterfuge.

Bruce had decided that he would play the benevolent landlord before they arrived at Gishe but the joy and relief of reaching the source made him even more generous than he had planned. He sent Woldo on to inform his subjects that he would be expecting no taxes and intended to pay for everything, whilst he observed the source. Thus: 'We found these news had circulated with great rapidity, and we met with a hearty welcome upon our arrival at the village.'

Cows, goats, spirits and bread were all produced by the shum and the servants started to prepare supper. Bruce made friends with the shum, who was known as Kefla Abay, or father of the Nile. About seventy years old, with a long beard, he dressed in hides which he wore under a large hooded cloak. His hereditary role was to guard the source and make sacrifices to the god within it. (The Guardian of the source is now a priest of the Ethiopian church rather than an animist. Many customs, not usually associated with Christianity, however, are still observed there.) Bruce was overjoyed by this and asked him many complicated questions about the visions which the guardian claimed to have. Soon though all thoughts of work were put to one side and the expedition members relaxed for an evening of drinking and debauchery: 'Our hearts were now perfectly at ease, and we passed a very merry evening. Strates, above all, endeavoured, with many a bumper of the good hydromel of Bure, to subdue the devil which he had swallowed in the enchanted water'.

Bruce went hunting and behaved in a manner that would have barred him from many a modern-day shooting party:

> The quantity of game, of all sorts, especially the deer kind, was, indeed, surprising; but though I was, as usual, a very successful sportsman, I was obliged, for want of help, to leave each deer where he fell. They sleep in the wild oats, and do not rise till you are about to tread upon them, and then stare at you for half a minute before they attempt to run off.

The shum offered Bruce a choice of his daughters – he claims as a housekeeper – and he chose Irepone as his 'nymph of the Nile'.

> She was about sixteen years of age, of a stature above the middle size, but she was remarkably genteel, and, colour apart, her features would have her a beauty in any country in Europe: she was, besides, very sprightly . . . [He gave her presents which she accepted with good grace] I often thought the head of the little savage would have turned with the possession of so much riches, and so great confidence, and it was impossible to be blinded, as not to see that I had already made great progress in her affections. [Bruce broke her heart when he left] She, more generous and noble in her sentiments than us, seemed to pay little attention to these that announced to her the separation from her friends; she tore her fine hair, which she had every day before braided in a newer and more graceful manner; she threw herself upon the ground in the house, and refused to see us mount on horseback, or take our leave, and came not to the door until we were already set out, then followed us with her good wishes and her eyes, as far as she could see or be heard.

There are two reasons why Bruce's bragging about his sexual conquests is important. Firstly, his sex appeal was essential to his survival: if he had not managed to charm so many women on his journey he would almost certainly have been killed. The Iteghe, Princess Esther and the other women he met during his march home protected him from their menfolk.

In this particular instance, however, he writes about his nymph of the Nile because it was something about which he could be absolutely truthful. In this entire episode he has specifically avoided mentioning his companion Balugani; hence, Strates and Irepone are given starring roles. It must have been hard for Bruce to write this part of the book. He was sincere when he told his beloved daughter, Janet, that 'the world is strangely mistaken in my character, by supposing I would condescend to write a romance for its amusement'. In this small but important part of a vast book, he emphasizes the romance for a reason.

The rest of the *Travels* are generally truthful reportage whilst this part has been manipulated to exclude Balugani. By writing in detail about Irepone and the tearful departure, he was able to return to the truth in the next chapter. Balugani, having been an important figure at the source – painting pictures of Bruce, Kefla Abay and others – could once again easily be ignored when Bruce embarks on telling the story of the march back to Gondar, his mission accomplished and the worries of the past two years behind him.

CHAPTER 9

THE HIGHLAND WARRIOR

Discovering the source of the Nile had not been an entirely simple task but, unluckily for Bruce, it was the easiest assignment he would have to undertake for some time. He was, after all, living in a country which had a policy of never allowing a visitor to leave. There was also a loose army between him and Gondar, a pretender on the throne and a swollen, unpassable river between him and his royal patrons. Before he had to face any of those horrors, however, he would have some help.

Shalaka Welled Amlac was 'one of the most powerful, resolute, and best attended robbers in all Maitsha' and he lived very close to the source. When Bruce had first arrived in Gondar, he had cured the bandit leader of a debilitating illness, clothed him and his servants (as was the custom) and sent him on his way. The brigand was therefore indebted to Bruce and could be relied on not only for safe haven but also for safe passage. He was not at his home when the travellers arrived but his appealing wife and daughters made them immediately at home. One of Fasil's wives was also there – 'the most beautiful and graceful of them all'. Cows were slaughtered and hydromel poured before their host returned to regale them with stories of his derring-do on both battle- and hunting-fields. It soon emerged that Shalaka Welled Amlac had been the devious guide who had led the king's Fit-Auraris to the treacherous ford in their retreat across the Nile a few months earlier. Despite the fact that he had, therefore, tried to drown them and the entire army, Bruce and his men had a magnificent evening and went to bed in the sure knowledge that the rules of

Abyssinian hospitality decreed that they would wake up alive in the morning.

True to form, Bruce did not sleep alone:

> The invariable custom of all Maitsha and the country of the Galla, of establishing a relationship by sleeping with a near of kin, was enlarged upon; and, as the young lady herself was present, and presented every horn of drink during this polite dispute concerning her person, I do not know whether it will not be thought a greater breach of delicacy to have refused than to have complied –
>
> > But what success Vanessa met
> > Is to the world a secret yet;
> > Can never to mankind be told,
> > Nor shall the conscious muse unfold.
>
> Fye upon the conscious muse, says Lord Orrery; and fye, too, say I: – A man of honour and gallantry should not permit himself such a hint as this, though the Red Sea was between him and his mistress.

The young Melectanea worked her spell on Bruce, such that he decided to stay another day, during which he planned to devote his time to 'satisfying the curiosity of our female friends'. Strates, however had not been so well looked after:

> 'We have nothing to do with people's manners,' said Strates 'as long as they are civil to us: as to this house, there is no doubt that the men are robbers and murderers, their women wh—es; but if they use us well while we are now here, and we are so lucky as to get to Gondar alive, let the devil take me if ever I seek again to be at Welled Abea Abbo.'

In between flirting with Melectanea and with Fasil's wife, Bruce found time to go hunting with his bandit friend. He paid off Woldo, his guide, and left him with Fasil's wife. Melectanea was showered with presents and 'Fasil's wife, on my first request, gave me a lock of fine hair from the root, which has ever since, and at this day does suspend a plummet of an ounce and half at the index of my three foot quadrant'. They left in good spirits the next morning with their host as their guide. In his company they would be able to pass unharmed through the troubled territory in front of them. Late in the day they reached the Nile where the two armies who were disputing the land let them pass without hindrance: Welled Amlac was treated with equal respect by both camps. Indeed, Bruce left him at the ford where the bandit was simultaneously feasting in the camps of both warring armies:

> He had been received with very great respect by the eastern body of combatants, and it is incredible with what expedition he swallowed near a pound of raw flesh, cut from the buttocks of the animal yet alive. After some horns of hydromel, he had passed to the other side, where he was received with still more affection, if possible, by Welletta Michael.

Bruce and his servants spent the night in the small village of Googue where the inhabitants allowed them to stay in one of their houses but refused to give them any food. It was so cold and wet that they did not venture outside the whole evening, but merely lit a fire and huddled round it. The unfriendliness of their hosts worked in their favour, however. When they woke up the next morning 'we found the whole village sick with the fever'. Had they been out carousing with the villages the night before, they would undoubtedly have succumbed. Bruce gave medicine to all his men and prepared to leave:

> The people, who saw the eagerness and confidence with which we swallowed this medicine, flocked about us demanding assistance. I confess I was so exasperated with their treatment of us, and especially that of lodging us in the infected house, that I constantly refused them their request, leaving them a prey to their distemper, to teach them another time more hospitality to strangers.

Since Bruce had already realized that this fever (his description suggests it may have been cerebral malaria) was fatal, he was teaching the villagers a very stern lesson which would do them little good for most of them would be dead before they next had any visitors. The explorers plodded on towards Gondar, their consciences untroubled. Constantly wet and travelling through diseased, bandit-ridden country, it was not the best of journeys: 'All the country from Googue is bare, unpleasant, unwholesome, and ill-watered. Those few streams that it has are now standing in pools, and are probably stagnant in January and February. The people too are more miserable than in any other part of Maitsha and Goutto.'

The people had good reason to be miserable. Forming the buffer zone between Ras Michael's and Fasil's territory, Maitsha and Goutto had been repeatedly razed – 'Ras Michael having everywhere destroyed their houses, and carried into slavery their wives and children, who have been sold to the Mahometan merchants, and transported to Masuah, and from thence to Arabia'.

The rest of their journey was unpleasant but uneventful. They ploughed through mud, skirted the skeletons of burnt-out villages and eventually arrived back at Gondar on 19 November. Fasil and his army were camped close to the Muslim town, Michael was not yet returned from Tigre and the Iteghe was living in fear of her life. Bruce ignored the protocol that decreed he should present himself to Fasil and went straight to Esther. As he approached Gondar he became increasingly guilty as he recalled last leaving her begging for a doctor. He had promised he would return as soon as he could yet instead had toyed with Fasil's wife and slept with several other women.

> I found that princess greatly recovered, as her anxiety about Fasil had ceased. She had admitted him to an audience, and he had communicated to her the engagement he was under to her husband, as also the conduct he intended to pursue in order to keep Gusho and Powussen from taking any effectual measures which might frustrate, or at least delay, the restoration of the king, and arrival of Ras Michael.

Whilst Bruce had been away, much had changed in Gondar. The rebel Woodage Asahel – the very mention of whose name had put fear into the minds of all during the last campaign – had come to Gondar and been rewarded by Fasil. Socinios, the new king, who did whatever he was told, had made Woodage Asahel Kasmati (governor) of Agow, Maitsha and Damot (Fasil's lands) whilst Fasil was away from his home province. Engineered by Fasil, this had given him an excuse to come to Gondar – putting the fear of God into the Iteghe – and to make his camp just outside. Plots were hatched by all and sundry and the town became a cauldron of gossip: would Fasil support Socinios or Tecla Haimanout. What would Michael do? Would he go into retirement or come back for a final clash with Fasil?

The town was in uproar:

> Troops flocked in from every quarter, as upon a signal given. Ayto Engedan, in discontent, with a thousand men, sat down near Gondar on the river Mogetch; his brother Aylo, at Emfras, about 15 miles further, with double that number; Ayto Confu, his cousin-german, with about 600 horse, lay above Koscam for the protection of Ozoro Esther, his mother, and the Iteghe his grandmother; all were in arms, though upon the defensive.

When Bruce first made contact with Ozoro Esther she was deep in conversation with Abba Salama the Acab Saat, the priest who, over the months, had caused him so many problems. Ayto Confu, Bruce's friend and Esther's son, arrived soon after and began to berate the spiritual leader of the Ethiopians for the uncharitable manner in which he had treated Bruce. It emerged that, not only had Abba Salama been speaking ill of the Scot, but he had even gone so far as to send troops to kill him: 'That pagan there' said Confu pointing at the bishop, 'who calls himself a Christian, did charitably recommend it to Fasil to rob or murder Yagoube, a stranger offending nobody'.

He had also sent the fearsome Woodage Asahel to carry off the attack but the bandit had, unknown to Bruce, been intercepted by his old friend the Lamb, who 'had slain and wounded the whole party, as dexterously as he had promised to us at our last interview'. Bruce had led a charmed life in his absence from Gondar. He had survived the machinations of the priest without even noticing, and had only once been seriously inconvenienced on his successful trip to the source, at the first meeting with Fasil. Both Ras Michael and the king had also suffered from the ill-judged pronouncements of the scheming bishop: they had both been excommunicated *in absentia*.

Bruce left the palace and inspected the cavalry with his old friend Confu as he listened to all that had occurred in Gondar during his absence: 'I resolved to remain at Koscam in the house the Iteghe had given me; as it was easy to see things were drawing to a crisis, which would inevitably end in blood'.

There was now a collection of rival courts at Gondar. Fasil – encamped outside with his army – still prevaricating about which side to support; Socinios – the new king, with his ever-dwindling band of followers; the Iteghe – surrounded by supporters of Tecla Haimanout and Ras Michael, but known to have flirted too long with Socinios. Bruce stayed with the Iteghe but tried to stay in communication with as many of the different camps as possible. At the end of November, Fasil came down on the side of Tecla Haimanout, even to the point where he claimed himself willing to support Michael's return to Gondar. Then, a few days later he pledged his allegiance to Socinios. Soon after Powussen, the governor of Begemdir, wreaked havoc on Ayto Aylo who was camped outside Emfras.

> Upon the first intelligence of this, Fasil proclaimed Tecla Haimanout king; and, striking his tents, sat down at Abba Samuel, a collection of villages about two miles from Gondar, inviting all people, that would escape the vengeance of Ras Michael, to come and join him and leave Gondar. From this he retreated near to Dingleber, on the side of the lake, and intercepted all provisions coming to Gondar, which occasioned a very great famine, and many poor people died.

In the midst of all this political cut and thrust, Bruce was desperate to return home but, with the country in such turmoil, he was unable to do so. Socinios and Abba Salama looted Bruce's house then demanded his attendance before roundly abusing him; the Iteghe had little time to see him and, stricken by terror, she was constantly plotting with others. It was a dreadful time to be in Gondar and with every day that passed it became more inevitable that the battle for power would be resolved only by the copious shedding of blood. On 15 December news reached the city that the king and Ras Michael had forded the Tacazze and were on their way back. Fearing the wrath of the vengeful tyrant who planned to restore Tecla Haimanout to his throne, the Iteghe fled with Socinios. Bruce stayed at Koscam hoping that his past friendship with the Ras would be remembered and that his recent association with Socinios and Fasil would be overlooked. It was a dangerous course of action but turned out to be the correct decision.

> On the 21st of December a message came to me from Ozoro Esther, desiring I would attend her son Confu to meet the king, as his Fit-Auraris had marked out the camp at Mariam-Ohha. Observing that I had a very indifferent knife, or dagger, in my girdle, (that which I had received from the king, being stolen, when my house was plundered), with her own hands she made me a present of a magnificent one, mounted with gold, which she had chosen with that intention, and laid upon the seat beside her. She told me she had already sent to acquaint her husband, Ras Michael, how much she had been obliged to me in his absence, both for my attention to her and her eldest son, who had been several times sick since his departure, and that I might expect to receive a kind reception.

By the time Bruce arrived at the centre of the camp, he had been joined by many friends, among them Yasine and a squadron of his own cavalry. He made first for the tent of the Ras, who was busy planning his return but was otherwise pleased to see him. The young king was besieged by well-wishers but also put Bruce's mind at rest: 'He smiled with great good nature, giving me first the back, and then the palm of his hand to kiss'.

The camp itself was in chaos: 'All Gondar, and the neighbouring towns and villages, had poured out their inhabitants to meet the king upon his return. The fear of Ras Michael was the cause of all this; and every one trembled, lest, by being absent, he should be thought a favourer of Socinios.'

They were justified in their terror, for Michael, after his great success during the rainy season, had regained all his renowned self-confidence. He would not be diffident when the time came to settle accounts. Anyone who had ever offended Michael had come to pay homage and seek forgiveness. Foremost among the penitent were the two Ethiopian bishops, Bruce's enemies, Abba Salama, the Itchegue (the premier monk and not Empress Mentuab, the Iteghe) and the Abuna himself. The Abuna was the spiritual head of the church and had only just arrived from Alexandria to administer to his far-flung flock. He had yet to learn a word of any Ethiopian language and could expect clemency. The other two, however, faced an uncertain future. They had excommunicated the king and the Ras in their absence and, although they had been partly forgiven on Esther's intervention they were still in great danger. Esther was influential but her word was by no means law.

Rather than enter Gondar the next day the king and the Ras camped outside as though they had it in mind to raze the town. Before their arrival Bruce had ridden out to be with the king and had there witnessed a scene that gave him little hope for what was to come. The carefree boy he had first known had coarsened during the long and dangerous months in Tigre. Whenever he appeared in public the king would wear a veil over his face and it was considered a great loss of dignity to be seen uncovered. Bruce watched the king crossing a river: as he did so, his cape caught on a kantuffa branch, whose vicious thorns tore off the veil. Having rearranged his headwear, the king called for the local shum who came bounding up with his son.

> There is always near the king, when he marches, an officer called Kanitz Kitzera, the executioner of the camp; he has upon the bole of his saddle a quantity of thongs made of bull-hide, rolled up very artificially; this is called the tarade. The king made a sign with his head, and another with his hand, without speaking; and two loops of the tarade were instantly thrown round the Shum and his son's neck, and they were both hoisted upon the same tree, the tarade cut, and the end made fast to a branch. They were both left hanging, but I thought so aukwardly, that they would not die for some minutes, and might surely have been saved had any one dared to cut them down; but fear had fallen upon every person who had not attended the king to Tigre.

Strangely, this relatively inoffensive story was another that no one believed when Bruce returned to England. Predictably and inaccurately, Walpole condemned it:

'Would you believe that the great Abyssinian, Mr Bruce,' he wrote to William Mason,

> whom Dr B. [Bruce had just contributed his first piece of writing to Dr Burney's *History of Music*] made me laugh by seriously calling

the *intrepid traveller*, has had the intrepidity to write a letter to the Doctor, which the latter has printed in his book, and in which he intrepidly tells lies of almost as large a magnitude as his story of the bramble, into which his Majesty of Abyssinia and his whole army were led by the fault of his general, and which bramble was so tenacious, that his Majesty could not disentangle himself without stripping to the skin and leaving his robes in it, and it being death in that country to procure or compass the Sovereign's nudity, the general lost his head for the error of his march.

This must have been infuriating for the explorer as the story was more than likely true. 'Cut the kantuffa' – the traditional command when the emperor was heading off into the bush – was still an oft-heard cry in Haile Selassie's time.

On a happier note, though, the story was appreciated by Bruce's later readers. Samuel Taylor Coleridge was born in 1772, the year that Bruce returned to Britain but, when he was at Cambridge, Bruce's *Travels* was a bestseller. According to John Lowes's *The Road To Xanadu*, 'There was one book of the day which everybody who read at all was reading – Bruce's *Travels to Discover the Source of the Nile*. It had been the topic of discussion in April 1794 . . .'

Coleridge is reported with Southey to have gambolled about Cambridge with a volume of Bruce's *Travels* under his arm and to have then used parts of the story in 'Kubla Khan'. When Bruce was close to the source he remarked that: In this plain, the Nile winds more in the space of four miles than, I believe, any river in the world; it makes above a hundred turns in that distance. This is thought to be the inspiration for 'five miles meandering with a mazy motion' but the comparisons become even more obvious:

> A damsel with a dulcimer
> In a vision once I saw:
> It was an Abyssinian maid,
> And on her dulcimer she played,
> Singing of Mount Abora.
> Could I revive within me
> Her symphony and song,
> To such a deep delight 'twould win me,
> That with music loud and long,

I would build that dome in air,
That sunny dome! those caves of ice!
And all who heard should see them there,
And all should cry, Beware! Beware!
His flashing eyes, his floating hair!
Weave a circle round him thrice,
And close your eyes with holy dread,
For he on honey-dew hath fed,
And drunk the milk of Paradise.*

That great literary scourge – 'the person on business from Porlock' – walked in at this point but despite the fact that Coleridge was reading Purchas (the seventeenth-century compiler of travel literature) as he fell asleep to dream his poem, Bruce was obviously a huge influence on the poet.

Bruce was greatly disturbed by the summary execution he had witnessed. He had seen the young king's eyes flash in a way that he had never seen before: 'The cruel beginning seemed to me an omen that violent resolutions had been taken, the execution of which was immediately to follow'.

His presentiments were confirmed when, on the army's arrival at Gondar, Michael assailed a travelling band of mummers. These people were paid to sing at weddings and when not thus occupied wandered around making up songs about current events in the hopes that people in the marketplace would pay them. They had emerged in force to welcome the army and were going through their paces in the deserted marketplace when the king and Ras Michael eventually arrived in the terror-struck city, unaware that Michael had been made aware of the treacherous songs they had sung in his absence. 'Confu and the king's household troops were before, and about 200 of the Sire horse were behind; on a signal made by the Ras, these horse turned short and fell upon the singers, and cut them all to pieces. In less than two minutes they were all laid dead upon the field.'

This was merely the start. Within half an hour of arriving,

*These last two lines were inspired by Sir John Mandeville, another great but unacknowledged British explorer. See Giles Milton's excellent *The Riddle and The Knight*.

Michael had convened the first trial – that of Abba Salama, the Acab Saat. Bruce witnessed the entire trial and even took part in it. Abba Salama put up a spirited defence, claiming that he had done no wrong and had every right to excommunicate whomsoever he wished.

> He said the Iteghe, with her brothers and Ayto Aylo, had all turned Franks, so had Gusho of Amhara; and that in order to make the country Catholic, they had sent for priests, who lived with them in confidence, as that Frank did, pointing to me; That it was against the law of the country that I should be suffered here.

Bruce took hideous and calculated revenge on the man who had plagued his life from his very first day in Gondar. When Ras Michael asked him what punishment would be meted out to the bishop in Britain, Bruce replied – '"High treason is punished with death in all the countries I have ever known." This I owed to Abba Salama', considered Bruce. His wish was soon granted:

> The unfortunate Acab Saat was immediately hurried away by the guards to the place of execution, which was a large tree before the king's gate, where uttering, to the very last moment, curses against the King, the Ras, and the Abuna, he suffered the death he very richly deserved, being hanged in the very vestments in which he used to sit before the king, without one ornament of his civil or sacerdotal preeminence having been taken from him before the execution.

The trials continued in a haze of brutality but one stood out from the others – that of Guebra Denghel – for, whilst Michael judged him, his daughter (who was also Michael's granddaughter) came to beg for clemency – 'The old tyrant threatened her with immediate death, spurned her away with his foot, and in her hearing ordered her father to be immediately hanged'.

This girl – Welletta Selassie – was only seventeen but had already endured more horror in her lifetime than anyone could bear. She had been betrothed to King Joas, whom Michael had killed, then to King Hannes, whom Michael had also killed. She was now to marry King Tecla Haimanout but died before she was able to do so: 'being strongly pressed to gratify the brutal inclinations of the

Ras, her grandfather, whom when she could not resist or avoid, she took poison . . . she had taken arsenic, having no other way to avoid committing so monstrous a crime as incest with the murderer of her father'.

In the midst of all this horror, Bruce also lost Balugani, his constant companion. Although he treated the memory of Balugani badly after his death, the loss of an educated European with whom he could discuss matters must have been devastating. The only reference to this, is a note in Bruce's commonplace book on 3 March saying: 'Found in my purse belonging to me in the custody of Luigi Balugani when he died 27 pst.' (Pst is an abbreviation of piastre, a unit of currency.)

This note was first discovered by Elisabeth Fairman, the curator of rare books at the Yale Center for British Art. It is not the kind that a murderer writes after having killed his servant, but it does confirm that Bruce was misleading about the date of Balugani's death.

Bruce was now on his own in apalling circumstances. The hypocritical explorer who had condoned the first killing in this welter of carnage and torture soon tired of the stench of death. Gondar had become a charnel house.

> Blood continued to be spilt as water day after day, till the Epiphany . . . The bodies of those killed by the sword were hewn to pieces and scattered about the streets, being denied burial. I was miserable, and almost driven to despair, at seeing my hunting dogs, twice let loose by the carelessness of my servants, bringing into the court-yard the head and arms of slaughtered men, and which I could no way prevent but by the destruction of the dogs themselves; the quantity of carrion, and the stench of it, brought down the hyaenas in hundreds from the neighbouring mountains; and, as few people in Gondar go out after it is dark, they enjoyed the streets by themselves, and seemed ready to dispute the possession of the city with its inhabitants . . . at last scarce ever went out, and nothing occupied my thoughts but how to escape from the bloody country by the way of Sennaar.

This gory description is unlikely to have been exaggerated. Even in modern-day Addis Ababa, it is hard to keep the hyenas at bay.

In 1991 I visited the scene of a huge explosion at an ammunition dump in which many had died. Vultures and hyenas dogged our every move. Bruce was obviously horrified by the bloodbath and the vivid description makes one confident of its veracity. There is a false note at the end, however. The fact that Michael had just subdued Tigre meant that his route home through Massawa would be simple. The Naybe would still be after him but Bruce was now well known and powerful enough to be able to thwart the Naybe's wishes and be on his way home by the route by which he had successfully come. Why go through Sennaar, a bloodthirsty kingdom which after many years' supremacy was now also being torn apart by savage ethnic strife? Sennaar, he knew, would make Gondar look like an oasis of peace.

If Bruce wanted to trace the route that the Ark is supposed to have taken from Jerusalem this was the only way he could go. To return via Massawa would be safer, shorter and easier. There was no reason to go through Sennaar except in search of the Ark. He had already considered entering Abyssinia by that route when he had the excuse of trying to find the source of the Nile. He had found it impossible. Now, though there was no obvious reason for doing so, he determined to try again. First, though, he needed the king's permission. On 1 January 1771 it was agreed that he could leave as soon as Gusho and Powussen had been defeated. He promised the king that if he was allowed to return home he would bring back an army to fight on the side of the king: 'that, if I could not pass by Sennaar, I should come by the way of the East Indies from Surat to Masuah, which, by how much time it was more tedious, was by so much more secure, than that by Sennaar'. It is worth noting that even Bruce – in an unguarded moment – believes that Sennaar is less safe from Massawa.

I cannot but hope, the impossibility of performing this oath extinguished the sin of breaking it; at any rate it was personal and the subsequent death of the king must have freed me from it; be that as it will, it had this good effect, that it greatly composed my mind for the time, as I now no longer considered myself as involved in that ancient and general rule of the country, Never to allow a stranger to return to his home.

Being free and able to go were two very different things. Having promised to await the outcome of the final confrontation between Gusho, Powussen, Fasil and Ras Michael, Bruce could do little else but observe the negotiations. Every day new messages came from the opposing camps, treaties were agreed and reneged upon and no one was any nearer to a resolution. The whole of Abyssinia was up in arms, yet little was actually being done.

Bruce soon found himself a new role. Amha Yasous, Prince of Shoa, arrived at Gondar in a great swirl of imperial pageantry with pots of gold, and even better, a feared cavalry regiment for Michael and the king. 'Amha Yasous with his thousand horse, presented himself before the door of the tent, and rode on till he was completely in it.'

Ostensibly, the Black Horse of Shoa (as the cavalry was named) were a present from the Prince of Shoa to his overlord – the King of Kings, Tecla Haimanout – but they were in fact rather more of a bribe to insure that Shoa, an all but independent kingdom, might stay that way. Bruce was immediately made commander of the Black Horse. He and the young Amha Yasous became close friends, which allowed the student of all things Abyssinian to brush up his Amharic and learn as much as he could about the ancient kingdom of Shoa without actually having to go there. (With the Tigrean Ras Michael in the ascendancy, Tigrinya was the principal language spoken at court in Bruce's time. Shoa is where the capital now is but – more relevantly to Bruce – was where the Solomonid line managed to survive while the Zagwe dynasty reigned in Lalibela.) 'All the Ozoros, or noble women at court, fell violently in love with Amha Yasous, as fame reported, except Ozoro Esther' (who was, of course, in love with another foreigner).

Messages and contradictory reports continued to arrive from the rival camps. Powussen reported that he had captured Socinios; Fasil sent word that he would come to the king's aid as soon as Ras Michael returned to Tigre. Others came to pay homage to the restored king, the least significant but most amusing of whom was Guanguol, a Galla commander.

He was a little, thin, cross-made man, of no apparent strength or swiftness, as far as could be conjectured; his legs and thighs being small and thin for his body, and his head large; he was of a yellow, unwholesome colour, not black nor brown; he had long hair, plaited and interwoven with the bowels of an oxen, and so knotted and twisted together as to render it impossible to distinguish the hair from the bowels, which hung down in long strings, part before his breast and part behind his shoulder, the most extraordinary ringlets I have ever seen. He had likewise a ring of guts hung about his neck, and several rounds of the same about his middle, which served as a girdle, below which was a short cotton cloth dipt in butter, and all his body was wet, and running down with the same; he seemed to be about fifty years of age, with a confident and insolent superiority painted in his face. In his country it seems when he appears in state, the beast he rides upon is a cow. He was then in full dress and ceremony, and mounted upon one, not of the largest sort, but which had monstrous horns.

The king sped laughing from the tent at the first sight of the offal-bearing cow so that when the little warrior dismounted he sat in the only available chair – the king's. He was beaten and hurled from the room by outraged courtiers since it was treason to sit on the king's chair. Pardoned – he could not have known otherwise – Guanguol was sent away from the camp and later killed by Ayto Confu for treachery unconnected with this incident, but the story of his arrival travelled far and wide. Bruce later encouraged an unfortunate dwarf to dress up like the Galla commander and repeat the episode as a charade for Ras Michael and anyone else who had not seen it. The incident became a source of great amusement in the grim atmosphere of the court. Guanguol exacted his revenge from beyond the grave: his descendants ruled Ethiopia for the next century.

By the end of March, the stalemate was becoming absurd. The armies of Gusho, Woodage Asahel, Fasil, Kasmati Ayabdar, Powussen and many more were exercising around Gondar trying to tempt the wily old general into an attack. The poor of the city were starving since no food could get past the gathering armies, there was little or no firewood, yet the diplomacy continued:

At last the cries of the people flying into Gondar, seeking protection from the cruelties of the rebels, determined the Ras to march out,

and set his all upon the fortune of the battle . . . Having previously
called in all his outposts, on the 13th of May he marched out of
Gondar, taking with him the king and Abuna, as also Ozoro Esther,
and Ozoro Altash her sister, and all the other ladies about the court,
who were in possession of the great fiefs of the crown, and whom
he obliged to personal attendance, as well as to bring the quota of
troops they were bound to by their respective tenures.

It was a vast army that set out from the imperial capital –
more than 30,000 foot soldiers and musketeers supported by 7500
medieval cavalry dressed in chain mail, they and their horses
covered in weighty, reinforced leather coats that would shield
them from the slings and arrows of any aggressors. The Tigrean
infantry – the most feared in the land – were armed to a man with
spears and shields, many wearing long-haired Colobus monkey
skins on their heads: Bruce himself wore a chain mail coat and a
tall helmet surmounted by a black and yellow horsehair plume.
This would have made him almost seven feet tall.

Upon the front of each helmet was a silver star, at least a white
metal one; and before the face, down to the top of the nose, a flap
of iron chain, made in the same manner as the coat of mail, but
only lighter, which served as a vizor. This was the most troublesome
part of the whole, it was hot and heavy, and constantly fretted the
cheek and nose, when either the man or the horse were in motion;
and therefore I always substituted a black silk net, which concealed
my colour better, and for the rest of my face I committed it to the
care of Providence.

Ras Michael commanded the van, whilst Bruce was in the centre
where the young king's command was monitored by the experienced and brave Guebra Mascal.

Bruce could bluster with the best of them but he had never
actually fought in a battle before, though of course he had witnessed the Battle of Crevelt when he was on his grand tour in
1758. In the battle to come Bruce would be expected to participate.
In Abyssinia there was much of the same battlefield chivalry that
was still prevalent in Europe – there was constant communication
between the two camps, and as in Europe the officers took their

wives and mistresses with them – and there were more than 10,000 women dancing attendance on Michael's warriors.

Serbraxos was to be of immense importance. The battle had been brewing for years and was to be utterly decisive: it would decide who would control the king. Ras Michael, Fasil, Gusho, Powussen, all had their fortunes invested in the outcome. Bruce soon found himself in the middle of it.

A strange rumour had spread through the country which augured that a decisive battle would be fought at Serbraxos and that from it would emerge a new emperor named Theodros: (It was because of this prophecy that 100 years later the emperor, who was later to kill himself after the British victory over his troops at Magdala, took the name Theodros.) This new king, said the prophecy, would then go on to rule peacefully for many years. In Abyssinia's superstitious climate it was thus logical that anyone spoiling for a fight should head straight for Serbraxos. But as Michael's army arrived, and before a proper battle could begin, their rear was attacked by the marauding Woodage Asahel and the large army that he had gathered about him. The baggage was saved only by the intervention of Bruce's friend and patient, Ayto Confu, who had disobeyed his orders to protect Gondar and had ventured out in search of battle.

Michael, infuriated by this unruliness, had sat outside his campaign tent, playing draughts and refusing to help his son, crying all the while that the boy should be allowed to win his spurs. The engagement lasted an hour and Confu did indeed prove himself, although he had to be helped by Bruce and some musketeers who acted with Michael's permission, and Ayto Engedan, who disobeyed orders to help the boy. Confu was wounded twice in the mêlée but honour was preserved when 126 pairs of testicles were hurled to the ground in front of the king. The first engagement at Serbraxos had been in specific breach of orders but it had at least been a victory.

Notwithstanding the natural hardness of his heart, and that the misfortune which had happened was in immediate disobedience of orders, Ras Michael shewed great sensibility at hearing that Confu was wounded; he came immediately to see him, a visit not according to etiquette, and gave him a slighter reproof than was expected for leaving his post in the town, as well as for fighting without his orders.

Bruce was commanded to take the wounded Confu back to Gondar and to see that the young nobleman was in good hands before returning. Accordingly, Bruce rode through the night and made sure Confu was properly cared for. Letters for Bruce and horses and armour for the king had arrived from Sennaar but Bruce had much to do before he rejoined the army. Two days later he set off again 'to the camp, taking twenty horse from Sanuda, and twenty from Confu, to escort the coats of mail and horses from Sennaar'.

Little had happened whilst he was away. The generals watched from hillsides the goings-on below as their respective troops tried to avoid clashing as they foraged for food and water. The only decisive action had been between some of Gusho's troops and Bruce's own cavalry from Ras el Feel which, in Bruce's absence, were commanded by Yasine. During the skirmish, Gusho's favourite horse had been captured by one of Bruce's men and, as was the custom, Gusho had immediately sent messages to the king petitioning for its return. This was deemed perfectly acceptable, whereon Yasine took the horse back to Gusho who 'cloathed Yasine magnificently, made him a present of another horse, and sent a very flattering message by him to me'. The entire campaign was fought throughout with a strange combination of appalling savagery and strict chivalry. Every day the opposing generals would make enquiries as to who (not simply the king) would be wearing what on the battlefield, not so that they could be targeted but so they could be protected from harm.

Later on the same day, the camp was struck and the army made its way along the plain to the hill of Serbraxos, a few miles further on. The king, attended by Bruce, reached the bottom of the hill safely without hindrance but Michael – who had gone on further with a third of the army – was set upon by Powussen's cavalry. Michael retreated before them and managed to lure them within range of his muskets, with lethal results. The elderly Ras lost his Fit-Auraris and 300 men in the fighting but the engagement could be judged a success since 900 of Powussen's men died on the field.

Meanwhile at the foot of the hill, the king was watering his horse when they were attacked by an attachment of Galla cavalry belonging to Gusho's uncle, Ayabdar. Bruce had his first taste of battle and it was a savage one; these troops were the late King Joas's bodyguard, and they had come to the field with scores to settle. The king ordered Bruce and the Black Horse forward and 'the Galla were all borne down, with little or no resistance, by the length of our pikes, and the superior weight of our horses, and those that were not slain were scattered over the plain'. Chaos ensued when the king's musketeers fired down into the throng from the top of the hill. They managed to kill seven of their own men and wound many others including Prince George, the king's younger brother. This small action was significant; having lost his Galla cavalry, Ayabdar retreated and earned the ire of all the other rebels, further splitting the loose, fractious alliance.

In the evening the Ras fell back and the entire army camped on Serbraxos, dominating the field where the decisive battle would be fought.

> This was the first battle of Serbraxos, which, though it contained nothing decisive, had still two very material consequences; as it so daunted the spirit of the Begemder horse [Powussen's men], that many chiefs of that country withdrew their troops and went home, whilst such discord was sown among the leaders, that I believe they never sincerely trusted one another afterwards; Gusho and Ayabdar, in particular, were known to correspond with the king daily.

Over the next two days messages passed back and forth between the armies, fever swept through the rebel army but streaming rain and increasing cold meant that all the armies were losing their will to fight. In fact, the whole affair was nearly concluded without the need to engage in battle at all. None of the rebels – well aware that he was a puppet – had anything against the king: it was the all-powerful Ras Michael whom they wished to overthrow so that they in turn could become the king's puppet masters. Rules of protocol, however, decreed that they could not do what Michael would have done: have their enemy murdered. Fortuitously, a Gurague robber nearly did that for them.

These Gurague,

all wear their hair very short, strip themselves stark-naked, and besmear themselves from head to foot with butter, or some sort of grease, whilst, along the outside of their arm, they tie a long, straight, two-edged, sharp-pointed knife, the handle reaching into the palm of their hand, and about four inches of the blade above the knob of their elbow, so that the whole blade is safe and inoffensive when the arm is extended; but when it is bent, about four inches projects, and is bare beyond the elbow joint; this being all prepared, they take a leafy faggot, such as the gatherers of fuel bring to camp, which they fasten to their middle by a string or withy, spreading it over to conceal or cover all their back, and then drawing in their legs, they lie down, in all appearance, as a faggot, and in the part of the camp they intend to rob, crawling slowly in the dark when they think they are unperceived, and lying still when there is any noise or movement near them: In case they find themselves discovered, they slip the faggot and run; and whatever part of them you seize escapes your fingers by reason of the grease. If you endeavour to clasp them, however, which is the only way left, the Gurague bends his elbow and strikes you with the knife, and you are mortally wounded.

One of two Gurague had made his way into Michael's tent and, when discovered, had murdered one of the Ras's servants in trying to effect his escape. The camp was in uproar and the next day was spent dealing with the endless messages from the opposing army denying responsibility for the attempted murder. Indeed, the Gurague and his companion made so many confessions in the course of their ensuing torture that it was never discovered whether one of the opposing generals had broken with protocol or not. Either way it delayed once more the impending battle. It was not until the following day – ten days after the king had left Gondar – that he eventually took to the field below Serbraxos and offered battle to the rebel army. It poured with rain and the offer was not taken up. In showing reticence the rebels made a tactical error. They had few firearms but many more men; thus, had they attacked during the storm, the Ras's men would not have been able to use their muskets and Michael would have been defeated.

Thanks to the unexpected arrival of a wandering herd of cattle, which solved the food shortage, the night was spent in feasting and drinking. Bruce taught his fellow officers how to make toasts and they drank countless horns of mead in perfecting the art.

I only went to the king's tent, where the company was dispersing, and kissed his hand, after which I retired. In my way home to my tent, I saw a faggot lying in the way, when the story of the Gurague came presently into my mind. I ordered some soldiers to separate it with their lances; but it had been brought for fuel, at least no Gurague was there.

The king was determined to take the field first, so after break-fasting early the army arrayed itself out on the valley floor.

The king's infantry was drawn up in one line, having a musketeer between every two men, with lances and shields. Immediately in the center was the black horse, and the Moors of Ras el Feel, with their libds [armoured ponchos that covered the man and horse entirely] disposed on each of their flanks. Immediately behind these was the king in person, with a large body of young nobility and great officers of state, about him. On the right and left flank of the line, a little in the rear, were all the rest of the king's horse, divided into two large bodies, Guebra Mascal hid in the bank on our left at right angles with the line, enfilading, as I have already said, the whole line of our infantry.

The army waited for the enemy to appear with their pretender, who had been named Theodros, to accord with the prophecy. The early morning sun and night wind had dried the ground on the plain but the hill behind them had been turned into a mire by the thousands camped upon it and now that all the trees had been cut down for firewood. They waited half an hour before the other camp stirred, and when they did it was a fearsome sight.

For the space of a minute, a thick cloud of dust (like the smoke of a large city fire) appeared on the side of Korreva, occasioned, as the day before, by the Begemder troops mounting on horseback; the ground where they were encamped being trodden into powder, by such a number of men and horse passing over it so often, and

now arised by the motion of the horses feet, was whirled round
by a very modest breeze, that blew steadily; it every minute
increased in darkness, and assumed various shapes and forms, of
towers, castles, and battlements, as fancy suggested.

Soon Powussen's men came out to meet the king and the two
armies faced off against each other across the plain. 'In the middle
of their cavalry . . . a large red flag was seen to rise, and was saluted
by the drums and trumpets of the whole army.' This was the flag
of the pretender Theodoros, under whose banner the rebel army
had decided to fight. At the sight of this Tecla Haimanout's
musicians started pounding their kettle drums in homage to their
king and Powussen's army took this as the signal to attack. The
heavy horse of Begemdir stormed towards Bruce and the king's
army only to be bowled over by Guebra Mascal's well-directed
musket fire. The loyalist line charged and hacked a way through
the middle of Powussen's army, dividing it in two. The king dived
into the gap and would have been split from his footsoldiers had
not the more experienced Kefla Yasous been covering his rear: 'A
common soldier in the king's household, busied in the vile practise
of mangling and spoiling the dead, found the red colours of king
Theodros lying upon the field, which he delivered me, upon
promise of a reward, and which I gave a servant of my own to
keep until after the engagement'.

The king meanwhile had been caught on a steep river bank
where he had lost his musicians to the enemy. He was in danger
of capture when his horse was seized and dragged by Sertza Denghel (a relation of Gusho's who was none the less loyal to the
king) down the bank and across the river. This infuriated the king
– who refused to retreat in front of the rebels – so much that he
broke his rescuer's front teeth with a lance. He was none the less
pulled to safety and the rest of his army, fearful for the king's safety
and neglecting their battle roles, were able to get back to work.
Powussen was wounded during an ill-fated charge and was seen
by both armies being carried from the battlefield. Soon after it
began to rain and both armies withdrew to their original positions.
Three thousand of the king's men had perished against 9000
on Powussen's side, but once again nothing had been decided.

Glorious though the last few hours had been for the young king, his own inexperience had led to no more than a Pyrrhic victory: 'This battle, though it was rather a victory than a defeat, had, however, upon the king's affairs, all the bad consequences of the latter, nor was there any thinking man who had confidence in them from that day forward'.

In the course of the battle Bruce had managed to have an argument with his old enemy, Guebra Mascal, which led to an absurd confrontation after the king and the great officers of state had been showered, in the time-honoured tradition, with the severed genitalia of the slain enemy by their troops. Having tended to as many of his wounded comrades as he could and seen to the health of all his men, Bruce went to the king, taking with him the red flag of Theodoros. He spread the colours on the carpet before the young king and sung the praises of the one man in the army who actively disliked him:

> So may all your majesty's enemies fall, as this arch rebel (the bearer of this) has fallen today . . . He was killed, as I suppose by a shot of Guebra Mascal, on the flank of our line . . . this day, my fortune has been to be near him during the whole of it, and I say it from certain inspection, that to the bravery and activity of Guebra Mascal every man in your left wing owes his life or liberty.

As Bruce was recounting this, Guebra Mascal himself rushed in to the king's presence claiming that Bruce was lying and that he, Guebra Mascal, had killed Theodoros. This was the second time that Guebra Mascal had humiliated himself over Bruce and it was left to his friends to drag him from the tent and explain what had happened. 'Guebra Mascal, now crying like a child, condemned himself for a malicious madman.' The two eventually made peace and the king forgave him. But Bruce retired to bed in low spirits, refusing even to go and see Esther before he did so. He knew that nothing had been resolved and that there was more senseless brutality to come. He slept well despite the noise of the trophy hunters with their castrating knives competing with the hyenas over the bodies of the dead and dying on the great plain below.

The next day was spent exchanging messages with the opposing camps and with Fasil, who still had not entered the fray. In the morning, Bruce and Guebra Mascal were called to Michael's tent where they were clothed appropriately by the Ras and sent to the king. They were nervous after the events of the night before, when the Ras had not deigned to speak to them; but to their surprise the king rewarded them both for their bravery – Guebra Mascal with lands and Bruce with a gold chain. They repaired to Michael's tent where the canny old general 'lifted up his head, smiled, and said, "well, are you friends now?"'

A few hours later there arrived on the field a man whose mere presence was to change the whole course of the battle: Ayto Tesfos, the governor of Samen, had come down from the Jew's Rock where he had defied Michael's rule since the murder of King Joas. He brought with him only 1000 men but the sight of these fellow Tigreans fighting on the other side had a devastating effect on the morale of Michael's army. 'There is a march peculiar to the troops of Tigre, which, when the drums of Tesfos beat at passing, a despondency seemed to fall on all the Tigran soldiers, greater than if ten thousand men of Amhara had joined the rebels.'

Tesfos immediately attacked a number of Kefla Yasous's men who were watering their horses and killed several, an act that demanded revenge. In the middle of the night Kefla Yasous led a retaliatory attack against Tesfos's men who had camped insultingly close to the king's army. Amid terrible confusion there was wholesale slaughter. Bruce managed to carry off a beautiful drinking horn which he brought back to England and later gave to Sir Thomas Dundas (his future father-in-law) 'to serve for a bugle-horn to the Fauconberg regiment'. When Powussen's men retaliated, they fell into a trap laid by Guebra Mascal and, when the sun rose the next morning, the dead were seen to be men of Begemdir and Lasta. The only member of the Black Horse to be injured was Bruce himself. Somewhat unglamorously, he suffered concussion when hit on the head by a rock, but it is to his credit that he mentions the absurd injury at all. In the morning came the dispiriting news that the rebels had been through Gondar – behind the king's army – and had taken Sanuda, Ayto Confu and Ayto Engedan prisoner. 'On the 24th, in the morning, a message arrived from Gusho to the king, desiring I might have liberty to come and bring medicines with me, for his whole family were ill with fever.'

In the bizarre atmosphere of the battle, where the opposing armies spent more time negotiating than fighting, this was deemed a perfectly normal request and Bruce refused only because of his sore head. In the afternoon the armies of Coque Abou Barea, Woodage Asahel, Heraclius, Mammo and Tesfos combined to attack the king's army. Entrenched on the lethally slippery hill, Michael had ordered the building of small walls for defensive purposes and that day it saved their lives: 'About noon, the hill was assaulted on all sides that were accessible, and the ancient spirit of the troops seemed to revive, upon seeing the enemy were the aggressors'. They managed to hold the hill but only with great effort and some humiliation. Woodage Asahel had been able to gallop through the emperor's camp and bow to the king's tent before being wounded and driven back with the rest of his men. Once again many had died and nothing had been resolved.

The next day, whilst the two armies licked their wounds, Bruce was given permission to cross the field of battle and tend to Gusho's family. Thus, he was able to see inside the opposing camp where the rebel army was suffering from some virulent but unspecified disease. He tended to Gusho's relations and enquired after his friends but was not allowed to see them. Miraculously, Gusho said that he had letters sent from Metical Aga for Bruce, one of which was from Captain Price, his friend in Jiddah. He was not allowed to see them, however, until the battle had been decided.

While Bruce was returning across no-man's-land, a mysterious stranger (claiming to be the servant of a friend) approached him and warned him that he should stay close to the king if he valued his life. He returned in pensive mood to see Ras Michael. The king was slightly unwell, and Bruce sent a message saying that he would not visit, for the king should get some rest: 'I thought he embraced this proposal willingly, Ozoro Esther having had a long conference with him the night before. I do not imagine the state of the realm had much share in the conversation,' noted the love-sick Bruce. Later in the day he repeated the message that he had received to the court. 'Stay close to Tecla Haimanout', he had been told. The king 'was violently agitated' by the news and linked it with the prophecy of another 'holy man'. 'As you value your life' said the king 'open not your mouth to man or woman, nor seem to take particular care about any thing.'

The armies never fought again. Powussen's soldiers were in a bad way. Disease was ravaging their ranks and they could not dislodge Ras Michael from his position on Serbraxos. The Ras had run out of food, his soldiers were losing their nerve and the enemy was harassing the road between them and Gondar. Some of Powussen's soldiers came in the night to steal mules and instead of merely shooting them the guards panicked and cried out that 'Fasil is coming'. Michael was even losing the support of his generals. On 28 May they decided independently that they must fall back on Gondar or lose the support of the army, and in order to do it safely they would have to conduct the retreat in the middle of the night. Ras Michael did not fear much but, bizarrely, he was terrified of the dark. He overcame his fear, however, so as to escape the burning humiliation of retreating in broad daylight. 'The Ras was now obliged to make a virtue of necessity; and it was given in orders, that the army should be ready to decamp at eight in the evening, but nobody should strike their tent before that hour on pain of death. The old general was ashamed to be seen, for the first time, flying before his enemies.'

The army made its way back to Gondar, slipping down the muddy sides of the mountain and scampering across the plain, and the rebels did not trouble to capture more than a few. They knew they had won. Bruce approached the city walls, riding with the king and Ras Michael:

> The whole road was now as smooth as a carpet; and we had scarce done speaking when Ras Michael's mule fell flat on the ground, and threw him upon his face in a small puddle of water. He was quickly lifted up unhurt, and set upon his mule again . . . the mule fell again, and threw the Ras another time in the dirt; on which a general murmur and groan was heard from all his attendants, for every body interpreted this as an omen that his power and fortune were gone from him for ever.

In later years Bruce's account was to be questioned again, this time by Salt in Lord Valentia's travels. Many others queried similarly whether Bruce had actually been at Serbraxos. Sir Walter Scott knew both men.

'I think Lord Valentia is rather inferior to Bruce,' wrote Scott in 1808:

> I know that surly Patagonian and though he may have romanced in matters where his own prowess was concerned yet I think no one could ever have described the battle of Serbraxos and the strange dispersion which afterwards took place, without having seen it. General Murray saw two Abyssinians in upper Egypt at the time of the Indian Army's being there, the elder of whom remembered Bruce as the commander of the Koccob horse . . . I therefore think the negative evidence as to his warlike and princely character good for little . . . a prince who left Bruce at home if he could have brought him out neglected the most able bodied associate you ever saw. Pendragon was a joke to him in size and muscle.

It was to a quiet and dispirited Gondar that 'Pendragon' and the king returned: no obeisant crowds to meet them, no mummers to sing their praises (perhaps cowed by the previous experiences of their kind at Michael's hands) and no sycophantic priests to curry favour. 'The king went directly to the palace, the Ras to his own house.' Bruce himself went home to check on his servants and store his baggage, but, feeling sorry for the abandoned king and remembering the whispered warning, soon went to the palace where he spent the night. 'The palace was quite deserted; even the king's slaves, of both sexes (fearing to be carried off to Begemder and Amhara) had hid themselves among the monks, and in the houses of private friends, so that the king was left with very few attendants.'

It seemed that Bruce's time in Gondar was to end in disaster. The people to whom he had allied himself were on the very brink of destruction, clinging pathetically to a capital that the rebels could not even be bothered to attack. Bruce had permission to leave now, but from a boy whose permission was no longer worth a great deal.

CHAPTER 10

ASTRONOMICAL SUCCESS

Bruce spent a cold night playing the faithful servant, asleep on a bull's hide in the palace. Although no one had come to greet the royal party on its arrival, the town was in fact full. All those that had fled to Fasil, who had been lurking in the background throughout the fighting, had returned on Gusho's promise that they would not be harmed. By nine o'clock the next morning, they were less sure of themselves. The rebel army, too, had marched during the night and by nine the town was entirely surrounded by the camps of the various commanders who were loosely allied against Ras Michael. Whilst Fasil, who had not fought at Serbraxos, was temporarily out of the picture, and Powussen was procrastinating, Gusho rushed to fill the gap. The people of Gondar were much more sophisticated than their countrymen since this was the only place in the realm that could then be called a city. They immediately looked to Gusho as their new leader as he was a courtly sophisticate who had been born and bred at Gondar. 'Powussen, and the rest, were looked upon as freebooters in their inclinations, at least by the townsmen; very little better than Michael, or his troops of Tigre' who had terrorized them for so long.

Michael and his army were trapped in Gondar and Gusho's immediate assumption of power was not even resisted by them. After more than fifty years as an unbeatable commander – feared throughout the realm – Michael lost his army without putting up a fight. The seventy-four-year-old's nephew and best general, Guebra Mascal, was the first to betray him. Only two days earlier he had been saving the skin of Michael and the king with his well-directed fire and faultless tactics. Now, 'he carried down to the place appointed, and surrendered, about 6,000 muskets, belonging to the Ras and his family. All the principal officers followed.' By midday almost every man in Michael's previously triumphant army had laid down his weapons and made camp under the watchful eye of Gusho's guards. 'Kefla Yasous alone, with about 400 men, had shut himself up in the church of Debra Berhan, where there was water, and he carried in sufficient provisions for several days.'

Even Kefla Yasous, though, was not going to help the betrayed tyrant. Having made a special treaty with Gusho, he merely refused to surrender with the common herd. By the end of the day, he had ordered most of his men to surrender their weapons and had been granted special concessions to retire – armed – to his own residence in Gondar with his weapons and bodyguard intact. Michael was left unattended and deserted in the palace of his office, watching as his power bled away:

> He played no more at drafts, by which game formerly he pretended to divine the issue of every affair of consequence, but gave his draft-board and men to a private friend; at the same time renouncing his pretended divinations, as deceitful and sinful, by the confidence he had placed in them.
>
> The next day, when he heard how ill his disarmed men were treated by the populace, when they were dismissed to Tigre, he burst into tears and cried out in great agony, 'Had I died before this, I had been happy!'

Bruce, meanwhile, stayed close to the king, who was behaving with great dignity as all those who had been mistreated in the past rushed to show their contempt for the fallen emperor: 'Some of the priests and monks, as is their custom, used certain liberties, and mixed a considerable degree of impertinence in their conversations . . . These he only answered with a severe look, but said nothing.'

Gusho put a stop to the insolence as soon as he heard of it, but he had not yet the measure of his new duties as Ras. On the first day he forgot his duty to send food to the king and his now tiny household. He would have to learn quickly if he wished to survive.

Messengers went to and from the palace but no one came to court save Bruce and a few elderly judges who were past playing games with the new and inexperienced Ras. Michael's once feared army was sent, defenceless, back to Tigre under light escort, through country that countless times over the last fifty years it had burned and pillaged. The local populace took their revenge by picking off the stragglers, stoning them and stripping them naked. Powussen, conscious that it could well have been his army in the same position, soon gave them Ayto Tesfos as an escort and made clear, by example, that anyone interfering with the defeated army would be punished.

In the transitional chaos the king was forgotten by all but Bruce and a few servants. During the period of instability, fourteen Galla came to the palace and began destroying the Venetian mirrors in the presence-chamber as the king watched from his throne. Bruce, though unarmed and outnumbered, feared for the king's life and was ready to intervene: 'We all three, therefore, got up and stood before the king, who made a gentle motion with his hand, as if to say, "Stay a little," or, "have patience".'

He was saved only by the timely intervention of Tensa Christos, a priest who had been given the job of policing Gondar but had almost arrived too late. Two of the Galla were executed and the rest whipped. 'These were all the executions which followed this great and sudden revolution; a proof of very exemplary moderation in the conquerors.'

On 1 June, Gusho and Powussen, forced by circumstances into a renewal of their alliance, came to see the Ras, still lurking in his palace, but no longer dressed in the 'insignia of command': they were met by the old hawk, disconcertingly clothed as a monk. 'From thence Gusho and Powussen went to the king's palace, where they did homage, and took the oaths of allegiance.' At last normality had been restored. Gusho was confirmed in the office of Ras which he had already assumed and, for the first time in his life, Tecla Haimanout took up the reins of power. Under Michael he had always been a puppet, yet with the rebel camp so divided he was able to assert his authority in a way that had never been possible when Michael, the man he called his 'father', had been in power.

On 4 June, Powussen arrived unexpectedly in Gondar, mounted Ras Michael on a mule and carried him away with his army back to Begemdir. Soon after the other armies began to make their way home before the rains made their returns impossible. 'Gusho took possession of the Ras's house and office' but all this was happening without force, which may have been effective in eighteenth-century Europe but was destined to failure in Abyssinia. The only person maintaining a semblance of order was Fasil. Had not Fasil been 'hovering with his army' the town would have fallen into anarchy since all the new officers of state were ruling without armies and had yet to assume the natural authority that accompanied their offices. Over the course of the month, the Iteghe returned from her self-imposed exile in Gojam to the plaudits of the Gondarenes, Socinios was brought back in chains and was sentenced to death, later commuted to perpetual slavery in the king's kitchens. (Even later, he was executed for stealing a chicken.) Yet if the battles of the last year had decided nothing, now neither did the peace.

At last, Fasil made his move. Coming to town at the head of the only army still in the field, he made straight for the palace to pay homage to the Iteghe and the king. He greeted Bruce like an old friend, astonishing the king who had been unable to charm the brutal general.

'I wish you would tell me, Yagoube,' said the king,

> how you reconcile all these people to you. It is a secret which will be of much more importance to me than to you. There is Gusho now, for example, so proud of his present fortune, that he scarcely will say a civil word to me; and Fasil has brought me a list of his own servants, whom he wants to make mine without asking my leave . . . yet he never sees you come into the room but he begins immediately joking and pleasant conversation.

The king was perceptive in noting this ease with people, one of the principal reasons why Bruce had survived so long. He seemed always to have the right word for the many people – generals, warlords, kings, sultans – he met in his travels. He was a master of courtly chivalry; strangely, among his own people this was one of his principal failings. Abroad, he was equal to anything, but in Britain he was invariably described as socially inept, rude and curmudgeonly. Fanny Burney, who often found him exasperating, was one of the few who managed to bring Bruce out of his shell:

> Except what I have written, almost ever word that he [Bruce] said was addressed *en badinage* to plague Bell [one of the Stranges' young daughters], or in diverting himself with Miss Strange's parrot. He seemed determined not to enter into conversation with the company in general, nor to speak upon any but trifling topics. It is pity, that a man who seems to have some generous feelings, that break out by starts, and who certainly is a man of learning and of humour, should be thus run away with by pride (and self-conceit).

From the court of Louis XV to that of the barbarian King of Sennaar, Bruce always managed to extricate himself with dignity whilst bending others to his will. When he returned to England, however, he left behind his courtly manners and behaved exactly as he wished. He was never treated well at the British court. For years he was a figure of fun, though much feared and always treated with respect to his face. According to a story corroborated by O. G. S. Crawford, an expert on Sudan, George III

> secreted the drawings which he had accepted from Bruce when the traveller's character and veracity became questioned. Later when Bruce had regained credit, search was made for the drawings, which was only ended when the King, in 'one of his short and partial suspensions from his sad calamity', sent for Barnard [the royal librarian] and told him where to find them.

As we heard earlier, Walpole added to his stories about Bruce: 'Remember this letter is only for your own private eye; I do not desire to be engaged in a controversy or a duel'.

In Gondar there was still a feeling of unease on the streets. After years of Michael's brutal rule, the citizens had come to respect him as well as to fear him. In his new role as Ras, Gusho was presumptuous and his authority soon came under threat. He treated the king and the old Iteghe, who had returned to Gondar at the king's invitation, with a marked lack of respect and he was soon using his office to make as much money as possible. He tried to do this through the force of his own personality – his army had returned to Amhara – but it was not sufficient. His allies were

charged for offices which they believed that they had won on the
battlefield. By 16 July, matters had come to a head. The people
of Gondar, who had known Gusho all his life, would put up with
him but the officers of state, the shums and the great noblemen
were outraged by his behaviour. Gusho, anticipating a crisis, made
the pretence that he had to take a pilgrimage to Saint Michael's
in Azazo as completion of a vow. 'And, accordingly, early in the
morning, he set out for that village, attended with thirty horse
and fifty musketeers.'

This was a mistake; particularly in regard to the size of the bodyguard. Ras Michael would have taken a bigger bodyguard to have a
bath. As Bruce had seen to his chagrin, Princess Esther took 300
men with her when she attended a banquet. The king seized his
opportunity. After a brief resistance and flight, Gusho was picked
up by a local shum on Tecla Haimanout's orders and was returned
to Gondar with his head shaven, a sign of humility: 'He was
cloathed in black, and was confined that same day (the first of
August) a close prisoner, and in irons, in a high, damp, uninhabited
tower of the king's house, without being pitied by either party'.

As this statecraft went on around him, Bruce had only one thing
on his mind – his return to the West – and he was still insistent
on travelling via Sennaar. From the border of Abyssinia, the entire
journey would take him through warring states that had never
before allowed a white man to pass and where he could rely on
no one for help. He had letters, but they were to people who
cared nothing for foreigners and were busy fighting for their own
lives. Metical Aga's servant, Mahomet Gibberti, was in Gondar
and would have made a perfect travelling companion had Bruce
decided to return through Massawa. Captain Price had gone to
considerable trouble to stay in touch with him and would support
any of Bruce's claims to British support if necessary. Despite the
fact that the French East India Company had just gone bankrupt
– causing Price appalling problems – he still worried about Bruce
and sent him long letters full of spelling mistakes (he was 'un
lettered' and wrote through an official secretary) in which he
enquired about the traveller and gave him news of Europe and
elsewhere. Even though Bruce only received two of his letters,
they must have offered a welcome glimpse of life outside the savage

kingdom. Bruce, however, was 'determined to attempt completing my journey through Sennaar and the desert'.

Yasine had brought Bruce a letter from Sennaar during the battle at Serbraxos in which the explorer had been told:

> that to come from Ras el Feel to Sennaar, was, for a white man like me, next to an absolute impossibility, connecting the danger of the way with the great hardships from the excessive heat of the climate, and want of food and water; that even arrived at Sennaar, I should be in the utmost danger from the soldiery, and the king's slaves, under no subordination, or government; and that, even if I was happy enough to escape there, the worst still remained, and no human power could convey, or protect me, in my remaining journey to Egypt through the great desert. I was therefore begged to lay all such intention aside as impossible, and either stay where I was, or return by Tigre, Masuah, and Arabia, the way by which I first entered Abyssinia. This was the severest of all blows to me, and threw me for some time into the lowest despondency; but it did not change my resolution, which was already taken, not to turn to the right or left, but either to complete my journey to Syene [Aswan], the frontier of Egypt, by Sennaar, and Nubia or perish in the attempt.

There is no reason why he should wish to take this route, save for the fact that he wanted to follow the presumed itinerary of the Ark. If we believe that Bruce's only object was to discover the source of the Nile then his grail quest was over. He was among friends in Abyssinia, even now in unsettled Tigre. If he went through Massawa with Metical Aga's servant, his safety was as good as guaranteed and regardless of that, now that he was the king's friend, the king could be relied upon to pressure the Naybe into assisting him. The journey to Massawa was 300 miles. Aswan was a thousand miles further.

> I told Metical Aga's servant the bad news I had got from Sennaar, and he agreed perfectly with the contents, adding, that the journey was not practicable; he declared they were so inhuman and so barbarous a race, that he would not attempt the journey, Mahometan as he was, for half the Indies. I begged him to say no more on

that head, but to produce from his master, Metical Aga at Mecca,
a letter to any man of consequence he knew at Sennaar.

Nothing could put Bruce off. Like a latter-day Parsifal, he prepared
for what was to be by far the most dangerous part of his journey.
He had mules, horses and servants who would help him in his
journey but had run perilously short of cash. He solved this problem by borrowing £300 from a Greek who was desperate to get
money out of the country. Bruce expressed astonishment that his
cheque reached England:

> It was the only piece of writing of any kind which found its way
> to its intended destination, though many had been written by me
> on different occasions which presented for Arabia; so that I will
> recommend to all travellers, for the future, to tack bills of exchange
> to their letters of greatest consequence, as a sure method of pre-
> venting their miscarriage.

The African Greeks were the eighteenth-century equivalent of
today's African Asians. Whilst controlling all trade, they were
always trying to send money home, and they always found a way
to do so. The same applies today to their successors. I once cashed
a British cheque with an Asian storekeeper in the Angolan highland
town of Huambo shortly before taking off from the airport. The
next day the city was surrounded by UNITA and besieged for
over a year. The cheque was presented in Leicester within a month.

Leaving was not an easy task for Bruce. Sickened and disgusted
by the brutality of the country, he was desperate to return home
and had the king's permission to do so. After saying farewell to
the king, his great love Esther, his friends from the Muslim town
and all the people who had helped him in his arduous journey,
he went to Koscam finally to take leave of his most constant patron,
the Iteghe. At the Iteghe's palace he found the usual collection of
priests, one of whom, Tensa Christos (who had earlier been given
the responsibility of policing Gondar), was strong and honourable
enough for Bruce to have admired. 'He was however, reputed a
person of great probity and sanctity of manners, and had been, on
all occasions, rather civil and friendly to me when we met.'

This priest asked leave to put one more question to the traveller, who puzzled him even after all Bruce's time at court – 'whether or not you really are a Frank, Catholic, or Jesuit?' For the last time the whole matter was gone into again in detail. It only ended when Bruce, wishing to leave, showed, once again, his hard-learned flair for diplomacy.

'And now, holy father,' he said, 'I have one, last favour, to ask of you, which is your forgiveness, if I have at any time offended you; your blessing, now that I am immediately to depart, if I have it not; and your prayers while on my long and dangerous journey, through countries of infidels and pagans.'

His wish was granted and for the last time he prostrated himself before the Iteghe and left the court.

> Twenty greasy monks, however, had placed themselves in my way as I went out, that they might have the credit of giving me my blessing likewise after Tensa Christos. As I had very little faith in the prayers of these drones, so I had some reluctance to kiss their greasy hands and sleeves; however, in running this disagreeable gauntlet, I gave them my blessing in English, – Lord send you a halter, as he did to Abba Salama (meaning the Acab Saat [who had been hanged with Bruce's wholehearted support]). But they, thinking that I was recommending them to the patriarch Abba Salama, pronounced at random, with great seeming devotion, their Amen, – So be it.

With this 'humorous Adieu' as Murray referred to it, Bruce left the medieval court of Abyssinia to commence his long journey back to the eighteenth century. He had been triumphantly successful at Gondar. Having learned the lessons of his near disastrous sojourn in Algiers he had handled his negotiations with the great officers of state in Abyssinia with considerable aplomb. When 'kingly arrogance' had been necessary he had employed it but he had also learned humility. He had prostrated himself before people he considered to be barbarians, kowtowed to bandits and even shown respect for priests. His skill in surviving cannot be underestimated. No foreigner, since Poncet in 1699, had ever been allowed to leave the court of the King of Kings. Bruce had not only survived, he had excelled.

His contribution to science and history was enormous. He had made extensive researches into Ethiopia's fascinating past, rediscovered the lost Book of Enoch, catalogued the flora and fauna of the unexplored highlands and monitored the progress of the weather and stars. Above all, he had taken advantage of the very latest technology to discover and map the source of the Nile. No longer was it, as Bruce put it, an 'opprobrium to geography'. Bruce left Gondar, not as an ordinary citizen, but as a lord of the bedchamber, cavalry commander, governor of Ras el Feel, and his favourite title, Lord of Geesh. He left behind him not just people he had domineered but friends.

> The several marks of goodness, friendship, and esteem, which I received at parting, are confined within my own breast, where they never shall be effaced, but continue to furnish me with the most agreeable reflections, since they were the fruit alone of personal merit, and of honest, steady, and upright behaviour. All who had attempted the same journey hitherto had met with disappointment, disgrace, or death; for my part, although I underwent every sort of toil, danger, and all manner of hardship, yet these were not confined to myself. I suffered always honourably, and in common with the rest of the state; and when sun-shiny days happened (for sun-shiny days there were, and very brilliant ones too), of these I was permitted freely to partake; and the most distinguished characters, both at court and in the army, were always ready to contribute, as far as possible, to promote what they thought or saw was the object of my pursuits or entertainment.

In the early morning of 28 December 1771, Bruce set off from Koscam on what was to be the most arduous and dangerous part of his journey. As he walked through the cedars that surrounded the palace towards Tcherkin and the plains below, Bruce pondered his future:

> All the disasters which I had been threatened with in the course of that journey, which I had thus begun, now presented themselves to my mind, and made, for a moment, a strong impression upon my spirits. But it was too late to draw back, the dye was cast, for

life or for death; home was before me, however distant; and if, through the protection of Providence, I should be fortunate enough to arrive there, I promised myself both ease and the applause of my country, and of all unprejudiced men of sense and learning in Europe, for having, by my own private efforts alone, compleated a discovery, which had from early ages, defied the address, industry and courage of all the world.

It was due to his extraordinary talent for making friends when he needed to that the first part of his journey – in contrast to the rest – would be one of the safest on which he had embarked. All the land between Gondar and Ras el Feel was owned by his friends and Ras el Feel was administered by Yasine under his own governorship. 'None of the inhabitants could possibly injure me in passing', mused the explorer as he walked unattended, at his own request, towards the border with Sudan.

He travelled first through the country of the Kemont (Quemant), an Agow sect similar to the Falashas: 'The people shewed great signs of uneasiness upon our first appearance, and much reluctance to admit us under their roofs . . . they hid all their pots and drinking vessels, lest they should be profaned by our using them'. A few stone-throwers interrupted their progress but were soon put off by the usual display of Western fire power. In the afternoon, though, came bad news. They learned from some fellow travellers that there was a squadron of rebellious Shangalla in the area intent on robbing their small caravan. It was difficult to be sure whether this was true or a scheme of the king's to make Bruce stay in Abyssinia for longer. They trusted it was the latter and continued their long walk through trees heavy with fruit. Bruce stayed close to his servants for their own peace of mind, walking through the bush with his rifle and shooting the pigeons which were later named after him by Joseph Banks and for which the Waalia area is famous.

In the evening of 1 January, Bruce returned from a shoot, his servant groaning under the strain of carrying the yellow-breasted pigeons his master had shot. They were approached by a man who claimed to be a servant of Ayto Confu, whom Bruce recognized from his days in Gondar. 'He had brought two mules, in case any of ours had been tired, and proposed the next morning I should set out with him alone for Tcherkin, where I should find Ayto Confu, and my baggage should follow me.' He was very insistent but Bruce refused to leave his servants when he was on a journey, believing in the fine but often neglected tradition of the British officer class, that he should ask them to do nothing he was not willing to do himself and that their safety was his constant responsibility.

'On the 2d of January, in the morning, by seven o'clock, having dressed my hair, and perfumed it according to the custom of the country, and put on clean clothes, with no other arms but my knife, and a pair of pistols at my girdle, I came out of the tent to mount my mule for Tcherkin.' (One shudders to think how he equipped himself when he wanted to be well-armed.)

When they arrived, the mysterious insistence of the servant became immediately explicable. 'I was then taken to an inner apartment, where to my great surprise, instead of Ayto Confu, I saw his mother, Ozoro Esther, sitting on a couch, and at her feet the secretary's daughter, the beautiful Tecla Mariam.'

Ozoro Esther had thrown a surprise going-away party for her lover. When Bruce expressed his astonishment, Esther replied: 'You would not stay with us, so we are going with you. Is there anything surprising in all this?'

They had a wonderful few days in the romantic palace, feasting on honey and hydromel by night and hunting elephant, rhinoceros and buffalo by day. High atop the 'enchanted mountain', away from the constraints of courtly life with only their close friends and servants, Bruce had such a fine time that he wished he could stay:

> There was nothing but rejoicing on all sides. Seven ladies, relations and companions of Ozoro Esther, came with Ayto Confu; and I confess this to have been one of the happiest moments of my life. I quite forgot the disastrous journey I had before me, and all the dangers that awaited me. I began even to regret being so far in my way to leave Abyssinia for ever.

The women were worried that the house would be stormed by the Shangalla if the men were seen to go out hunting during the day but nothing could put Ayto Confu off his sport. 'Though we were all happy to our wish in this enchanted mountain, the active spirit of Ayto Confu could not rest.'

The local Agageer tribe were famed throughout the empire for their skill at hunting elephant and Confu had been looking forward to the chase. Accordingly the men left a squadron guarding the house before going out into the fields. Bruce was astonished by the talents of the Agageers who scampered around on horses in front of the elephants, two to a mount. One hunter would bait the elephant from the front whilst the other jumped off and sped round the back, wielding a long sword. This latter would try and get close to the rear legs and chop the unfortunate victim's tendon, thus crippling the beast in order that they might kill it in safety.

After two weeks abandoned to 'mirth and festivity', Bruce had to continue his march and Ozoro Esther had to return to Gondar. Bruce makes no mention of the pain of his departure but one can tell from the frequent references to Esther in his *Travels* that he had truly loved his princess. It must have been with a heavy heart that he mounted the camel sent to him by Yasine and made his way through the 'thickest and most impenetrable woods I ever saw' away from his lover and out of her life for ever. He knew as he left that he would never hear from her again and that her future – as the wife of a disgraced dictator in a country torn by turmoil – was far from certain.

They travelled through what should have been friendly country, but even then had difficulties. Abyssinia was in so much turmoil that loyal subjects such as Gimbaro, the chief of Sancaho, defied etiquette and refused to send provisions to the travellers:

> Gimbaro . . . was the tallest and stoutest man of his nation; about six feet six inches high [thus even taller than Bruce], and strongly made in proportion; hunted always on foot; and was said, among his people, to have singly killed elephants with one blow of his spear. The features of his face might well be called hideous . . . [he] seemed to be a picture of those Cannibal giants, which we read of, inhabiting enchanted castles, in the fairy tales.

Outraged by Gimbaro's treatment of his party, Bruce stormed into his presence, armed to the teeth and flanked by two servants wielding ships' blunderbusses. The naked giant, who was sitting in a long trophy room worthy of a mid-western big game hunter, surrounded by rhino horns and elephant hides, soon acquiesced to Bruce's wishes and provided him with camels, bread and honey. They parted without bloodshed, Bruce promising to return the next year to hunt rhinoceros. It was the last time that Bruce would be able to get away with such cavalier behaviour. They were soon to arrive in Hor-Cacamoot, the capital of his own government, Ras el Feel, but from then onwards the fact that he was the king's stranger would become a hindrance rather than an asset.

In the baking plain ('The sun, by the thermometer, sometimes exceeded 130'), the border between Abyssinia and the myriad kingdoms of Sudan, Bruce once more succumbed to dysentery while Yasine prepared the way ahead. He was cured by a new method:

> Sometime before I left Gondar I had been threatened with an attack of the dysentery. At my arrival at Hor-Cacamoot it grew worse and had many unpromising symptoms when I was cured by the advice and application of a common Shangalla by means of a shrub called Wooginios growing very common in these parts the manner of using which he taught me.

The plant – classified by Joseph Banks of the Royal Society on Bruce's return – is officially known as *Brucea antidysenterica*.

The ailing Scot was about to depart Ethiopian shum country and enter Arabic sheikh country. He had sent medicines, letters and firmans ahead of him but his safety could be guaranteed nowhere. Fidele, the Sheikh of Atbara, had promised him safety but another sheikh (who Bruce had reason to trust) warned against putting himself into Fidele's hands. Bruce set off for Teawa with the confidence of a man who had taken all practicable precautions but knew not what lay ahead. A servant of Yasine's would be posing as someone else in Teawa and would act as a messenger if Bruce came across any trouble. Insistent on leaving by this bizarre route, there was little else that Bruce could do to safeguard his life.

The climate had changed from the often bitter cold of the highlands of Abyssinia. Their road had been almost entirely down-hill from Gondar and the temperature had changed accordingly.

It made the going harder for, unable to rely on rivers for water, they had to carry their own water in ox skins known as girbas – 'the edges sewed together very artificially by a double seam, which does not let out water, much resembling that upon the best English cricket-balls'. 'Surf el Shekh is the boundary of Ras el Feel. Here I took an affectionate leave of my friend Yasine, who, with all his attendants, shewed, at parting, that love and attachment, they had constantly preserved to me since our first acquaintance.'

Bruce had first met Yasine on the boat from Jiddah to Massawa when they had endured near shipwreck. They had been through many travails together: both could have been killed by the Naybe or on the long journey to Gondar; they had fought side by side at Serbraxos and advanced each other's fortunes at every opportunity. It was appropriate that Yasine should be the last Abyssinian to bid farewell to Bruce: 'At parting, I gave the faithful Yasine one of my horses and my coat of mail . . . Yasine, like an old traveller, called the whole company together, and obliged them to repeat the Fedtah, the Prayer of Peace'.

The prayer succeeded in keeping the natives under control but the animals required a little more application. As they plunged through thick forest (its foliage burnt back by the locals thus affording no shade but much cover for predators), besieged by kantuffa and plagued by lack of water, their every move was dogged by ravenous hyenas and lions. This was a problem since they did not wish to draw attention to themselves by using their firearms. When a lion ate one of their asses and a hyena attacked a servant, however, drastic measures were called for. Out came the ships' blunderbusses each of which 'had fifty small bullets' and off went their oppressors. They marched on to Rashid unmolested by anything but the elements. They were now in the domain of the simoom, a baking hot wind that whirled round the caravan as it marched relentlessly on.

All but myself, fell mortally sick with the quantity of poisonous vapour that they had imbibed. I apprehend, from Rashid to Imserrha is about five miles, and though it is one of the most dangerous halting places between Ras el Feel and Sennaar, yet we were so enervated, our stomachs so weak, and our head-achs so violent, that we could not pitch our tent, but each wrapping himself in his cloak, resigned himself immediately to sleep, under the cool shade of the large trees, invited by the pleasant breeze, which seemed to be merely local, confined to this small grove, created probably by the vicinity of water, and the agitation we had occasioned in it.

The simoom was to become a major hindrance in the march. It is not, of course, a pestilential wind, bearing disease, but it is immensely hot and nags and wails at travellers to this day. Like the mistral or the scirocco, its very constancy drives people insane. For the time being Bruce remained relatively immune to it but, whilst his servants slept, an opportunistic thief stole away with one of their mules and disappeared into the forest. It was the first of many thefts on the long march back to civilization that would drain Bruce's already strained resources. On their sixth day out of Ras el Feel, they had still not encountered anyone on the road but knew that Arabs were nearby from traces that they found at a well where the girbas were refilled. They became lost in a wood whilst trying to avoid them. 'Here we were terrified to find that the water in our girbas was entirely gone; whether by the evaporation of the hot wind, or otherwise, I know not.'

So far from a cricket pitch it was unlikely that anyone had tampered with the seams. It would have been akin to suicide. Despite the number of trees in the area, they were in arid country and entirely reliant on the water that they could carry between wells. Wells too were dangerous for there they could fall easy prey to bandits. Notwithstanding, Bruce led his men from the forest in search of a well – 'I really then began to think we were lost'. Gasping for breath they marched all morning until by sheer luck they found a well and fell upon the water. 'The effect of this hurry was very soon seen. Two Abyssinian Moors, a man and a woman, died after drinking.'

Bruce, rather more sensibly, cooled himself down first and took small sips before drinking 'till I was completely satisfied'. The well marked the end of the burnt forest through which they had been travelling and with it all hope of shelter. They abandoned their dead to the hyenas and began their march across the scorched plains. 'The thermometer, slung under the camel, in the shade of the girba of water, had yet, nevertheless, varied within these three hours from 111° to 119.5.'

The journey became increasingly nightmarish as they neared their first destination, Teawa. That day, they arrived in a village:

> whose inhabitants had all perished of hunger the year before; their wretched bones being all unburied and scattered upon the surface of the ground where the village formerly stood. We encamped among the bones of the dead; no space could be found free from them; and, on the 23d, at six in the morning, full of horror at this miserable spectacle, we set out for Teawa; this was the seventh day out from Ras el Feel.

Later that evening they arrived in Teawa and fell under the control of Fidele, the Sheikh of Atbara. Throughout his time in Abyssinia, Bruce had provided medicine for the sheikh by way of Yasine. The two had corresponded amicably and Bruce believed that in Fidele he had an ally. Added to this, he had vast experience of dealing with Arab chieftains from his previous travels and his sojourn as consul at Algiers. Indeed, he was much better prepared for manipulating Arab sheikhs than he was Christian emperors. Yet Fidele's very existence was precarious. Once-great Sennaar itself was rent by internal strife and the entire region was terrorized by a band of warlike nomads, the Daveina. Fidele's small kingdom was composed of only 1200 men, 'naked, miserable, and despicable Arabs, like the rest of those that live in villages, who are much inferior in courage to the Arabs that live in tents'.

Because of this, and the warnings of the Sheikh of the Nile (the tribe not the river) at Hor-Cacamoot, Bruce had taken the extra precaution of having a servant spy on them from afar in order that he might send messages to Yasine if the caravan should fall into trouble. His prudence would pay off.

From their first meeting, it became clear that Bruce had put too much faith in Sheikh Fidele, a treacherous drunk who punctuated his demands for money only with lies about the state of the road to Sennaar. The camels with which he had agreed to provide Bruce were, he claimed, fifteen days march away in the desert. Bruce immediately sent a message to Yasine via the servant and bided his time, treating the wives of the sheikh for various diseases and Fidele for appalling hangovers. 'Bring him a vomit' was the almost constant demand of Fidele's servants, at which Bruce would appear in the drunkard's palace bearing cups of the emetic ipecacuanha.

Bruce's caravan had more firearms than the entire town so they did not fear attack from that quarter. They were very worried, however, about their house: 'We were now apprehensive of fire, things were come to such an extremity; and as our house was composed of nothing but dry canes, it seemed the only obvious way of destroying us'.

By 10 April, matters had come to a head. Bruce had received no replies to his letters and he feared that his messenger had been intercepted. Sheikh Fidele was becoming more and more insistent that Bruce should give him money or die in Teawa. The traveller for once was cautious, calming down his own servants, who were all for fighting their way out of the town. He did not have enough money to pay the ransom but he did not want to sour relations with the divan at Sennaar, which would be easily influenced by the desert chieftain. Bruce visited the sheikh, unsure of anything other than that he must stand up to him:

> considered at last, that we could not escape from his hands; and that the only way to avoid the danger was to brave it . . . It was resolved to go armed, for fear of the worst; but to conceal our weapons, so as to give no umbrage. I had a small Brescian blunderbuss, about 22 inches in the barrel, which had a joint in the stock, so that it folded double. It hung by an iron hook to a thin belt under my left arm, close to my side quite unperceived, like a cutlass. I likewise took a pair of pistols in my girdle, and my knife as usual. All these were perfectly covered by my burnoose.

Bruce was ushered into an audience room by a boy slave where he greeted the inebriated sheikh and told him that he had brought his emetic. ' "D—n you and the vomit too" says he with great passion, "I want money, and not poison. Where are your piastres?" '

Bruce once more stated that he had no money and that he had come in his role as doctor, but the sheikh would not give in and, trembling with fury, unsheathed his sword and threw the scabbard at Bruce's feet. The interview was not going well.

> I now stept one pace backwards, and dropt the burnoose behind me, holding the little blunderbuss in my hand, without taking it off the belt. I said in a firm tone of voice, 'This is my answer: I am not a man, as I have told you before, to die like a beast by the hand of a drunkard; on your life, I charge you, stir not from your sofa.' I had no need to give this injunction; he heard the noise which the closing of the joint in the stock of the blunderbuss made, and thought I had cocked it, and was instantly to fire. He let the sword drop, and threw himself on his back on the sofa, crying, 'For God's sake, Hakim, I was but jesting.'

Bruce's descendent in the male line, the Earl of Elgin and Kincardine has an excellent collection of Bruceana at his home, only a few miles from Kinnaird. Amongst the paintings, notes and letters he also has a telescope, a strange pair of sleeping trousers complete with feet and the blunderbuss described in this scene. He kindly allowed me to play with it. It is a weapon which only a man of Bruce's stature could describe as 'little' and it has a peculiarly satisfying click. Having seen and heard it, Fidele's cowering seems eminently sensible.

Although this dramatic scene, which ended in Bruce returning home safely to bed, showed Fidele that the Scot was not a man to be taken lightly, it did not do a great deal to hasten Bruce's departure. If anything, it made the sheikh more cautious. There was, however good news awaiting him at their inflammable house. The Sheikh of Beyla, a man whom Bruce knew he could rely upon, had sent a messenger to inquire after him, and with the message-bearer, two holy men who would intercede with Fidele on Bruce's behalf. It emerged that this would have happened much earlier had Fidele not sent false despatches to the effect that Bruce had already left by another route. Bruce went to sleep worrying about how his aggressive behaviour of the evening might affect their chances. He was soon to find out. He was awoken by a messenger, a servant of Fidele's wives, with whom, as usual, he had made a good impression: 'They advised me to be upon my guard, for the Shekh was absolutely resolved to take a severe revenge upon us all'.

Bruce and his men had spent the last week crippled with diarrhoea and he was concerned that Fidele was trying to poison them. When the pains became more severe he brought up the matter with the servant who had first warned them to be on their guard. She laughed and told him this was impossible since she prepared all the food. The water had caused their stomach aches, as happened to all visitors to Teawa. Relieved in mind, but rather too much in body, Bruce spent Sunday studying the stars and working out the coordinates of the prison town whilst the two holy men, who had just arrived, tried to persuade Fidele to allow the caravan to continue. 'I had, indeed, an inclination to observe the approaching eclipse; but as I knew perfectly the situation of Teawa with regard to Ras el Feel, I thought I might spare myself this unnecessary trouble, and only make use of the eclipse to frighten Fidele as part of the punishment he so amply deserved.'

News had arrived of fighting on the border between Ras el Feel and Fidele's fiefdom and no one could be sure what had sparked it. Fidele insisted that it could have nothing to do with Bruce since he had been forbidden from sending any messages. Bruce, however, prompted by one of the holy men, insisted that he had sent messages to Yasine and that this was doubtless the cause of the troubles. Fidele refused to believe it but his fellow sheikhs were by now becoming angry with him: the last thing they wanted was a war with Abyssinia. All had been peaceful on that front since an ill-fated invasion by Yasous II and both sides saw the benefits of the peace. Bruce claimed that he had sent messages not only to Yasine but also to Mecca and other parts of the Muslim world, complaining of his treatment at the sheikh's hands. Fidele insisted that this was not possible, thus giving Bruce the perfect opportunity to show off his magical powers.

'Well then' said I, 'the difficulty is only to know if he is informed of this at Mecca. Friday, the 17th, is your festival. If the afternoon of that shall pass like those of common days, I am a worthless man and an impostor; but if on that day, after el'asser [four o'clock], a sign be seen in the heavens that shall be thought by all of you unusual and extraordinary, then am I an innocent man, and Fidele's designs against me are known to the world, at Sennaar, at Mecca, at Cairo, and at Gondar, and every where else, and will not be pleasing either to God or man.'

With that Bruce quit the audience chamber leaving Fidele at the mercy of the mullahs and the sheikhs who opposed his treatment of the traveller. Bruce was confident that his celestial trickery combined with the intervention of the sheikhs, who had arrived to discuss the border troubles, would secure his speedy release. More messengers had arrived, this time from Sennaar, demanding that Bruce be allowed to move on. These Fidele could not ignore and he sent word that the caravan should prepare to leave. Bruce and his party did so cautiously, doubting that this was the end of the matter and fearing that they should inevitably be intercepted on the road.

By the morning of the seventeenth, camels had been prepared and girbas filled with water for the travellers' journey but final permission for their departure had yet to be given. Servants of Yasine and the Sheikh of Beyla were camped outside the town, monitoring the progress of the negotiations. This was considered rude to the point of being a 'declaration of enmity' since Fidele had already offered them food, which is a declaration of peace. It was, though, a fair example of the relationship between the Abyssinian (though Muslim) Yasine and his Arab neighbour.

Having made his preparations for departure, Bruce relaxed and waited for Fidele to get his comeuppance.

I knew I could not be far wrong, having seen in the ephemerides the hour the eclipse was to begin . . . There was to be a total eclipse of the moon. I did not tell them at first, till the moon having arisen, the shade appeared some way advanced upon the disk. 'Now! look at that,' said I; 'in some time after this the moon shall be so totally swallowed up in darkness, that a small light shall only be seen in the edges.' They were frightened at the denunciation, rather than at anything they observed, till a little before the eclipse became total a violent apprehension then fell upon them all; and the women from their apartments began to howl, as they do on all melancholy occasions of misfortune, or death. They were in the inner square. 'Now,' continued I, 'I have kept my word; it will soon be clear again and will do no harm to man or beast.'

So, having unwittingly inspired Rider Haggard, Mark Twain, Hergé and countless others, Bruce retired to bed before, permission having been granted, leaving the next night for Beyla. There he could expect a better reception from the Sheikh of Beyla and tales of his wizardry would go before them. They had been encouraged by the mullah at Teawa to make their way to Beyla as fast as possible where they would be well received, and where the mullah himself would join them the next night. They should on no account tarry along the way, he urged them, a challenge Bruce found easy to meet since they were travelling by night to escape the heat of the day, and there was little to distract them. Bruce's description of the landscape is still very apt 200 years later. 'Our journey, for the first seven hours, was through a barren, bare, and sandy plain, without finding a vestige of any living creature, without water, and without grass, a country that seemed under the immediate curse of heaven.

They arrived safely at Beyla and, in marked contrast to their reception at Teawa, were met by the sheikh at the city gates. He showered them with food and drink and 'the whole company was full of joy'. Unfortunately, Bruce was still feeling unwell and retired immediately to bed. The sheikh would only give presents and would take none in return for he felt greatly indebted to Bruce, Hakim Yagoube, who with typical foresight had been sending soap pills to the sheikh for the last year. They had been most efficacious, almost completely curing the sheikh's gallstones. Bruce's medical studies in Aleppo had not only kept him alive on numerous occasions but, by enabling him to cure others, had allowed him to overcome countless other obstacles. All the later explorers – from David Livingstone to Samuel Baker – followed Bruce's example of studying a rudimentary form of medicine and found it equally fruitful.

Unfortunately, Bruce was in a hurry to leave Beyla, a place he found agreeable. It was not untypical. So often he found himself delayed for months in dangerous, unpleasant places, and having to race through the agreeable ones at high speed. Beyla was one of the latter. He was back on the road to Sennaar within two days, marching through 'a very pleasant, flat, country'. For three days they continued their leisurely walk before they encountered a new danger:

> We had scarcely advanced two miles into the plain, when we were enclosed by a violent whirlwind, or what is called at sea the water-spout . . . The unfortunate camel . . . was lifted and thrown down at a considerable distance, and several of its ribs broken. Although, as far as I could guess, I was not near the centre, it whirled me off my feet, and threw me down upon my face, so as to make my nose gush out with blood.

They were looked after by the local tribe – the Nuba – who helped them to recover. A tribe of moon worshippers, looked down on by almost everyone who came into contact with them, they were very hospitable and gave the travellers everything they could need: 'I had seldom, in my life, upon a journey, passed a more comfortable night,' claimed Bruce.

At the Nuba village they were met by representatives of Sheikh Adelan – the prime minister of Sennaar – who greeted them warmly and told Bruce that he should stay outside the city until given permission to enter. The environment may have started to conspire against Bruce but the same could not be said of the natives. Having escaped from the clutches of Sheikh Fidele they had experienced nothing but kindness on a road which they had been warned would be very dangerous. Bruce became optimistic about Sennaar. He should not have done. When they had been given leave to enter they took the ferry across the Nile to the ancient city. The fragile boat was attacked by voracious crocodiles, an omen of things to come.

CHAPTER 11

FLIGHT TO EGYPT

In the spring of 1772 Sennaar was suffering the death throes of the formerly invincible Fung dynasty that had ruled there since 1515. No white man had visited it since the unfortunate du Roule had been butchered in 1705 but Bruce hoped to fare better for he believed himself to be on good terms with Sheikh Adelan who held a similar position to that of Ras Michael in Abyssinia.

Bruce's optimism seemed to be justified when he first arrived for they were taken immediately to 'a very spacious good house belonging to the Sheikh himself' and were provided with food from the sheikh's table. Adelan's house, like those of the other important people, was of two storeys but the majority of those in the town were built of clay and had only one floor. As was his wont, Bruce set up his observatory on the top floor before settling down to await news from Adelan. He had been advised to wait, before seeing the king, until he had been briefed by the sheikh but the sheikh did not act fast enough. The next morning Bruce was called – unprepared – to an audience of King Ismain. He was impressed by the grandeur of the one-storey palace, though it did seem to be somewhat unfurnished, save for the principal rooms: 'The king was sitting upon a mattress, laid on the ground, which was likely covered with a Persian carpet, and round him was a number of cushions of Venetian cloth of gold'.

The first interview was a little unsettling but seemed to go well. He told King Ismain that he was a 'travelling dervish' and the king seemed to believe him. Later in the evening, however, he was recalled and found the king naked – 'a servant was rubbing him over with very stinking butter or grease' which turned out to be elephant fat.

His toilet being finished, I then produced my present, which I told him the king of Abyssinia had sent him, hoping that, according to the faith and custom of nations, he would not only protect me while here, but send me safely and speedily out of his dominions into Egypt. He answered, There was a time when he could have done all this, and more, but those time were changed. Sennaar was in ruins and not like it once was.

Crumbling government was not the only problem in Sennaar at the time. It was once more the rainy season and the people of the fertile south were escaping to the desert in order to escape the dreaded tsetse fly. As Bruce observed from *his* house, *their* houses – abandoned until the 'winged assassins' died – were following them: 'The whole stream was covered with wreck of houses, canes, wooden bowls and platters, living camels and cattle, and several dead ones passed Sennaar, hurried along by the current with great velocity'.

The war against the tsetse fly – the carrier of sleeping sickness – had gone on since ancient times and continues to this day. The roads were therefore packed with potential robbers waiting to prey on the people moving their livestock away from the tsetse. This made it difficult for Bruce to stay in contact with Sheikh Adelan – for the warlord was camped away from Sennaar – and it was a week before Bruce could make the three and a half mile journey to Adelan's stronghold. Surrounded by 400 of his Black Horse of Sennaar, the sheikh was levying taxes on everyone fleeing the tsetse. Bruce, by now a former cavalry officer himself, was delighted by both the commander and his men.

A steel shirt of mail hung upon each man's quarters, opposite to his horse, and by it an antelope's skin, made soft like shamoy, with which it was covered from the dew of the night. A head-piece of copper, without crest or plumage, was suspended by a lace above the shirt of mail, and was the most picturesque part of the trophy. To these was added an enormous broad-sword, in a red leather scabbard; and upon the pommel hung two thick gloves, not divided into fingers as ours, but like hedgers gloves, their fingers in one poke . . . no body of horse could ever be more magnificently disposed under the direction of any Christian power.

It was not simply the cavalry that Bruce admired; he and Adelan – both no-nonsense men of action, who were adept at courtly behaviour but preferred life in the field – struck up an instant rapport. Adelan's reputation had gone before him: 'Adelan, in war, was a fair-player, and gave every body his chance. He was the first man always that entered among the enemy, and the last to leave them, and he never changed his horse'.

The sheikh was sitting on a tree stump, admiring his troops, when Bruce arrived. 'Upon my coming near him, he got up; "You that are a horseman" says he without any salutation, "what would your king of Habesh give for these horses?" "What king," answered I, in the same tone, "would not give any price for such horses, if he knew their value?"'

The pair breakfasted before Bruce went back to Sennaar 'very well pleased with my reception at Aira'. 'I had not seen, since I left Gondar, a man so open and frank in his manners, and who spoke, without disguise, what apparently he had in his heart,' he wrote of Adelan.

The king and Adelan were very close to war. Bruce's inclination was to side with Adelan but he was living in Sennaar rather than Aira, and weak or not, a king was a king. The king, however, claimed he was unable to vouch for Bruce's safety. Matters improved, Bruce believed, when he was asked to cure the king's wives of various ailments, for:

All acquaintance with the fair sex had hitherto been to my advantage. I must confess, however, that calling these the fair sex is not preserving a precision in terms . . . One of these, who, I found, was the favourite, was about six feet high, and corpulent beyond all proportion. She seemed to me, next to the elephant and rhinoceros, the largest living creature I had met with her. – Her features were like those of a Negro; a ring of gold passed through her under lip, and weighed it down, till, like a flap, it covered her chin, and left her teeth bare, which were very small and fine. –

The inside of her lip she had made black with antimony. Her ears reached down to her shoulders, and had the appearance of wings.

There were fifty similarly built wives for Bruce to tend and they all wanted bleeding and vomiting. It was not a pleasant afternoon. By the end of it,

> The room was overflowed with an effusion of royal blood . . . and the floor of the room received all the evacuations. It was most prodigiously hot, and the horrid, black figures, moaning and groaning with sickness all around me, gave me, I think, some slight idea of the punishment in the world below. My mortifications, however, did not stop there.

Soon the women started removing their clothing. Bruce 'could not but observe that the breasts of each of them reached the length of their knees'. But even that was not the end of it. They insisted that Bruce followed suit and then started poking him and reacting in disgust to his white skin. When Bruce was eventually allowed to leave, his luck had not turned. He was robbed on the way home.

Soon Bruce was well and truly immobilized in Sennaar. Adelan was living outside the city where he and other armies were hovering like confident vultures over the rotting corpse of Sennaar, too preoccupied with their own affairs to be much concerned with a European traveller. The king did not know what to do with him, and either ignored him or occasionally asked for money in a rather desultory manner. Bruce was unloved and unwanted: his only friend in the town was the lonely and morose executioner – Achmet Sid el Coom.

Achmet had a bizarre role that was meant to ensure good government but was not very successful in doing so. A relation of the king, he was employed to kill all the king's brothers at the time of his coronation and to be ready to kill the king whenever a council of elders ordered him to do so. Every morning Achmet, who 'seemed by strange accident, to be one of the gentlest spirits of any that it was my misfortune to converse with at Sennaar' had to attend the king in case there was any execution to be carried out.

> Achmet Sid el Coom, the present licensed regicide, and resident in Ismain's palace, had murdered the late King Nasser, and two of

his sons that were well grown, besides a child at his mother's breast; and he was expecting every day to confer the same favour upon Ismain; though at present there was no malice on the one part, nor jealousy on the other; and I believe both of them had a guess of what was likely to happen.

Bruce spent a great deal of time with Achmet, learning as much as he could about Sennaar, so much so that he dared not walk through the town unless well guarded. Suffering in the intense heat – 119° in the shade – he made a copy of the list of the Fung kings which Achmet provided. This was not like the Kebra Negast, or Glory of Kings, the beautifully bound book that Bruce brought back from Abyssinia; instead it was the ultimate primary source, the one document that Achmet always had to hand – 'the hangman's roll'. Bruce also inspected the crops that grew in great profusion around Sennaar, though livestock faced a different fate. The annual flight to the desert was an absolute necessity: 'No horse, mule, ass, or any beast of burden, will breed, or even live at Sennaar, or many miles around it. Poultry does not live there. Neither dog nor cat, sheep nor bullock, can be preserved a season there. They must go all, every half year, to the sands'.

The heat was the main problem. Bruce found it 'excessive hot', far outreaching the temperatures at Massawa, and spent his time trying to move as little as possible. The residents had a different technique; they swapped their winter wives for summer ones: 'The Arabs, from choice, cohabit only with Negro women in the hot months of summer, on account of the remarkable coolness of their skins, in which they are said to differ from the Arab women'.

For once, Bruce seemed to be sleeping alone and thus had no such choice. He did, however, have another perennial problem – he was running out of money. Some years earlier he had arranged to cash a cheque with a trader called Hagi Belal. They had corresponded at Gondar and Hagi Belal had accepted Bruce's guarantees but now that he needed money he was unable to get any. He was stranded with nothing of value except the 'magnificent gold chain' that Tecla Haimanout had given him at Serbraxos. Without money, even if he could get away from Sennaar, he would be unable to buy the camels, water and provisions that he would need for his journey across the desert. In addition, Adelan had left his station at Arai and since his departure food had stopped being delivered to Bruce's house. He needed money for food immediately. The only solution was to sell the gold chain to Hagi Belal. Having bought all he needed, 'I received back six links, the miserable remains of one hundred and eighty four, of which my noble chain once consisted'.

At the end of August, after three months of enforced inactivity, two events took place that were to affect Bruce's future. First Mahomet Towash, a holy man who was leading a pilgrimage to Mecca, came through Sennaar and offered to join forces with Bruce. He jumped at the opportunity for there was safety both in numbers and in the fact that Towash was 'accounted sacred, and regarded with a certain religious awe'. All was prepared for departure when news came that Mahomet Towash had left without them. He had been ordered by the king to continue without Bruce. Frustrated at this obstruction, Bruce and his small party sat up late discussing their misfortune.

The second event was a sudden attack on Bruce's house by a mob led by another of the king's servants. The intruders forced the outer gate and had reached the courtyard before a show of weapons persuaded them to desist. On top of the disaster of the morning, this was enough to make them despair but in fact it greatly eased their departure. Mahomet had committed a grave error in trying to attack Bruce, for he was lodged in Sheikh Adelan's house, and this was taken as a personal insult to the most powerful man in the country. Immediately a price was put on Mahomet's head and Bruce at last became useful to the king. Mahomet was a royal favourite so King Ismain agreed with Bruce that if he interceded with Adelan on Mahomet's behalf *he* would be allowed to leave Sennaar. 'I charge you when you see him' said the king 'to ask for Mahomet's life, or a considerable deal of blame will fall upon you. When you return back I will send him to conduct you to the frontiers of Egypt.'

Bruce, who had no intention of ever returning, leaped at this offer and arranged matters accordingly with Adelan. On 6 September, he at last left Sennaar and set out to follow the blue river to what is now Khartoum. They would be marching upon the 'most frequented road in the kingdom' where they should be reasonably safe against attack. 'We flattered ourselves, that once disengaged from this bad step, the greatest part of our sufferings was over; for we apprehended nothing but from men, and, with very great reason, thought we had seen the worst of them.'

And for a while their presumptions of safety were justified. They travelled through pleasant woods and fields, his servants and travelling companions on foot with the baggage camels, Bruce astride a riding camel. The irrigated land on the banks of the Nile was infested with tsetse fly for the first stage of their journey but they were soon beyond its range. All along their route, Adelan had sent messages to the local chiefs instructing them to treat Bruce with respect and they learned from one of these chiefs that Yasine and 'the Moorish troops from Ras el Feel had burnt Teawa'. Bruce's cavalry had taken revenge for his treatment by Fidele even after he had left their country. They continued onwards at the leisurely pace of fifteen miles a day: 'Nothing could be more beautiful than the country we passed that day, partly covered with very pleasant woods, and partly in lawns, with a few fine scattered trees'.

The road they travelled was always 'parallel with the Nile' but often they had to cross it at the various ferries along the way, where Bruce would enquire into the local customs. The only unfriendly people they encountered were terrified of firearms. 'The report of a gun, even at a distance, will make a hundred of them fly and hide themselves. We gave them several volleys of blunderbusses, and double barrelled guns.' Fellow travellers coming in the other direction gave them news of trouble ahead but for the time being the journey home could not have been easier.

At Halfaia – now the centre of modern-day Khartoum – 'a large, handsome and pleasant town, although built with clay' he discovered that 'the people here eat cats, also the river horse [hippopotamus] and the crocodile'. Bruce always tried to avoid eating crocodile, but tells us that it tastes like 'conger eel' (though chicken is nearer the mark). They spent what must have been a very depressing week in Halfaia. The unorthodox nature of the food would not have bothered Bruce at all. It was the water that was the problem:

The river Abiad, which is larger than the Nile, joins it there. Still the Nile preserves the name of Bahar el Azergue, or the Blue River, which it got at Sennaar . . . The Abiad is a very deep river; it runs dead and with little inclination, and preserves its stream always undiminished, because, rising in latitudes where there are continual rains, it, therefore, suffers not the decrease the Nile does by the six months dry weather.

In point of fact this is the confluence of the Blue and White Niles: Bruce glosses over it in one short paragraph. Perhaps this is unsurprising; this enormous river threatened to destroy all his claims of having found the true source of the Nile. While he was there, as he freely admits, the white river was at its height and the blue was only just preparing to become a torrent. (At Khartoum one can clearly see the line between the two for they travel through different soil, which is the reason for their different colours.) Bruce visited the confluence, and as he observes the White Nile was the larger. Even if reaching the source of the Nile was not his only object, it was certainly an achievement of which he wished to be proud. To find another large river flowing into the Nile must have been utterly devastating. He was not to know that on average the Blue Nile provides five-sixths of the water in the true Nile and that most of the water from the White Nile disperses in the (then as now) fiercely contested swamps of southern Sudan. Bruce's description of the confluence is often cited as an example of his perfidy, but this is unfair. He does at least write about it, rather than avoiding the subject all together. Bruce continued his march onwards towards Chendi where he had a letter recommending him to the queen from one of the chiefs who had helped them earlier in the journey. 'It was so sultry at the end of August and beginning of September, that many people dropt down dead with heat, both in the town and villages round it; but it is now said to be much cooler, though the thermometer at noon was once so high as 119°.'

Chendi had once been a town of significance when it had been a regular stopping point for caravans using the great trade routes across Africa. It had recently fallen into disrepair, however, as the eternal fighting between the desert Arabs and the impending collapse of the Fung dynasty in Sennaar had drastically reduced the traffic. In the distant past, as Bruce suggested and later archaeologists have confirmed, Meroe – a capital of the ancient Egyptians – was once the farthest outpost of the Axumite empire.

This fact has often been overlooked, perhaps because Bruce could not himself confirm it. He explains his calculations of latitude and longitude, compares them with those of Pliny, Ptolemy and Strabo and describes the ruins he discovers but goes no further than 'It is impossible to avoid risquing a guess that this is the ancient city of Meroe'.

At Chendi he found the people greatly exercised that Venus was then visible in their skies during daylight hours. Bruce attempted to turn this to his advantage by demonstrating his telescopes and claiming that it was a good omen.

He also found a mysterious queen with whom to dally. Being a good Muslim, Sittina conducted their first audience from behind a screen from which Bruce tried to coax her. They had pleasant conversation but she refused to show herself until the next day when she,

> appeared magnificently dressed, with a kind of round cap of solid gold upon the crown of her head, all beat very thin, and hung round with sequins; with a variety of gold chains, solitaires, and necklaces of the same metal, about her neck. Her hair was plaited in ten or twelve small divisions like tails, which hung down below her waist, and over her was thrown a common cotton white garment. She had a purple silk stole, or scarf, hung very gracefully upon her back, brought again round her waist, without covering her shoulders or arms. Upon her wrists she had two bracelets, like handcuffs, about half an inch thick, and two gold manacles of the same at her feet, fully an inch diameter.

Daringly Bruce kissed her hand, to marvellous effect. The interview ended with Sittina demanding that 'while you stay, let me see you every day, and, if you want any thing, send by a servant of mine'.

There had been bad news at the audience, too. Mahomet Towash, he discovered, had been through Chendi before him and – on the orders of the King of Sennaar – had taken all the hybeers, or guides, with him. This put Bruce in a predicament. Until then he had no need of guides – they had been able to follow the river – but he now intended to cross the desert rather than follow the Nile in the vast loop that it makes on its way to Egypt. To do that he needed guides to point out the wells and to protect him from the desert Arabs who made their living by preying on caravans.

And then, as if out of nowhere, a naked Arab named Idris appeared who 'had been sick at Chendi for some months' and was willing to guide Bruce's party. This made the explorer suspicious, given that Towash had reputedly requisitioned all the guides. After close interrogation it emerged that Idris was heavily in debt and had been divested of his clothes and camels by his creditors. Deducing that anyone helplessly in debt could not be all bad, Bruce agreed to pay off Idris's creditors and redeem his property. Idris 'was to shew me the way to Egypt, and he was there to be recompensed, according to his behaviour'. He told his fellow travellers of their new plans and set off in search of food and water for the journey. 'I prepared now to leave Chendi, but first returned to my benefactress, Sittina, thanks for all her favours. She had called for Idris, and given him very positive instructions, mixt with threats, if he misbehaved.'

They set off on the evening of 20 October for Gooz, the last town before the real desert begins, and during the night passed the ancient ruins of Meroe. Five days later, they reached the river which Bruce had known in Ethiopia as the Tacazze but by now had become the Atbara, a major tributary of the Nile. Another day's march and they were in Gooz where Idris was immediately arrested. He had debts, it appeared, in every town.

In Gooz, they made their final preparations for their crossing of the great Nubian Desert. Like Chendi, Gooz was a town of former pomp but presently reduced circumstances. It too had suffered from the collapse of desert trade. It was none the less, still a hotbed of gossip where they could gather useful information for their desert crossing while at the same time be spied on by the rapacious Bishareen whose role in life it was to harrass people such as them. Bruce bought back his guide once again, reclothed him, and the pitiful little party committed itself to the journey ahead. Bruce was no longer travelling in the style to which he had become accustomed. Of the original party only Bruce had been robust enough to survive thus far. This next step of the journey, however, would tax the strength of Hercules. Bruce supervised their preparations minutely. There were not enough of them to carry emergency rations. They would have enough water and food only if there were no accidents or thefts. The smallest mistake would inevitably result in death.

> There were Ismael the Turk, two Greek servants besides Georgis, who was almost blind and useless; two Barbarins, who took care of the camels, Idris, and a young man, a relation of his, who joined him at Barbar, to return home; in all nine persons, eight only of whom were effective. We were all well armed with blunderbusses, swords, pistols, and double barrelled guns, except Idris and his lad, who had lances, the only arms they could use. Five or six naked wretches of the Turcorory joined us at the watering place.

Appropriately enough it was at the foot of the Mountain of Thirst that they greased, tested and filled their water skins. It must have been with a strangely ambivalent feeling that Bruce bade farewell to the Nile for what he believed would be the last time: 'While the camels were loading, I bathed myself with infinite pleasure for a long half hour in the Nile; and thus took leave of my old acquaintance, very doubtful if we should ever meet again'.

The quest for the source of the Nile had occupied his waking hours for years. He had risked all to solve the 'opprobrium of geographers' and then, having succeeded, he was confronted by the confluence at Halfaia. In his heart he knew that the riddle would not be solved until someone had followed the other 'larger' branch. Characteristically, he shrugged off the disappointment and led his little band of followers into the desert.

On the very first night they discovered their greatest mistake. They had as much food as they could carry, they had plenty of water and courage enough but they had overlooked one thing: 'Our shoes, that had needed constant repair, were become at last absolutely useless, and the hard ground, from the time we passed Amour, had worn the skin off in several places, so that our feet were very much inflamed by the burning sand'.

Soft European feet would not last for long on the burning sands of the Nubian Desert where every step would be acute agony. Like the strange lizards that inhabit the oases, Bruce would have to hop from foot to foot, even when at rest, to stop the skin burning down to the very bone. It could not have been a worse start. They continued onwards, making their way from wadi to wadi whilst the constantly shifting desert changed around them. They travelled 'slowly ... our feet being sore and swollen', occasionally stopping to gaze in awe-filled terror at the 'pillars of sand' that dogged their steps. Looking far out across the desert they could at one time see eleven of those small whirlwinds racing across the desert floor, sucking up more sand into their vortexes before collapsing 'as if struck with a large cannon shot'.

After a restless night spent dreaming about the horrors of the day before, they awoke to find that they had been almost covered in sand and that one of their four skins of water was all but empty: one of the Turcorories had been helping himself to their precious water whilst Hagi Ismael slept. Matters did not improve when the already disheartened party saw in the clear light of dawn that they would once more be plagued by whirlwinds.

> They began, immediately after sun-rise, like a thick wood, and almost darkened the sun: His rays shining through them for near an hour, gave them an appearance of pillars of fire. Our people now became desperate: The Greeks shrieked out, and said it was the day of judgment. Ismael pronounced it to be hell, and the Turcorories, that the world was on fire.

Terrifying as this sight was, the 'pillars of fire' never actually intercepted their path and the day went better than could have been expected. Bruce's feet, however, were now swollen and cracked, making it increasingly difficult for him to keep up. It was thus with great relief that they came in sight of a hillock called Chiggre where they knew there would be water. As they contemplated the welcome sight of the peak of the hill, just perceptible over the long curve of desert that lay ahead of them,

> Idris cried out, with a loud voice, Fall upon your faces, for here is the simoom! I saw from the S.E. a haze come, in colour like the purple part of the rainbow, but not so compressed or thick. It

did not occupy twenty yards in breadth, and was about twelve feet high from the ground. It was a kind of blush upon the air, and it moved very rapidly, for I scarce could turn to fall upon the ground with my head to the northward, when I felt the heat of its current plainly upon my face. We all lay flat on the ground, as if dead, till Idris told us it was blown over. The meteor, or purple haze, which I saw, was indeed passed, but the light air that still blew was of heat to threaten suffocation.

They had experienced the simoom before on their way from Ras el Feel and had survived its searing heat, but they were now in the middle of the desert. They had previously believed that it was impossible to get any hotter, yet here they had been assaulted by a wind that burned the very skin off their faces. Bruce was faced with the task of restoring the morale of his group, which had fallen into 'an universal despondency': 'I bade them attend to me, who had nearly lost my voice to the simoom, and desired them to look at my face, so swelled as scarcely to permit me to see; my feet swelled and inflamed, and bleeding with many wounds'.

If he could continue, he exhorted them, then so could they. He ordered that every man should have a gourd more water than was usual and that they should concentrate their minds on the 'bare, black, and sharp point of the rock Chiggre, wherein was the well at which we were to fill our girbas, and thereby banish the fear of dying of thirst in the desert'. For five long hours the simoom continued as they marched across the desert. After thirteen hours, though, they arrived at the well and fell upon the water with something akin to religious fervour. It was too much for the Turcorory, however, two of whom died within twelve hours. There was no grazing there, so they fed the camels (they had not eaten for three days) with the dora bread that all desert travellers relied upon. This strange powdered bread swelled to twice its size when added to water and in terms of space and weight was the most economical food to take with them. The wells at Chiggre had attracted a number of migratory partridge which, to their immense frustration, they dared not shoot for fear of attracting bandits. Bruce set up his quadrant so that he could mark the desert watering-hole on his map for future travellers and was interrupted by an antelope so tame that it seemed to him that it was like some sort of friendly spirit: 'It seemed so interested in what I was doing, that I began to think it might perhaps be my good genius, which had come to visit, protect, and encourage me, in the desperate situation in which I then was'.

The antelope too avoided the pot – though it would have been simple to kill silently – so they went to sleep no longer thirsty but having eaten only the sour reconstituted bread they had brought with them. Only six days from the edge of the desert yet already two of their party had died and everyone else seemed in varying stages of decay. It was with a sense of dread for the coming day that they spent another freezing night after the fiery temperatures of the day. Their senses would not be disappointed. 'A little before eleven we were again terrified by an army (as it seemed) of sand pillars.'

Bruce had become more relaxed about these phenomena, largely because, despite a camel being rudely deposited in another part of the desert earlier in their journey, they had not recently been threatened by them on this stage: 'But it was otherwise with the simoom; we all of us were firmly persuaded that another passage of the purple meteor over us would be attended with our deaths'.

On the evening of the eighteenth they were at last able to feed their now tiring camels for they came across a little stand of acacia bushes at El Cowie, a small oasis in the blank sands of the unending desert. Then they marched on to Terfowey, where they found more trees and even grass. 'We had this day enjoyed, as it were, a holiday, free from the terrors of the sand, or dreadful influence of the simoom.' Bruce's idea of a holiday is strange: he had spent the day walking on feet which were 'now swelled to a monstrous size, and everywhere inflamed and excoriated'.

As Bruce sat nursing his feet and guarding the camels, he heard a clink from the padlocked chains that hobbled their pack animals. He 'rose, and cried in a threatening tone' but was not answered. He and Mahomet, Idris's nephew, searched the ground and found footsteps in the sand around the camels and a link broken on one of the camel's chains. There was a thief about, and Bruce suspected that they would be attacked at dawn:

> We were in the middle of the most barren, inhospitable desert in
> the world, and it was with the utmost difficulty that, from day to
> day, we could carry wherewithal to assuage our thirst. We had
> with us the only bread it was possible to procure for some hundred
> miles; lances and swords were not necessary to destroy us; the
> bursting or tearing of a girba, the lameness or death of a camel, a
> thorn or a sprain in the foot, which might disable us from walking,
> were as certain death to us as a shot from a cannon.

They had to see off the anticipated morning's assault or perish.
Bruce gathered his men around him and explained his plan:

> Our only chance then remaining was, that their number might be
> so small, that, by our great superiority in firearms and in courage,
> we might turn the misfortune upon the aggressors, deprive them
> of their camels and means of carrying water, and leave them, scat-
> tered in the desert, to that death, which either they or we, without
> alternative, must suffer.

'God is great! Let them come' shouted the motley collection of
men before choosing their places on the perimeter and aiming
their blunderbusses, pistols and rifles into the gloom. They sat
there all night, alert to any movement, but at dawn there was no
attack so Bruce and Ismael went to scout around. They soon
discovered that, rather than being surrounded by a savage horde
of Bishareen, they had in fact been robbed by a single Bishareen,
an emaciated man camped with his wife and child at the other
side of the rocks. Bruce and Ismael burst in upon the pathetic
scene and held a sword to the man's throat. Maintaining this
threatening posture, Bruce interrogated the man at length. Fearing
imminent death, the man spat out his confession. He had been
with a party of thirty men who had set upon the caravan of
Mahomet Towash in the desert and slaughtered it to a man. His
camels had become lame, he claimed, and he had been forced to
camp in the desert, hoping that a traveller would pass from whom
he would be able to steal a camel. Noting this Bruce then went
to the man's wife, whom he had kept apart from her husband, to
ascertain the truth of the story. Ever the gentleman, he put his
sword to her throat and demanded her corroboration: 'If you do

not improve by telling the truth, I will first slay your child with my own hand before your face, and then order you all cruelly put to death together'.

This terrifying display proved effective and the woman confirmed her husband's story in every detail. She then begged for her husband's life and that of her child. Bruce relented: 'I found myself so much moved, and my tears came so fast, that it was in vain to endeavour to carry on a farce under such tragical appearances.'

He lowered his sword, overcome with the realization that they were safe. They were not surrounded by the Bishareen and, moreover, by not travelling with the unfortunate Mahomet Towash, they had escaped the destruction of his caravan. If the king of Sennaar had not forced them to venture alone into the desert, they would indubitably have been killed by the Bishareen. The travellers now knew where they stood. They had interrogated their captives thoroughly and were confident that there were no Bishareen nearby. The problem remained of what to do with their prisoners. Leave them, and every desert Arab would soon know of their whereabouts; take them, and they would slow down the march and consume valuable supplies. Death seemed the only solution, and the sobbing Bruce was the only man who was against inflicting it.

His powerful defence of the robbers won the day. It was decided that they would take the man along with them, handcuffed to one of the Barbarins, to serve as an extra guide; the woman and child would be left at the oasis with the lame camels to provide milk for the child. Bruce ordered that the camels be hamstrung so that the women would be unable to leave until rescued. He even gave her twelve handfuls of his valuable bread to prevent her from starving.

With a sense of righteousness and equipped with an extra guide – who, if necessary, could speak for them if they came across his fellow Bishareen – Bruce led his party once more into the forbidding desert. At about twelve o'clock the simoom hit them again and continued unabated till three. At their resting place that evening one of the camels died of a combination of starvation and exhaustion. Having butchered it and taken the meat for drying, they plodded on the next day – every step an agonizing one for

the crippled Bruce – to the next well at Naibey. There they were
greeted by a sorry sight: the bodies of two camels and their owner
lay by the side of the well. 'No vermin had touched it, as in this
whole desert there is neither worm, fly, nor any thing that has the
breath of life.'

The days started to merge in to one. They marched across sharp
rocks which tore not only at the men's feet but also at the camels';
they were blasted with sand by whirlwinds and regularly, every
afternoon, the simoom descended upon them, sapping their
strength still further. They managed to find more bushes for the
camels to eat but not before another died. One of the Turcorory
went mad and had to be abandoned to the vengeful desert. 'Silence,
and a desperate kind of indifference about life, were the immediate
effect upon us.' They arrived at another well – Umarack – on the
twenty-second.

> I here began to provide for the worst. I saw the fate of our camels
> approaching, and that our men grew weak in proportion; our
> bread, too, began to fail us, although we had plenty of camel's
> flesh in its stead; our water, although in all appearance we were to
> find it more frequently than in the beginning of our journey, was
> nevertheless brackish, and scarcely served the purpose to quench
> our thirst; and, above all, the dreadful simoom had perfectly exhaus-
> ted our strength, and brought upon us a degree of cowardice and
> languor that we struggled with in vain . . . our camels were now
> reduced to five and it did not seem that these were capable of
> continuing their journey much longer.

Bruce threw away all the mineral samples and dead birds that he
had collected in his travels and the party began to carry their own
water and food, realizing that they could not rely on the camels
for much longer. They discovered the body of Mahomet Towash
– 'stript naked, and lying on his face unburied' – and must have
almost envied him his speedy death. They marched on, remorseless, past the bodies of the dead who had been left to die of thirst
by the Bishareen who had attacked Mahomet Towash's caravan.
In the evening they came to another well, this one guarded by a
solitary duck. It was initially a good omen, but their hopes were
shattered when it flew off to the west, thus showing that the Nile

was closer to the west (where it made, until the advent of the Aswan dam, a great loop) than it was at Aswan in the north, where they were heading.

On the twenty-third, Bruce had to bribe Ismael and Georgis to continue. *In extremis*, they wished to be abandoned to their fate in the desert, but were persuaded only when Bruce said they might ride the camels, something no one had done on the whole march. It did the camels no good. Two more long days of agonizing marching across the burning sands brought them, gasping, to the well at Haimer where they were frightened by a party of Arabs coming from Aswan. They made a pact and shared food as a sign of peace but neither party could help the other. At least Bruce's initial fears had been unfounded, however. The Arabs were fellow-travellers, not the bandits he had expected. By the twenty-seventh:

> We were now very near a crisis, one way or the other. Our bread was consumed, so that we had not sufficient for one day more; and although we had camel's flesh, yet, by living so long on bread and water, an invincible repugnance arose either to smell or taste it . . . Georgis had lost one eye and was nearly blind in the other . . . I had supported the wounds in my feet with a patience very uncommon, yet they were arrived at a height as to be perfectly intolerable, and, as I apprehended, on the point of mortification . . . a quantity of lymph oozed continually . . . we determined to throw away the quadrant, telescopes and timekeeper, and save our lives, by riding the camels alternately.

The next morning, not one of the camels would move – 'Every way we turned death now stared us in the face'. They slaughtered the camels and managed to extract another four gallons of water from the reservoirs inside the beasts, but they scarcely had the strength to walk, let alone carry their provisions. Bruce bandaged his feet and ignored the vast pile of baggage which contained his astronomical equipment, his notebooks, hundreds of paintings, the Kebra Negast, the lost Book of Enoch, his journal, his books – everything he valued in the world. All the fruits of his travels – the minute measurements, the maps he had drawn and the docu ments he had collected – were left to the mercy of robbers or to the sands, whichever got to them first. They marched on, Georgis stumbling in the haze of his failing sight, Ismael crippled by age and exhaustion, and Bruce, his feet bleeding through the bandages that covered them, leaving damp footprints in the sand. They managed only five hours that day before collapsing in the darkness.

The next day they marched on towards a distant hill. Bruce forged ahead, dragging his crippled feet only by willpower. He reached the top alone and could see only a few trees ahead, no river to the west or the north. He sank to the floor unable to comprehend a way forward. They had no bread left and could scarcely carry enough water to last a morning. The game was up: 'The evening was still, so that sitting down and covering my eyes with my hands, not to be diverted by external objects, I listened and heard distinctly the noise of waters, which I supposed to be the cataract, but it seemed to be to the southward of us, as if we had passed it. I was, however, fully satisfied that it was the Nile.'

At the very point of giving up hope, Bruce had heard the sound of water. They had made it. It was with a long lost spring in his all but broken stride that Bruce stumbled back down the hill to tell his friends. He could not see the Nile but he could at least hear it. It must therefore be close:

> A cry of joy followed this annunciation. Christians, Moors, and Turks, all burst into floods of tears, kissing and embracing one another, and thanking God for his mercy in this deliverance; and unanimously in token of gratitude, and in acknowledgement of my constant attention to them in the whole long journey, saluting me with the name of Abou Ferege, Father Foresight, the only reward it was in their power to give.

On 29 November, after twenty days of the most appalling deprivation and suffering, they arrived in Aswan. They could not have survived another day.

Aswan was civilization – the first place Bruce had been for quite some time which had regular communication with the outside world – but it was a while before the exhausted traveller was able to enjoy it. Having drunk from the Nile which he had never expected to see again, Bruce lay down under a palm tree and collapsed into a 'profound sleep'. Ismael, though, was soon picked out by some comrades on account of his green turban (which, despite the rest of his tattered outfit, identified him both as a janissary and as a descendant of the prophet Mohammed) and was taken to the Aga. He told his new friends to go and find Bruce: 'Go,' says Ismael, 'to the palm-trees and when you find the tallest man you ever saw in your life, more ragged and dirty than I am, call him Yagoube, and desire him to come along with you to the Aga.'

Within a few minutes – and with much of the town following them in the style of a Greek chorus – Bruce and his servants were attending an audience with the Aga. They were immediately given a house, food, water and new clothing but Bruce's first concern was not for his body but for his equipment: 'It is the first favour I am to ask of you, when I shall have rested myself two days, to allow me to get fresh camels, to go in search of my letters and baggage.'

It was to be a little longer than two days (he was unable to eat anything solid before then) but, as soon as he could mount a camel, Bruce returned to the fearsome desert that had so nearly cost him his life. He left with an escort and a number of pack camels to retrace his steps but had little hope of success. On the second day, however: 'We had the unspeakable satisfaction to find our quadrant and whole baggage; and by them the bodies of our slaughtered camels'.

In abandoning his baggage to the desert in those last desperate days Bruce had given up everything that had made his journey of value. He was thus understandably overjoyed when he was able to retrieve his notes and paintings. Incredibly, he had not lost a thing since the shipwreck all those years ago when he had first attempted to visit Crete. (They did, though, very nearly come to grief again: on Bruce's return to Europe, the ship's captain tried to throw the whole lot overboard during a storm.) Since leaving Abyssinia, Bruce had possessed little money. He had sold his beloved chain in Sennaar and, by the time they arrived in Aswan, every penny had been spent on camels, guards and provisions for him and his servants. Aswan was the first town in the Ottoman Empire where Bruce could write a small cheque. He obtained a little money and bought camels and clothes for Idris, their guide, and for the Bishareen who had first tried to rob him in the desert and then served them faithfully for the rest of the journey: 'Though rich beyond his hopes, and so very lately our enemy, the poor fellow, with tears in his eyes, declared, if I would permit him, he would only go back and deliver up what I had given him to his family, and return to me at Syene, and follow me as my servant wherever I should go.'

Only through the submission of this cheque would Drummond's, his bank in London, ultimately discover that their wealthy client was still alive, for they had heard nothing of him for years. The first rumours of his survival would gradually be confirmed but, as Bruce made his final descent of the Nile, it was difficult to persuade anyone that he was who he claimed to be. Confined to the boat which he and his travelling companions used as a hospital ship, he tried to obtain food, drink and medicine from the monks at the monastery at Furshout. They, however, refused to believe Bruce's servant: they had heard that Bruce had died on the Red Sea or even at the hands of robbers in Abyssinia. Either way they elected to believe that Bruce was most certainly dead and his servant was sent packing. Bruce was unable to confound the sceptics personally. The combination of malaria, a guinea worm in his already battered leg and the fact that they had a great deal of brandy on board meant that he had difficulty walking. Thus they sailed on to Cairo – hungry:

> On the 10th of January 1773, we arrived at the convent of St George, all of us, as I thought, worse in health and spirits than the day we came out of the desert. Nobody knew us at the convent, either by our face or our language, and it was by a kind of force that we entered. Ismael and the Copht went straight to the Bey, [This was the son-in-law of Bruce's friend, Ali Bey, who had declared himself an independent sultan in Bruce's absence, shortly before being ousted. Ali Bey was at that time trying to recruit a new army.] and I, with great difficulty, had interest enough to send to the Patriarch and my merchants at Cairo, by employing the only two piastres I had in my pocket.

Bruce fell asleep at the monastery in the hope that he would be awoken by news from the Patriarch and, with luck, food and drink. He was penniless, extremely ill and dressed as an impoverished dervish. Only two hours later he was startled from his dreams by a squadron of soldiers with orders to bring him before the Bey.

They treated him with a marked lack of respect, beating him as much as the unsaddled mule they forced him to ride through the city to the Bey's palace. It was in this state that Bruce appeared before the Bey, almost fainting from the pain in his feet and the fever in his head: 'Though it was late, he was in full dress, his girdle, turban, and handle of his dagger, all shining with the finest brilliants, and a finer sprig of diamonds upon his turban than what I had seen his father-in-law wear, once when I was with him'.

The Bey immediately apologized for the behaviour of his men and thanked the traveller for looking after Ismael in the desert, and for delivering him back safely to the janissary at Cairo from which he had been parted for so long (Ismael had originally gone to Abyssinia to accompany the new Abuna). He gave Bruce a purse of cash and was much impressed by his refusal to accept it: 'Julian and Rosa, the first house in Cairo, will furnish me with what money I require; besides, I am in the service of the greatest king in Europe, who would not fail to supply me abundantly if my necessities required it, as I am travelling for his service'.

Even in his acute distress, Bruce remembered that he should never oblige himself to anyone at all if possible, for by accepting money he would lose his status. The Bey promised Bruce he would do whatever the traveller desired, which allowed the Scot to perform a service for his friends Price and Thornhill at Jiddah. And he extracted a firman from the Bey that allowed British ships to come all the way up the Red Sea to Suez where they would pay only an eight per cent duty rather than the twelve per cent demanded at Jiddah. Bruce considered this one of his greatest achievements and was hurt that he received no official recognition for his efforts. He did, however, receive the plaudits of the men for whom he had done it – the India captains. Bruce heard in 1775 from Captain William Scott who asked: 'Please send me the draft [you] made of the Red Sea particularly between Suez and Jiddah; Thornhill sent a ship to Suez from Bengal this year. That ship has returned and has succeeded pretty well'.

After a few weeks recovering in Cairo, Bruce heard that the Bey was leaving to fight his father-in-law who had amassed a new army and was threatening to attack: 'I went therefore the last time to the Bey, who pressed me very much to go to the camp with him. I was sufficiently cured, however, of any more Don Quixote undertakings.'

It was a cure that would last the rest of his life. On 25 March 1773 he arrived in Marseilles and apart from a marked preference for settling arguments by duelling, he would never purposely risk his life again. The beloved quadrant – balanced by a weight suspended on the lock of Fasil's wife's hair – which had accompanied Bruce throughout his travels, was thus returned to its place of manufacture.

CHAPTER 12

THE ROVER'S RETURN

Bruce's arrival at Marseilles was the cause of great excitement. France's most respected sages flocked to the southern port to meet the man who had advanced European learning to such an extent. First among them was the Comte de Buffon, without whose help it would have been impossible for Bruce to have completed his travels to his satisfaction: it was Buffon who had interceded with Choiseul, and through him to the king, for Bruce to be given a quadrant. The traveller was immensely popular. Not only did he have many interesting stories to tell the naturalists, antiquarians and enlightened aristocrats who flocked around him but he had also brought back many presents. To Buffon – whose vast *Histoire Naturelle* was the first book of its kind – he brought giraffe skins, seeds and his extensive knowledge of African flora and fauna. Buffon would remain a friend long after Bruce had discarded the others and would reward the Scot with a fulsome acknowledgement in his seminal work on natural history. Bruce returned the favour by describing Buffon as 'the Pliny of Modern Europe' in his *Travels*.

Bruce had been away from Britain for eleven years, yet he did not rush home. He was sick – the guinea worm which had become embedded in his shin had been broken by a servant trying to extract it and the resultant putrefaction was causing him considerable pain. Guinea worms usually burrow into one's feet and grow there. They are removed by being wrapped round a match and pulled out. If broken in this process, however, they can rot and cause all sorts of ills. One doctor he consulted wanted to amputate the leg but Bruce refused, preferring his own treatment and, eventually, a course of salt baths, which cured him over a year later: 'To limp through the remains of life, after having escaped so many dangers, was hard, – so much so, that the loss of life itself seemed more desirable'.

Bruce was also exhausted by the general privations of the last few years and the taxing desert crossing to Aswan. He would have difficulty with his breathing – he sounded rather like a pair of bellows – for the rest of his life. He put this down to his near-drowning on the way to Crete, in conjunction with his childhood illness, yet never complained of it during his travels in Africa. His reception in France, however, would have been his main motiv-ation for staying in Europe. This was a country where he had long been addressed as *chevalier* and where he was treated with respect by all he met. France, it seemed, was a great deal more enlightened than his homeland and was hungry for knowledge, even if it came from a citizen of the enemy.

After staying a while with Buffon at Marseilles, where he enjoyed the fawning of Journu de Montagny and Alexandre Guys, academician and secretary to the king respectively, Bruce went to Paris where he was courted by dukes and intellectuals and almost immediately received at the court of Louis XV. The court was then ruled by the Dauphin because of the king's illness but it was Louis XV (who was to die the next year) who had given Bruce the necessary equipment to make his journey and to him Bruce felt a lasting gratitude. He gave the king many exotic presents – a copy of the apocryphal Book of Enoch, many seeds and cuttings (stored in glass bulbs that miraculously survived the journey) for the gardens at Versailles and Abyssinian books aplenty. The plants were bedded at the '*jardin royal à Paris, le magnifique jardin de Trianon, le jardin de Perpignan et de Montpelier*'. Their offspring can still be seen today. Long after Bruce had returned to Britain he continued to receive letters from both the king's and the Dauphin's gardeners, giving him detailed news on the progress of his plants. They stopped only when the National Convention took a fatal cutting of the Dauphin, by then Louis XVI, in 1793. Bruce – a firm believer in kings – reacted badly to this news. According to John Kay, the Scottish caricaturist who heard the anecdote from William

Graham's housekeeper: 'Mr Bruce retained such a strong remembrance of the kindness shown him by Louis XVI, that when he heard of the King's tragical end, in January 1793, his feelings were so much overpowered that he cried like a child'.

Whilst Bruce was enjoying his triumph in Paris, news was slowly filtering out to his British friends that the unstoppable Scot had risen from the dead. His end had been reported in many different forms: drowning in the Red Sea, murder at Gondar, a riding accident in Arabia Felix. The one thing all had agreed upon was that Bruce was dead. To a few Bruce's Lazarus-like appearance was an unpleasant surprise (his family for example, was trying to get hold of his property) but for many it was cause for celebration. Congratulatory letters began to reach Paris. Even one of Bruce's former colleagues, John Murat, wrote, 'I most sincerely congratulate you on your surprising escape from so many dangers, your surmounting so many difficulties cannot fail to afford you future pleasing reflections.'

The academies of Europe rushed to enrol him (Berlin, Boulogne, Marseilles, Bologna and Cartona in the first six months) in much the same way, perhaps, as universities fought to give honorary degrees to Neil Armstrong after he first stepped on the moon. Bruce took pleasure in receiving the kind of recognition that he had always anticipated. Women threw themselves at him despite the prophylactic effect of his suppurating leg. There survive letters from French paramours in three different hands from this period: 'Your eyes and your heart tell me, dear Brus, that you love me' is typical.

As Bruce's leg did not seem to be healing he decided to visit the medicinal baths of Poretta in Bologna which were owned by Luigi Balugani's patron, Ranuzzi. They eased the pain without entirely curing him. Italy, however, was useful for finding help in finishing the paintings that he had brought back from Africa. He could also visit his friends. Rome and indeed the whole of Italy was then so overflowing with English *milordi*, that, short of going home, it was the best place to see his compatriots. He went first to Bologna where he stayed with Ranuzzi, and hired four painters to finish the paintings of ruins that he had been carrying about with him for the last few years. They inserted the figures and landscapes to the architectural works.

Bruce was made an academician in Bologna. Balugani had suggested this course of action in a letter to his *alma mater*, but soon things became a little unpleasant. Bruce was, as we have seen, very hazy about the date and circumstances of Balugani's death; he was miserly about rendering Balugani's back pay to his relations and he seemed to be taking undue credit for work that the artist's former teachers could clearly recognize as their pupil's. Rumours began to circulate that Bruce had killed the young Italian. Bruce, however, did have artistic talent of his own; he was not entirely reliant upon Balugani. The Paesto paintings which were executed before Bruce hired Balugani have been condemned by some art historians but are charming enough. There is a radiant painting of a fish at Broomhall which is certainly by Bruce and almost swims off the paper. The fact that it was usual to have paintings 'finished' creates doubt as to the authenticity of many other eighteenth-century paintings. Bruce's treatment of Balugani is perfectly understandable. He hired the artist to paint pictures and therefore could do with them what he liked, Ranuzzi felt the same; he never criticized Bruce but welcomed him to his home. Such approval silenced the critics and thus Bruce left Bologna for Florence, satisfied at his reception and pleased with the work that was now finished.

He stayed with Horace Mann, whom he had first met when awaiting his orders for Algiers, and was painted with him in Zoffany's marvellous *The Tribuna of the Uffizi Gallery*. Zoffany obviously knew Bruce well for he painted the returned explorer standing at the foot of the Venus de' Medici with a smirk on his face that seems to announce that Bruce had sacrificed to that very Venus only minutes earlier.

At an opera house in Florence Bruce had a fateful chance meeting: he encountered Margaret Murray, the girl he had left behind in Scotland clutching his miniature by Victoria Stern. She was no longer attached to that miniature but was instead clutching a small Italian marquis, the Marchese Accoramboni, who had become her husband. With the twisted logic of a man who had bedded most of the eligible (and many of the ineligible) women in Arabia, Abyssinia and France, Bruce flew into a towering rage. The marchioness, meanwhile, had fainted and had been taken home to recover from seeing her long-dead fiancé. The angry Bruce immediately set off for Rome whence Margaret and her husband had fled, ignoring the pleas of his friends ringing in his ears. Horace Mann amongst others wrote him an impassioned letter advising him against the folly but Bruce demanded satisfaction. 'I am your equal, Marquis, in every respect' he wrote to the Marchese Accoramboni:

> and God alone can do me justice for the injury which you have done me. Full of innocence, and with a clear conscience, I commit my revenge to him, and draw my sword against you with confidence inspired by the reflection of having done my duty, and by a sense of the injustice and violence which I have suffered from you without any reason.
>
> At half past nine, (French reckoning) I come to your gate in my carriage; if it does not please you, let your own be ready; and let us go together to determine which is the more easy, to injure a man in his absence, or to defend it when he is present.

The effete aristocrat reacted swiftly to this absurd letter and immediately sent a grovelling reply – which Bruce accepted – thus freeing himself from the necessity of fighting an expert swordsman who was approximately a foot taller than him and built like a house:

> When the marriage with Miss M., at present my wife, was arranged, it was never mentioned to me that there was a promise made to you, otherwise that connection should not have taken place.
>
> With regard to yourself, on my honour, I have never spoken to you in any manner, as you were entirely unknown to me. On which account, if I can serve you, command me. With the profoundest respect, I sign myself, your most obedient humble servant.

Astonishingly but perhaps unsurprisingly, whilst all this was going on Bruce was conducting yet another relationship in nearby Bologna. Only six days later Bruce – 'Carissimo mio Brus' – received a letter from one Marianna Sarti of Bologna saying that he must marry her if he wanted her to return his affection.

Sadly for the great traveller, this somewhat ridiculous story was the first thing many Britons heard of the man who claimed to have found the source of the Nile. Still, he did not return home.

He had many friends in Rome and the Duc d'Aiguillon had given him an introduction, through Cardinal Berni, to the Pope. Clement XIV was not only the scourge of the Jesuits (something Bruce would heartily applaud) but he was also the secular monarch of the Papal States and, as we know, Bruce loved a king.

It was spring of the next year before he returned to Paris and Marseilles for two months and from there to England. He was still a curiosity rather than a laughing stock in Marseilles. There he met the glamorous and well-connected Duchess of Northumberland who was surprised at how civilized Bruce was. 'At my return home,' she wrote in her diary:

> Mr Bruce the great Traveller, came and drank Tea with me. He by no means answer'd the idea which I had form'd to myself of him. I had figured to myself a figure with a vast Beard as long as Liotard's [a notably hirsute artist], a Turban & a flowing Turkish Robe, but instead I saw enter a fresh well looking man in a Scarlet Coat embroidered with Gold, a White Feather in his Hat and a Chin as smooth as a Billiard Ball. He was very polite but I confess I was not so much entertained with his Conversation as I expected to have been.

As a returning consul bearing gifts for the king, Bruce had arranged, through Joseph Banks and Johann Zoffany, that he would not have to pay duty on any of the goods he was bringing back. Thus his baggage was ordered by the head of customs in London to be 'immediately sent to the warehouses here under the seal of office without being unpacked, opened or otherwise disturbed'. This was an impressive way to return but the respect with which he was treated would not last for long. On 21 June 1774 he at last arrived in London after twelve years abroad. He was no longer the slightly aimless unknown who had left England but an imposing forty-four-year-old with a face worn by years in the tropics, a wheezing but none the less vast barrel of a chest, and a mine of fascinating stories: 'He was a large man' said the printmaker, Cradock, 'and, in an evening, rather splendidly dressed. He had a most extraordinary complaint which could not well be accounted for; when he attempted to speak, his whole stomach suddenly seemed to heave like an organ bellows.'

Almost as soon as Bruce returned, the remorseless gossip Horace Walpole fired off a letter to Mann in Tuscany, telling him of Bruce's arrival. Mann was not nearly as punctilious a correspondent as Walpole and hence had not told his friend of his acquaintance with Bruce. 'I am sorry all Europe will not furnish me with another paragraph', he wrote after a particularly scurrilous page about aristocratic goings-on:

> Africa is indeed coming into fashion. There is just returned a Mr Bruce, who had lived three years in the Court of Abyssinia, and breakfasted every morning with the maids of honour on live oxen. Otaheite and Mr Banks are quite forgotten; but Mr Bruce I suppose will order a live sheep for supper at Almack's, and ask whom he can help to a piece of the shoulder. Oh yes, we shall have negro butchers, and French cooks will be laid aside.

Bruce had indeed arrived in London at a time when it was over-flowing with glamorous characters. Joseph Banks had just returned from Cook's voyage to the South Seas with the aforementioned Otaheite, an unfortunate Tahitian who was being paraded around London's salons. (Bruce felt very sorry for the Polynesian, whose real name was Oomai, on the basis that he would be disbelieved in exactly the same way as Bruce himself was. Oomai was returned – laden with presents – to the South Seas by Captain Cook where he was killed by his jealous compatriots on his native Huahine island.) Banks and Cook, however (who had the entire crews of the *Endeavour* and the *Resolution* to corroborate their stories), were believed, whereas Bruce soon became a figure of fun.

England had changed since Bruce's departure. London was enjoying a period of great prosperity as the Industrial Revolution gained momentum; Wilkes's supporters had been rioting and putting the fear of God into the aristocracy, the French were still the enemy but the battlefield had changed. The Bostonians had given their tea party the year before; Gin Lane was no longer and in fact the first pavements had been built outside Bruce's house in Westminster. His friends were overjoyed to see him and showered him in praise: they had heard nothing of him for the four years prior to his arrival in Marseilles and had presumed him dead, as had the rest of London. For a short period he was the talk of the town and a great catch for London hostesses. The king gave him an audience and accepted the paintings of ruins which he had commissioned so long ago; Lord North, the Prime Minister, invited him to dine; he met Joseph Banks and was elected a Fellow of the Royal Society. The newspapers wrote about him and his every anecdote seemed to be published as soon as it was uttered. By the end of his first year back in Britain, a two-volume account of his travels had already been published in Germany – without his permission. The gossip, too, started almost immediately: 'When I first came home' claimed Bruce 'it was with great pleasure, I gratified the curiosity of the whole world, by showing them each what they fancied most curious'.

His pleasure soon turned to fury. No one criticized him openly but he rapidly began to realize that he was not believed. His stories were too outlandish and his manner too frightening. Nor was he being given the preferment that he had been led to expect. Having lived as a nobleman in the East and in Africa, France and Italy he had presumed that he would be given at least a baronetcy on his return. The late Lord Halifax had earlier intimated that he would be ennobled for his troubles. Instead, the king had accepted his paintings but had neither paid him nor advanced him. In fact, it would be nearly three years, at the end of 1776, before Bruce was paid the £6000 he eventually received for the paintings.

Within a few months of his triumphant return, Bruce had decamped to Scotland to lick his wounds. This was not entirely in a fit of pique: he had other reasons for returning to Kinnaird, not least that it was home; a home, however, that was under threat due to his long disappearance. Presuming the traveller to be dead, Bruce's relations had started legal proceedings which would allow them to inherit Kinnaird House and its valuable land. Bruce's rage heightened when he discovered that, contrary to his instructions of a dozen year earlier, the tenant farmers and miners had not been evicted and the Carron iron works and collieries that he had done so much to disguise before his departure were now completely ruining the view from the house. They had also transformed his home town: the busy but essentially agricultural Falkirk he had left behind was now a sooty and grimy industrial mess. He settled down to a period of sustained litigation and rebuilding.

One can imagine how the proud Scot felt as he settled back into life at Kinnaird. He had suffered appalling hardships and battled against terrifying odds to discover the source of the Nile for his country, yet here he was, without honours from the king and a figure of fun. After his adulation on the continent it must have been a crushing reception. Finding the source should have been an event of enormous significance. The riddle of the Nile had plagued everyone from Nero to Herodotus, Cambyses to Darius, Prince Henry the Navigator to Ptolemy the Geographer. Now he, 'a mere private Briton' had solved it yet no one would give him the credit he deserved. He was seen as slightly dubious and, indeed, laughable. Exactly the same would happen to Speke of the Nile 100 years later when, in strikingly similar words, he really did resolve what Bruce believed he had resolved – 'the first geographical desideratum of many thousand years to ascertain, and the ambition of the first monarchs of the world to unravel'. Most galling for Bruce must have been the way in which the members of Cook's expedition – undertaken with the backing of the crown – were being honoured by all and sundry. Bruce's achievements were entirely comparable and had been accomplished at much higher personal expense – spiritual, physical and financial.

Haughty and hurt, 'the Great Lyon' vented his spleen upon the Carron Company and his tenants. R. H. Campbell, a historian of the Carron Company, states that it 'would have been difficult to find a more impossibly difficult laird'. A digest of the local paper – the *Falkirk Herald* – gives an example of the type of man that the Carron Company was dealing with. Some engineers had been called to Kinnaird to try and settle a dispute between Bruce and the company. They soon became frustrated with the intractable laird:

> The engineer said that if Mr Bruce was not afraid he might go down [the mines] and satisfy himself on the point by personal investigation. The word 'afraid' startled the ear of the traveller, whose commanding figure and bold demeanour had been the chief means of bringing him through so many dangers. 'Afraid!' said he, in his magnificent way. 'Sir, do you think I would be afraid to go down into my own mines?' He immediately proposed to go down

with them next day . . . down he went with his corps of engineers
. . . leading the Abyssinian such a dance as never traveller danced
before . . . At one place the engineers passed through an aperture
barely wide enough for themselves, who were men of moderate
size, but which was evidently too narrow for Bruce . . . he was
too proud to own himself defeated – tried the aperture, and fairly
stuck in it. They had to pull him out by the head and shoulders,
and a sore pull it was . . . Nevertheless, up to the last moment he
maintained his usual composure; and the only remark he now made
that seemed to denote his feelings was that he did not think that
the wastes had been so dirty.

Inevitably, the stubborn explorer won his cases, though two
went as far as the House of Lords before they were settled. Legal
disputes were not his only pastimes. In nearby Edinburgh was the
Freemason's lodge that he had joined with William Graham in
1753. At Canongate Kilwinning Lodge No. 2 he would have been
treated with great respect. All there would have been overjoyed
to see him for he had brought back from Abyssinia the apocryphal
Book of Enoch, a work of immense importance to 'the Craft' that
had been lost for centuries. (Enoch is thought to be one of the
father's of Freemasonry. He is said to have taught the Masons how
to build, thus for Masons, many of whom are convinced that they
built the pyramids, he is a significant figure.) We can only surmise
what other exciting things Bruce had to tell his confrères – perhaps
that the Ark was safe and well in Ethiopia, that he was unable to
get his hands on it but also that he was sure nobody else could.
The Ark, he could tell them, would remain safely in Ethiopia's
mountain fastness for no one was ever allowed to approach it and
every man in Ethiopia would die before letting it fall into the
hands of a foreigner.

In Edinburgh he spent time with all the Enlightenment figures
living in the city; the New Town was under construction and he
had his eye on a property; David Hume was still alive and surrounded by savants. Edinburgh was developing into one of the
most dynamic cities in the world, at the forefront of thought,
architecture and literature. There Bruce met for the first time
a man who was to be one of his most influential critics – the

Anglicized Scot James Boswell. They were both members of Kilwinning Lodge yet actually met at the Court of Session. Boswell pursued Bruce to his lodgings in Milne Square and interviewed him for the *London Magazine*. Bruce was a tricky man to interview, already wary of all inquiries: Boswell likened digging information from him 'as from a flinty rock with pickaxes' and compared him unfavourably with Joseph Banks, the President of the Royal Society, upon his own return from distant seas. 'All extraordinary travellers are a kind of shows;' claimed Boswell 'a kind of wild beasts. Banks and Bruce however were animals very different from one another. Banks was an elephant, quite placid and gentle, allowing you to get on his back and play with his proboscis; Bruce, a tiger that growled whenever your approached him.'

Bruce had made a serious error in not trying to charm Boswell, who had enormous influence and was very capable of discrediting him. He had two reasons for doing so. He worshipped Samuel Johnson – then considered the expert on Abyssinia thanks to *Rasselas* and his translation of Father Lobo – and Bruce's thoughts on Abyssinia were diametrically opposed to Johnson's. Christopher Hibbert in his 1971 *Personal History of Samuel Johnson*, says '*Rasselas*, following upon his translation of *Lobo's Travels*, gained for Johnson an undeserved reputation as an authority on Ethiopia. His expressed doubt that the explorer, James Bruce, had ever even entered the country contributed much, therefore, to Bruce's early failure to gain credence for his exploits.'

More importantly, though, Boswell's own pride would have been pricked by his compatriot. Until that time, Boswell – who we now only associate with Johnson – had been known as 'Corsican' Boswell, due to a book he had written about his travels in the wild mountains of Corsica. 'Corsican' Boswell does not compare well with 'Abyssinian' Bruce and this nickname problem could well have sparked their animosity.

In the winter of 1774 Bruce did not of course neglect his love life. He fell heavily for a poet and neighbour, Lady Anne Lindsay. He experienced competition, however, from the Earl of Rosebery. After being refused (they both failed: Lady Anne remained a spinster for another twenty years) he set off back to London where he hoped he might find someone willing to sponsor the publication of the extensive collection of paintings which he had kept for himself rather than give to the king. Plate-making was a very expensive process and, although he could afford it, Bruce sought the flattery of sponsorship. He sustained his grudge against Rosebery whilst in London, joking (prophetically, for Bruce would die in a similar manner) to Fanny Burney that, 'I shall bribe his servant to tie a cord across his staircase some night, and as I daresay he is never at the expense of allowing himself a candle to walk up and down, he must necessarily break his neck'.

It is through the diaries and letters of Fanny Burney that we know the details of how Bruce spent his time in this period. Fanny Burney would die at ninety-two, a novelist and lady-in-waiting. Best remembered for her gruesomely vivid description of her own mastectomy, she was at this point, however, a frothy twenty-three-year-old besotted with the glamorous explorer. She does not let her fantasies cloud her judgement, however, and gives excellent descriptions of Bruce which provide an insight into why he had so many enemies, whilst still acknowledging his charms. They met through their mutual friends the Stranges to whom Bruce had moved closer in fashionable Leicester Fields (George III had lived there until his coronation). In between showing 'his collection of curiosities' to people he thought might sponsor the publication of the prints, Bruce spent hours in the company of the Stranges by whom he was much beloved. For someone so anxious to avoid social intercourse, the houses of the Stranges and the Burneys in nearby Castle and St Martin's streets respectively were odd places to visit since they were two of the most fashionable in London. Bruce was as likely to meet Garrick, Reynolds or Boswell in either house as he was to take a quiet cup of tea with Isabella Strange. His later animosity towards Johnson and Boswell must have been a problem, too, for Johnson was inordinately fond of the Burneys: 'I love all of that breed' said Johnson 'whom I can be said to know, and one or two whom I hardly know, I love upon credit'.

When Fanny and Bruce first met, he had already written his piece about Abyssinian lyres for Dr Burney's *History of Music* (Burney had begged Mrs Strange for an introduction) but they had another link beyond this and the Stranges – the Burneys were themselves a cosmopolitan travelling family. Fanny's brother Charles had been to the South Seas with Captain Cook; he would later command Cook's ship after the navigator's death in Hawaii and attain the rank of admiral. Her father had written what may be described as a musical travel book about his journeys in the more obscure parts of Europe. Fanny herself would marry a French marshall. The Burneys could be relied on not to disbelieve all Bruce's stories in the way that untravelled listeners did. Fanny, though, was not blind to Bruce's faults. She gives a vivid description of him in early 1775:

I had yesterday the honour of drinking tea in company with *His Abyssinian Majesty* Mr Bruce; for so Mrs Strange calls Mr Bruce . . . He has been acquainted intimately with Mrs Strange all his life, and is very much attached to her and her family. He seldom passes a day without visiting her; but Miss Strange who has told me of many of his singularities, says that he is generally put into a *pet* when they have any company, as his excessive haughtiness prevents his being sociable with them and makes him think them impertinant if they take the liberty to speak to him. Indeed, she told me he has been very ill-used by the curiosity, which previous to his provocation, he *did* satisfy, for many people gathered anecdotes and observations from him and printed them. This . . . as he intends . . . to publish his travels himself, was most abominably provoking. It is not enough to say, that this put him *upon his guard*, it has really made him shy of being asked how he does? or, what's o'clock? Haughty by nature, his extraordinary travels, and perhaps his long resistance among savages have contributed to render him one of the most imperious of men; he is indeed by far the most so, that I ever saw. He is more than six feet high, is extremely well proportioned in shape, and has a handsome and expressive face. If his vanity is half as great as his pride, he would certainly become more courteous, if he knew how much smiles become him, for when he is pleased to soften the severity of his countenance, and to suffer his features to relax into smiling, he is quite another creature.

In order to try and hawk his paintings, Bruce did occasionally have to leave the confines of the Stranges's home and, whenever he did, there was always a reaction, generally to his detriment. He showed his pictures to Lord North, the Duke of Gloucester, Doctors Banks and Solander at the British Museum (to which, together with the Bodleian Library in Oxford, he lent most of his manuscripts) yet whilst all publicly admired them no one would help him publish. Dr Johnson completely failed to see the charming side of Bruce's character when they met on April Fool's Day at 'Single Speech' Hamilton's house in Lincoln's Inn. The great arbiter of almost everything immediately took against Bruce, whether from jealousy over their relative authority on Abyssinia or merely from personal animosity, we will never know: 'He is not a distinct relater' he told Boswell. In Bruce, 'I did not perceive any superiority of understanding.'

Worse was to come. Johnson eventually began to let it be known that he did not believe Bruce had been to Abyssinia at all. Boswell records, 'when he first conversed with Mr Bruce, the Abyssinian traveller, he was very much inclined to believe he had been there; but that he had afterwards altered his opinion'.

Many others joined Johnson's side. Baron de Tott, the traveller, weighed in from Cairo, claiming that Bruce had never been to Gishe Abbay; soon the feckless Edward Wortley Montagu was doing the same; an anonymous academician from Bologna claimed in print that Bruce had painted none of the views he had given to the king. Bruce's manner so discouraged people that even those who should have known better doubted his word. Horace Walpole found it most amusing to write the traveller off as a total fraud. Before he went to Scotland, he had become a sort of standing joke in Walpole's fashionable Richmond/Twickenham set. In 1774 Walpole signed off a letter: 'In this wavering situation I wish you good night, and hope I shall wake tomorrow as resolute as Hercules or Mr Bruce'.

In fact, even after he returned to Scotland, his pictures unpublished and his pride severely damaged, Bruce's spirit would linger on in London as the butt of jokes. When his article in Burney's *History of Music* was published, the gossips roared back into action. It was said that he had 'lie[d] himself into £7,000' when he was eventually paid for his paintings and his consulship in 1780. Adventures of Baron Münchausen were dedicated to him and books continued to be published in which the most remarkable stories he had told were relayed to the public for someone else's profit.

Furious and hurt, he laid low at Kinnaird where he continued the renovations of his house and settled down to find himself a wife. He stumbled upon one next door, a Dundas – after which family many Edinburgh streets are named – and married her on 20 May 1776. Mary Dundas was the daughter of one of Bruce's neighbours, Sir Thomas Dundas, with whom the irascible traveller had been feuding for years. Despite having much in common – both their parents had frittered away their son's inheritances; both had been to Rome and indeed been painted by the same artist (Pompeo Batoni's portrait of Dundas is a swaggering masterpiece, sadly Bruce's rather dull) and both despised the Carron Company – they had never got on. Bruce had sued Dundas's father, Lawrence, and won at least once. The marriage healed the inter-familial wounds and the two men joined forces to torment the iron works on which both their fortunes depended. By all accounts the marriage was blissfully happy despite the difference in age – Mary had been born in the year that Bruce's first wife had died. They had three children, one of whom died young, and Bruce settled down to life as a country laird. He built an observatory on the roof of Kinnaird and rode around his estate on a huge Clydesdale horse for whose well being his tenants became increasingly concerned as their landlord's girth began to compete with his mount's.

Friends came to visit him but even the dearest and most steadfast had to be careful. Even 'Single Speech' Hamilton saw Bruce's sharper side. Colonel Head who knew Bruce's daughter and wrote his biography in the early nineteenth century, recalled one incident:

> One evening at Kinnaird, he [Hamilton] said, 'Bruce! To convince the world of your power of drawing, you need only draw us now something in as good a style as those drawings of yours which they say have been done for you by Balugani, your Italian artist.' 'Gerard!' replied Bruce, very gravely, 'you made one fine speech, and the world doubted its being your own composition, but, if you will stand up now here, and make another speech as good, we shall believe it to have been your own.'

His childhood friend William Graham still lived at nearby Airth; he had friends in and around Edinburgh and he spent a great deal of time at Ardwhillery, his estate in Monteith. This he bought because of its startling similarity with the highlands of Ethiopia which he missed increasingly as he grew older. For the next ten years he had a happy life, spending almost all his time at home with his family. At last he had found a relatively healthy companion who was unlikely to be executed and who had survived the honeymoon. He spent some time translating the Book of Enoch from the Ethiopic and visited the lodge when he was in Edinburgh. He continued his lifelong love affair with hunting and also showed an interest in local affairs. In conjunction with local landowners he built Bank Street in Falkirk and forced the Carron Company into paying much of the bill. He wrote to London occasionally, keeping in touch with his metropolitan friends Hamilton, Barrington and the Stranges who kept him up to date with the goings-on there. From Joseph Banks, who was classifying the plants which Bruce had discovered, he heard of other travellers' adventures. Mainly he indulged in endless correspondence with his neighbours and the building of a museum at Kinnaird to show off his 'curiosities'. The museum soon began to receive a steady trickle of visitors to whom he would display the exhibits: 'We went and saw the Pale Abyssinian Bruce's curiosities – a great number of drawings of birds and fishes,' wrote one underwhelmed visitor.

John Lettice wrote about the museum in a travel book about his Scottish tour. He was obviously teased by the retired explorer:

> Before we departed Mr Bruce obligingly accompanied us to an enclosure in his park, to show us his Abyssinian sheep. They are entirely white, except their heads which are black. Their tales are large, and, indeed, the animal is larger than our common sheep. They are extremely tame, and often very frolicksome. The three or four remaining in the possession of Mr Bruce are unfortunately all males. One of them bred with a she-goat but the offspring died.

The sheep described sound suspiciously like undocked Suffolk Blacks and, since we know that Bruce nearly starved to death on his return through the desert, it seems highly unlikely that any stray sheep would have survived the journey uneaten. Other visitors did not get treated so well. One who doubted that raw meat was fit for consumption was forced to eat a raw steak by the irascible laird.

For a few years, Bruce's friends continued to write from the Continent. Journu de Montagny pleaded that 'all of Europe is awaiting' a record of his adventures, Buffon and his friends from the Levant all asked him to write about his travels but the laird was content with life. Even the love letters, which had appeared every now and then from France and Italy, ceased having been left unanswered by the now happily married Bruce. In 1785, however, tragedy struck once more. His beloved young wife Mary died (probably of tuberculosis) leaving him with two young children and nothing to do. He was initially shattered: once again someone he loved had been taken from him. After a few months of mourning, though, Bruce's life took on purpose once more. He threw himself into action with a gusto he had not known for fifteen years.

First he decided he would secure the baronetcy he felt he deserved. He wrote to the Marquess of Aylesbury (a Brudenell-Bruce, he was a distant cousin) and asked him to petition the king. Aylesbury agreed to do this but, before anything could be done about it, the king went mad again. The prime minister (by now William Pitt the Younger – all Bruce's champions of the early days were dead, their children in power) did not even reply to the letter. His friends rallied round, however, and suggested that he should now write the long-awaited book of his travels. Most vociferous among these was Daines Barrington, the old Harrovian schoolfriend who had advised Gilbert White to publish his *Natural History and Antiquities of Selborne*. He would be very helpful with the eventual publication of the book which Bruce tried to administer from Scotland whilst using Barrington as a London agent.

In 1786 Bruce hired a secretary, William Logan, who would remain with him until his death, and together they sat down to write the book that would become the *Travels*. It was an arduous and complicated process. Bruce had recorded everything that he had seen and done in notebooks, journals and, when he had run out of books, on long strips of paper bought in Gondar. The entire collection was in an appalling mess. He set out to write down everything he knew about Abyssinia, the Sudan and the Red Sea but much of the time he relied on his memory and this showed in the book when it was eventually published.

Benjamin Latrobe, the pastor of the Moravian church in London's Fetter Lane, claims to have spent a year as his amanuensis and to have been paid only five guineas for the job. He wrote after Bruce's death:

> This was a task which required the most persevering attention, as well as a great quickness of pen, as he himself, seated in an easy chair, had nothing to do but crowd his ideas upon me, and he was very impatient if I did not keep pace with him. In this manner I attended him every morning before eight o'clock and was frequently detained until nine at night, during which time I had no intermission of labour unless when he was under the necessity of devoting some time to a friend that called upon him, or he chanced to fall asleep in the midst of his dictating, or during the time for dinner, for breakfast and tea were expected to make no interruption to the business. I believe that during the whole time of my attendance I did not miss above four or five days without doing more or less for him.

This sounds like the Bruce of whom we have grown so accustomed – treating Latrobe with the same disrespect as he did Balugani. However, it is a very unlikely story. For a start, we know from an extant receipt that Bruce knew Latrobe long before and indeed had given him £10 for 'the furtherance of the gospel among the heathens'. Bruce, therefore, was reasonably generous. The original manuscript of the book has evidence of three hands – Bruce's, Logan's (Bruce's secretary) and another, presumably Latrobe's – but the vast majority is written by Bruce. This suggests firstly that it is the original: having two secretaries at his disposal, he would have hardly copied it personally. Secondly, it shows that Bruce wrote with more care than was previously thought. It seems likely that Latrobe did help in some way but that, having been poorly paid, he was pressing his claim for more money from the estate.

The writing of the *Travels* was no easy task. The sections about his own time in Abyssinia would have been easy enough but as well as this he had to translate from the Ethiopic the Kebra Negast which is inserted into the book. His descriptions of plants, animals,

the state of trade and the locations of clean water wells on the
Red Sea coast also had to be checked meticulously or rendered
worthless. He managed to finish the whole five volumes quarto
(including plates) by the spring of 1788, less than two years after
he had started. The haste does show somewhat and the second
and third editions prepared by Bruce and finished after his death
by the brilliant orientalist Alexander Murray are much better than
the first. The original, though, was a magnificent book. Bruce
sent it first to Daines Barrington who was immediately excited by
his friend's work:

> I have, this morning, finished your journey from Masuah to Gon-
> dar, and shall continue to observe your injunction of making no
> observations till you carry me back to Cairo. I shall venture, how-
> ever, to say, that you have interested me most thoroughly with
> regard to what relates to that unfrequented country, where I now
> find myself perfectly at home.

Barrington was scarcely going to write back to Bruce that he
did not like the book. He did, however, immediately identify what
is so extraordinary about the *Travels*. He found himself 'perfectly at
home'; this is the great triumph of the book. It describes a very
foreign culture which seems to stem from a different century from
Barrington's; yet, Bruce describes the human aspect of the drama
with such excellence that it is simple to imagine oneself there.
Actually walking through the vaulted castles where Bruce conducted his love affairs and watched the goings-on at court is an extraordinary experience for anyone who knows his book well. Hugh
Blair, the great Enlightenment figure, was likewise entranced when
he was allowed to see the manuscript. He suggested that Bruce
should have Lord of Geesh added to his coat of arms and praised
the book to the skies: 'You make one absolutely in love with your
great favourite Ozoro Esther. Have you never heard a word of
what is become of her and your other old friends there?' he asked.
    In fact, Bruce had heard a little of Abyssinia a few years earlier
when the Indian Captain William Scott wrote informing him that
he had assisted a prince of the Royal Blood who had been robbed
on his way to Jerusalem and that Tecla Haimanout was dead. This,

though, was all that he had ever learned of his beloved Abyssinia and its princesses after his departure.

Buoyed up by the positive reactions of his friends, Bruce sped into action, preparing his book for the press. So busy was he that he did not join the newly formed African Association, although Daines Barrington kept him up to date with its proceedings. It was important to Bruce that the book should be produced in Scotland but at the same time he wanted it to be perfect. The great book of exploration of the time was Cook's *Voyages* and Bruce went to considerable lengths to make sure his looked similar. He demanded 'paper such as Cook's voyages' and was unable to find the correct ink until May 1789: 'A barrel of ink was sent by yesterday's waggon directed to James Ferrier Esq., it is strong and such as Cooke's Voyage was printed with.'

His attention to detail was rewarded when the splendid looking book was eventually published in 1790, a trifling eighteen years after he had quit Abyssinia. Beginning with a lengthy dedication to the king, it was an overnight bestseller, almost selling out in the first thirty-six hours; it had been translated into French and German by the end of the year. The epic introduction anticipated and condemned any criticism:

> I do solemnly declare to the public in general, that I never will refute or answer any cavils, captious or idle objections, such as every new publication seems unavoidably to give birth to, nor ever reply to those witticisms and criticisms that appear in newspapers and periodical writings. What I have written I have written. My readers have before them, in the present volumes, all that I shall ever say, directly or indirectly, upon the subject; and I do, without one moment's anxiety, trust my defence to an impartial, well-informed and judicious public.

He was far too trusting. The book sold magnificently but, had bestseller lists existed, Bruce's great and truthful account of his travels would have been number one on the *fiction* list. Readers loved it but presumed that the vast majority was a figment of Bruce's imagination.

They were helped in their presumption by the reviews which were often savage. Almost immediately, the *Travels* were described as 'more wonderful than those of Sinbad the sailor and perhaps as true'. His friends rushed to contradict them: 'When I wrote last' said John Douglas, Bishop of Carlisle 'I could not have supposed it possible that any of our periodical critics would treat you with the very illiberal abuse that disgraced the *Monthly Review* for June.'

Critical though they were, no one could deny the fact that it was a marvellous read. The *Critical Review* of 1790 pondered all the reviews and criticisms, studied the book at great length (almost 100 closely printed pages) and came to its own conclusions:

> Mr Bruce's credit has more than once been questioned; and these travels have openly been called the fictions of a lively imagination, a tale built on report, a building raised on the foundations of neglected publications, and accounts collected at Alexandria, Cairo and Algiers. Those who dared not proceed so far, have attacked his style, his reasoning, and his opinions, and even doubted whether he has yet seen the head of the Nile, the object of his travels and the subject of his boast. With the work in our hands, we have patiently examined every objection, we have followed some disputed passages which our own observation has pointed out, and with every publication relating to Abyssinia before us, we have examined the whole question. It is needless to be minute on every particular passage; we shall prefer giving the result of our enquiries ... It remains then to examine, whether any of these surprising events are inconsistent with the observations of nature, or the narratives of other travellers; we cannot discover any inconsistencies or contradictions of either kind; and we have little hesitation in saying that, in general, this work is entitled to credit and applause ... On the whole, we have been highly gratified in the perusal of this author's travels, and we have endeavoured to convey the pleasure and the instruction to our readers, in a series of extensive articles.

Scarcely ringing praise but at least a measured opinion, Bruce did not mind this kind of review. It was the vicious and often anonymous side-swipes that irritated him. John Kay, Isaac Cruikshank and many lesser known artists published insulting cartoons; more editions of Münchausen were dedicated to him; Peter Pindar (the famous satirist John Woolcot's pseudonym), published a bestselling 'complimentary epistle to James Bruce Esq. The Abyssinian Traveller' in which he made Bruce sound ridiculous. Sniping, anonymous letters were published in the papers: 'Sir, Mr Bruce has travelled far, and seemed determined to come home laden with a full cargo of the marvellous, whatever else he might leave behind him. Münchausen, Sir, was a great traveller also, but the Abyssinian researcher has beat him hollow even in his own line' appeared pseudonymously in the *St James's Chronicle*.

Edward Wortley Montagu wrote a letter to the *European Magazine* casting doubt on Bruce's claims. Even the ageing Horace Walpole remembered the fun he had had at Bruce's expense: 'It is the most absurd, obscure, and tiresome book I know,' he wrote, having become marooned in the first volume. For once, he had a point: much of the first volume comprises Bruce's rambling dedication to the king.

To the ire of Bruce's critics, the book was the talk of the town – indeed of Europe. Pirated editions began to appear, edited down to a more manageable length. They too sold very well and gave Bruce something on which to vent his spleen. Whilst preparing a second edition in octavo, on the advice of his friends Bruce went back to one of his great loves – litigation. He tried to sue his publishers in Scotland whom he believe had not paid him his due. He managed to have unauthorized copies burnt in Ireland and to halt their appearance in England. Using the copyright law recently fashioned by Hogarth, Bruce was able to safeguard what had since the death of his wife been his only love – the *Travels*. He scarcely left Kinnaird after the publication of his book, preferring to spend time with his beloved daughter who worshipped him. He entertained a lot and ate a great deal.

Samuel Walker, who drew the maps for the *Travels*, asserted 'that Bruce was latterly so large and heavy a man, that, in getting into his carriage [he could no longer ride a horse] it bent sideways with his weight'.

'Bruce in his latter years,' says his entry in *Eminent Scotsmen*, 'lost much of his capabilities of enjoying life by his prodigious corpulence. We have been told that at this period of his life he was enlarged to such a degree as almost to appear monstrous. His appearance was all the more striking, when, as was his frequent custom, he assumed an Eastern habit and turban.'

On 26 April 1794 his prodigious weight was to be his undoing. Manoeuvring himself down the stairs of Kinnaird on his tiny size seven feet, he fell over and landed with the full weight of his vast body on his head. He was dead by morning.

GREAT SCOT

On May Day 1794, James Bruce was buried beside his wife in Larbert churchyard where his ancestor had preached and where many of his Masonic colleagues had been buried. His is one of few graves that is not decorated with skulls, crossbones and set squares. Instead, in the corner of the lonely car park stands a cast-iron obelisk overlooking an industrial estate. On it are written the words:

In this tomb are deposited the remains
of
James Bruce Esq., of Kinnaird,
who died on the 27th of April, 1794,
in the 64th year of his age.

His life was spent in performing
useful and splendid actions.
He explored many distant regions.
He discovered the sources of the Nile.
He traversed the deserts of Nubia.

He was an affectionate husband,
an indulgent parent,
an ardent lover of his country.

By the unanimous voice of mankind,
his name is enrolled with those
who were conspicuous
for genius, for valour, and for virtue.

The last stanza was and remains untrue. Then few believed him and now few have heard of him.

Shortly before his death, Bruce told his daughter Janet, 'I shall not live to witness it; but you probably will see the truth of all I have written completely and decisively confirmed'.

He was a reliable prophet, for over the last 200 years his influence has been far-reaching and his narrative has been confirmed in all its important details. He is still virtually unknown but those who do know his work respect it enormously, to the point where our greatest living Ethiopist, Edward Ullendorf, can describe him thus: 'James Bruce rekindled the flame [of interest in Ethiopia], and the stimulus he gave to Ethiopian scholarship became the decisive basis on which all else is built'.

Alexander Murray, the great self-taught orientalist, was the first man to study Bruce's work and, although he had not travelled, he was eminently qualified for the job. He spoke and read countless languages, seeming to learn them with the same fortuitous aptitude as did Bruce. James, Bruce's son, engaged Murray to sort out the papers at Kinnaird and edit the second edition of the *Travels*. Murray took scholarship very seriously, yet although he accused Bruce of laziness and vanity he could find little that was actually false. He was furious when Lord Valentia – who got no further than Massawa – tried to denigrate Bruce's memory:

> The language of Lord Valentia's 'travels' with respect to Mr Bruce, is, I think, a great deal too like what occurs in books written by new adventurers in discovery [he wrote to Henry Salt, Valentia's assistant, who had made more progress than his master]. He gives Bruce the lie direct, and uses terms far too broad, even if they had been sanctioned by an absolute certainty of that traveller's falsehood . . . I, though the editor of his works account myself in no respect obliged to defend him, or any man, in their wilful or accidental errors. I wish merely that the real merits of his labours should be known and made certain.

Salt was the first person after Bruce to get anywhere near Ethiopia, in 1804 and again in 1809. Whilst working for Valentia, he seemed to be under orders to disprove everything that Bruce had said, but even when nit-picking about events that took place forty years before he arrived he experienced some difficulty. He is even kinder after his second visit. C. F. Beckingham wrote a short life of Bruce at the beginning of his 1964 edition of the *Travels* for the Edinburgh University Press in which he quotes Sir Walter Scott:

> Salt is Bruce's most authoritative and most damaging critic but his assessment of his reliability was far more favourable than is often supposed. In 1815 Scott wrote to Lady Abercorn:

> 'We have Salt, the Abyssinian traveller here [Edinburgh] just now, a remarkably pleasant conversible man . . . He corroborated my old acquaintance Bruce in all his material facts, although he thinks that he considerably exaggerated his personal consequence and exploits, and interpolated much of what regards his voyage in the Red Sea.'

Despite all those who have tried over the centuries, no one has yet managed to discredit Bruce. He exaggerates stories but what traveller does not? His dates are sometimes wrong and he occasionally puts things in their wrong sequence but what explorer has not? His claims and predictions have stood up remarkably well to the test of time. Perham and Simmons wrote in *African Discovery*: 'Bruce was the first great scientific explorer of Africa, the first to go out there neither for trade, nor for war, nor to hoist a flag, nor for the Glory of God, but from curiosity – to find out the truth about the source of the Nile.'

He was a true man of the Enlightenment and this is what Bruce's critics seemed unable to appreciate. And he put ideas into action. Bruce marched off to Abyssinia with the same insouciance that others undertook the Grand Tour. He explored somewhere more interesting than his contemporaries dared and ended up discovering the source of the Nile, a riddle that had been plaguing the world for millennia. To those who lacked the gumption to achieve half that Bruce did, it would have been easier to laugh at him than admire him. Linguists would have been infuriated by the man who merely had to land in a country to be able to speak its language; astronomers enraged that his calculations of the source's location were only twenty minutes out.

Bruce took as much equipment as he could with him so that

his journey would be a useful one but he did not have squadrons of biologists, botanists and cartographers dancing attendance upon him. He merely learned as much as he could about all those subjects and then did it himself. He was remarkably good at all he attempted. His maps were subsequently used by the army, his descriptions of plants formed the basis of all early learning about African flora. Where he knew he was deficient – in drawing, for example – he took an assistant and returned with beautiful paintings. Whatever happened to Balugani, it is his master who had the vision to employ him and to instruct him.

When Bruce returned to Britain he was almost universally sneered at; 'lion faced and chicken hearted critics' doubted his word. It maddened him but he reacted by refusing to talk about his travels, thus leaving the denigrators with nothing to vilify. He was blissfully happy living with his family in Scotland, going to the Lodge occasionally where his friends knew that he had performed many 'useful and splendid actions', and hunting on his beautiful estate. He was too self-confident to let his critics discourage him. He knew what he had achieved and he was content. He had spent twelve exciting and dangerous years, pitting his wits against overwhelming odds and he had succeeded in doing all that he had set out to do. He had also fallen in love and more importantly *been* loved, sown more wild oats than any man deserves to and had many 'sun-shiny days'.

Widowed and approaching his dotage, Bruce at last wrote the book of his travels. The task gave him two years of infinite pleasure and has given measureless joy and inspiration to others since his death. When he wrote the book, he was able to sit back and remember the glorious things he had done in Africa and the Levant and reflect upon a life, not of thwarted ambition but of triumphant success. No one had helped him to achieve the astonishing feats he performed in his thirties. They were all done on his own merit – of that he could be justly proud. By rights he should be remembered as one of our greatest explorers – the father of nineteenth century exploration and the one with the purest motives – but instead, through an unhappy combination of circumstances, he is all but forgotten.

There is one man whose achievements in the field of African

exploration have never been doubted; to him I leave the last word. He saw through the jealousies of Bruce's eighteenth-century critics and shared the credit with the Pale Abyssinian for all that he had achieved:

'Old Nile played the theorists a pretty prank by having his springs five hundred miles south of them all! I call mine a contribution, because it is just a hundred years since Bruce, a greater traveller than any of us, visited Abyssinia, and having discovered the sources of the Blue Nile, he thought he had solved the ancient problem.

David Livingstone, 1868.

BIBLIOGRAPHY

Abir, M., *Ethiopia: The Era of the Princes, the Challenge of Islam and the Re-unification of the Christian Empire 1768–1855*. London: 1968
——*Ethiopia and the Red Sea*. London: 1980
Abu Salih, *Churches and Monasteries of Egypt and Some Neighbouring Countries*. Oxford: 1895
Addison, Charles Greenstreet, *The History of the Knights Templars, the Temple Church, and the Temple*. London: Longman & Co., 1842
Alvares, Francisco, *The Prester John of the Indies*. London: Hakluyt Society, 1961
Alvarez, Alfonso, *The Portuguese Embassy to Abyssinia*. London: Hakluyt Society, 1964
Alvarez, González Francisco, *Narrative of the Portuguese Embassy to Abyssinia, 1520–1527*, 1881
Baker, Sir Samuel White, *The Nile Tributaries of Abyssinia And the Sword Hunters of the Hamran Arabs*. London: Macmillan, 1908
——*The Nile Tributaries of Abyssinia*. Camden: Briar Patch Press, 1987
Banks, R. E. R., *Sir Joseph Banks: A Global Perspective*. London: 1832
Barrow, G. W. S., *Robert Bruce and the Community of the Realm of Scotland*. London: Eyre & Spottiswoode, 1965
——*Robert the Bruce and the Scottish Identity*. Edinburgh: Saltire Society, 1984
Battuta, Ibn, *Travels in Asia and Africa, 1325–1354*. London: Routledge, 1929
Beckingham, C. F., *The Achievements of Prester John*. London: School of Oriental and African Studies, 1966
——*Prester John, The Mongols and the Ten Lost Tribes*. Aldershot. Variorum, 1996

————, and Huntingford, G. W. B., *Some Records of Ethiopia –
1593–1646*. London: Hakluyt Society, 1954

Beinecke Rare Book and Manuscript Library, Catalogue of the Papers
of James Boswell at Yale University. New Haven: Yale University
Press, 1993

Belai, Giday, *Ethiopian Civilization*. Addis Ababa: University Press, 1992

Beston, Henry. J., *The Book of Gallant Vagabonds*. New York: George
H. Doran: 1925

Bidder, Irmgard, *Lalibela*. London: Thames and Hudson, 1959

Boswell, James, *An Account of Corsica: The Journal of a Tour to that
Island, and Memoirs of Pascal Paoli by James Boswell, Esq.; illustrated
with a new and accurate map of Corsica*. Glasgow: Printed by Robert
and Andrew Foulis for Edward and Charles Dilly in the Poultry,
1768

————*Life of Johnson*, Oxford: Oxford University Press, 1934–50

————*Boswell for the Defence, 1769–1774*. London: William Heinemann,
1960

Brady, F. James, *Boswell: The Later Years 1769–1795*. London: William
Heinemann, 1984

Breasted, J. H., *A History of Egypt*. New York: 1905

Brown, Peter Hume, *Scotland, A Concise History*. Glasgow: 1992

Bruce, James, *Travels to Discover the Source of the Nile in the Years 1768,
1769, 1770, 1771, 1772 & 1773*. Edinburgh: 1790

————*Travels to Discover the Source of the Nile in the Years 1768, 1769,
1770, 1771, 1772 & 1773*. Edinburgh: 1804–5

————*Travels to Discover the Source of the Nile in the Years 1768, 1769,
1770, 1771, 1772 & 1773*. Edinburgh: 1813

————*Travels to Discover the Source of the Nile* . . . Selected and edited with
an introduction by C. F. Beckingham. (Abridgement based on the text
of the 2nd edition.) Edinburgh: Edinburgh University Press, 1964

Buckle, Henry James, *On Scotland and the Scottish Intellect*. Chicago:
1970

Budge, Sir E. A. Wallis, *A History of Ethiopia, Nubia and Abyssinia*.
London: 1928

————*The Queen of Sheba and Her Only Son Menyelek*. London: 1922

Buffon, Georges Leclerc, Comte de Buffon, *Histoire Naturelle*, vol. 18.
Paris: 1775

Burney, Fanny, *Memoirs of Madame d'Arblay*. New York: J. Mowatt
and Co., 1844

————*The Early Diary of Frances Burney*, edited by Annie Raine Ellis.
London: G. Bell and Sons, 1913

——The Journals and Letters of Fanny Burney (Madame d'Arblay). Oxford: Clarendon Press, 1972–84

——Selected Letters and Journals, edited by Joyce Hemlow. Oxford: Clarendon Press, 1986

Buxton, D., The Abyssinians. London: 1970

Campbell, G. A., The Knights Templar. New York: AMS Press, 1980

Campbell, R. H., The Rise and Fall of Scottish Industry. Edinburgh: Donald, 1980

Campbell, R. H., and Skinner, Andrew S., The Origins and Nature of the Scottish Enlightenment. Edinburgh: Donald, 1982

Caraman, Philip, The Lost Empire: The Story of the Jesuits in Ethiopia, 1555–1634. Notre Dame: University of Notre Dame Press, 1985

Chambers, Robert, A Biographical Dictionary of Eminent Scotsmen. Glasgow: Blackie & Son, 1832–5

Cheesman, R. E., Lake Tana and the Blue Nile. London: Macmillan, 1936

Chitnis, A., and C., The Scottish Enlightenment and Early Victorian English Society. London: 1986

Clarke, John, The Life and Times of George III. London: Weidenfeld & Nicolson, 1972

Colin, Gérard, Le Synaxaire Ethiopien. Turnhout: Brepols, 1987

Cook, James, A voyage of the Pacific Ocean. Undertaken, by the command of His Majesty, for making discoveries in the Northern hemisphere, to determine the position and extent of the west side of North America; its distance from Asia; and the practicability of a northern passage to Europe. Performed under the direction of Captains Cook, Clerke, and Gore, in His Majesty's ships the Resolution and Discovery, in the years 1776, 1777, 1778, 1779 and 1780. Vols I and II written by Captain James Cook, F.R.S. Vol. III by Captain James King, L.L.D. and F.R.S. Illustrated with maps and charts, from the original drawings made by Lieut. Henry Roberts . . . with a great variety of portraits . . . views . . . and historical representations . . . drawn by Mr. Webber . . . Published by order of the Lords commissioner of the Admiralty. London: Printed by W. and A. Strahan, for G. Nicol, & T. Cadell, 1784

Colley, Linda, Britons: Forging the Nation, 1707–1837. New Haven: Yale University Press, 1992

Cooley, William Desborough, Claudius Ptolemy and the Nile: or, an inquiry into that geographer's real merits and speculative errors, his knowledge of eastern Africa, and the authenticity of the Mountains of the Moon. London: John W. Parker & Son, 1854

Crawford, Osbert Guy Stanhope, Castles and Churches in the Middle

Nile Region. Khartoum: Sudan Antiquities Service. (Occasional Papers, no. 2.), 1953

——*Ethiopian Itineraries, circa 1400–1524. Including those collected by Alessandro Zorzi at Venice in the years 1519–24,* edited by O. G. S. Crawford. Cambridge: Cambridge University Press (Hakluyt Society), 1958

——*The Fung Kingdom of Sennar. With a Geographical Account of the Middle Nile Region.* Gloucester: John Bellows, 1951

Cumming, Duncan, Sir, *The Gentleman Savage: The Life of Mansfield Parkyns, 1823–1894.* London: Century, 1987

Dennistoun, James, *Memoirs of Sir Robert Strange, Knt., Engraver . . . and of his brother-in-law Andrew Lumisden, private secretary to the Stuart princes.* London: Longman, Brown, Green, 1855

Devine, T. M., and Mitchison, Rosalind (eds), *People and Society in Scotland: Social History of Modern Scotland,* vol. 1, 1760–1830. Edinburgh: Edinburgh University Press, 1988

Doresse, Jean, *L'Empire du Prêtre Jean.* Paris: 1957

Easson, David Edward, *Medieval Religious Houses, Scotland.* London: Longmans, Green & Co., 1957

Eden, Frederic, *The Nile Without a Dragoman.* London, 1871

Enoch, Book of Enoch the prophet: an apocryphal production, supposed for ages to have been lost; but discovered at the close of the last century in Abyssinia; now first translated from an Ethiopic MS. In the Bodleian Library, Oxford, Oxford: S. Collingwood, 1838

Farmer, David Hugh, *The Oxford Dictionary of Saints.* Oxford: Oxford University Press, 1992

Farrer, R., *Biographical Dictionary of Medallists.* London: 1904

Faucher, Jean André, *Dictionnaire historique des francs-maçons du XVIIIe siècle à nos jours.* Paris: Librarie Académique Perrin, 1988

Fellows, O., and Milliken, S., *Buffon.* New York: Twayne, 1972

Fisher, Godfrey, *Barbary Legend.* Oxford: Clarendon Press, 1957

Flad, Martin J., *A Short Description of the Falasha and Kamants in Abyssinia, together with an outline of the elements and a vocabulary of the Falasha-Language.* Basel: Reprinted at the Mission-Press, 1866

Fowler, Montague, *Christian Egypt: Past, Present, and Future.* London: Church Newspaper Co., 1901

Friedmann, Daniel, *Les Enfants de la reine de Saba: les Juifs d'Ethiopie (Falachas: histoire, exode et intégration).* Paris: Editions Métailié: Diffusion Seuil, 1994

Garnett, R., James Bruce in *The Dictionary of National Biography.* London: 1921–2

Geddes, Michael, *The Church-History of Ethiopia*. London: 1696

George III, King of Great Britain and Ireland, *The Correspondence of King George the Third. From 1760 to December 1783* . . . arranged and edited by Sir John Fortescue, etc. London: Frank Cass & Co., 1967

George, Mary Dorothy, *Catalogue of Personal and Political Satires*. London: 1938

Gerster, Georg, *Churches in Rock*. London: Phaidon, 1970

Gilmour, Ian, *Riot, Risings and Revolution: Governance and Violence in Eighteenth-Century England*. London: 1992

Gobat, Samuel, *The Journal of a Three Years' Residence in Abyssinia: in furtherance of the objects of the Church Missionary Society to which is prefixed, A brief history of the church of Abyssinia by Rev. Professor Lee*. London: Hatchard, 1834

Graham, Henry, *The Social Life of Scotland in the Eighteenth Century*. London: 1937

Great Britain, War Office Intelligence Division, Routes in Abyssinia, London: HMSO, 1867

Hallett, Robin, *Records of the African Association, 1783–1831*. London: Nelson, 1964

——*The Penetration of Africa. European Enterprise and Exploration Principally in Northern and Western Africa up to 1830*. London: Routledge & Kegan Paul, 1965

Hamilton, H., *An Economic History of Scotland in the Eighteenth Century*. Oxford: Clarendon Press, 1963

Hancock, Graham, *The Sign and the Seal: The Quest for the Lost Ark of the Covenant*. London: William Heinemann, 1992

Harvie, Christopher, *Scotland and Nationalism: Scottish Society and Politics, 1707–1977*. London: 1977

Hassen, Mohammed, *The Oromo of Ethiopia: A History*. Cambridge, 1990

Hayes, A. J., *The Source of the Blue Nile*. London: Smith, Elder and Co., 1905

Head, F. B. *The Life of Bruce, the African Traveller*. London: John Murray, 1836

Hepper, F. Nigel, 'On the botany of James Bruce's expedition to the source of the Nile 1768–1773'. London: *Journal of the Society for Bibliography of Natural History*, 1980

Hibbert, Christopher, *Africa Explored*. London: Allen Lane, 1982

——*The Personal History of Samuel Johnson*. Harmondsworth: Penguin Books, 1984

——*The English: A Social History 1066–1945*. London: Grafton, 1987

Holt, P. M., *Egypt and the Fertile Crescent 1516–1922: A Political History*. London: Longman, 1966

Horne, Alex, *King Solomon's Temple in Masonic Tradition*. London: Aquarian Press, 1972

Hoskins, George Alexander, *Travels in Ethiopia Above the Second Cataract of the Nile etc*. London: Longman, 1835

Houtsma, M. T., *The Encyclopaedia of Islam*. Leiden: 1913–38

Hulton, P. F., Hepper, F. Nigel, and Friis, Ib, *Luigi Balugani's Drawings of African Plants*. New Haven: 1991

Huntingford, G. W. B., *The Galla of Ethiopia*. London: 1955

——*The Periplus of the Eythrean Sea*. London: 1980

——*The Historical Georgraphy of Ethiopia from the First Century AD to 1704*. Oxford: Published for the British Academy by Oxford University Press, 1989

Hyatt, Harry Middleton, *The Church of Abyssinia*. London: Luzac, 1928

Johnson, Samuel, *Rasselas, The Prince of Abissinia. A Tale*. London: R. & J. Dodsley, 1759

Jones, A. H. M., and Monroe, Elizabeth, *A History of Ethiopia*. Oxford: Clarendon Press, 1968

Kaplan, Steven, *The Beta Israel (Falasha) in Ethiopia: From Earliest Times to the Twentieth Century*. New York: New York University Press, 1992

Kaplan, Steven, Parfitt, Tudor, and Trevisan Semi, Emanuela, 'Between Africa and Zion'. *Proceedings of the First International Congress of the Society for the Study of Ethiopian Jewry*. Jerusalem: Ben-Zvi Institute, 1995

Kay, John, *A Descriptive Catalogue of Original Portraits*. Edinburgh: H. Paton, 1836

Keay, John, and Julia, *Collins Encyclopaedia of Scotland*. London: Collins, 1994

Kenny, Virginia C. *The Country-House Ethos in English Literature 1688–1750. Themes of Personal Retreat and National Expansion*. Brighton: Harvester Press, 1984

Kessler, David, *The Falashas: The Forgotten Jews of Ethiopia*. London: George Allen & Unwin, 1982

Knoop, Douglas, *The Scottish Mason and the Mason World* (microform). Manchester: Manchester University Press, 1939

Kobischanov, Y. M. *Axum*. London: 1979

Lenman, Bruce, *Integration, Enlightenment and Industrialization: Scotland, 1746–1832*. London: Edward Arnold, 1981

Littmann, E., *The Legend of the Queen of Sheba in the Tradition of Axum.* Leiden, 1904

Lobo, Jerónimo, *Itineraria. A voyage to Abyssinia, by Father Jerome Lobo . . . Containing the history, natural, civil, and ecclesiastical, of that remote and unfrequented country, continued down to the beginning of the eighteenth century: with fifteen dissertations on various subjects, relating to the antiquities, government, religion, manners, and natural history of Abyssinia.* By M. Le Grand. Translated from the French by Samuel Johnson, LL.D. To which are added, various other tracts by the same author, not published by Sir John Hawkins or Mr. Stockdale. London: Elliot and Kay, 1789.

——*Itinerário.* English (translated by Donald M. Lockhart; from the Portuguese text established and edited by M. G. da Costa; with an introduction and notes by C. F. Beckingham). London: Hakluyt Society, 1984

London Magazine, 1775

Love, James, Local Antiquarian Notes and Queries. Reprinted from the *Falkirk Herald*. Falkirk: F. Johnston & Co., 1908–28

Lowes, John Livingston, *The Road to Xanadu: A Study in the Ways of the Imagination.* Princeton: Princeton University Press, 1986

Ludolphus, J., *A New History of Ethiopia.* London: 1684

Lythe, Samuel George Edgar, *An Economic History of Scotland, 1100–1939.* Glasgow: Blackie, 1975

Mackenzie, Allan, *History of the Lodge Canongate Kilwinning No. 2.* Edinburgh: James Hogg, 1888

Mackie, J. D., *A History of Scotland.* London: Penguin Books, 1964

Marcus, Harold G., *A History of Ethiopia.* Berkeley: University of California Press, 1994

Marsden-Smedley, Philip, *A Far Country: Travels in Ethiopia.* London: Century, 1990

Massie, Allan, *101 Great Scots.* Edinburgh: 1987

McCoy, Robert, *A Dictionary of Freemasonry: A Compendium of Masonic History, Symbolism, Rituals, Literature, and Myth.* New York: Bell, 1989

McCrindle, J. W. (ed.), *The Christian Topography of Cosmas, an Egyptian Monk.* London: 1897

Mclaren, Moray, *Understanding the Scots: A Guide for South Britons and Other Foreigners.* London: 1956

Melly, George, *Khartoum and the Blue and White Niles.* London: 1851

Milkias, Paulos, *Ethiopia: A Comprehensive Bibliography.* Boston: G. K. Hall, 1989

Moorehead, Alan, *The White Nile*. London: Hamish Hamilton, 1960
——*The Blue Nile*. London: Hamish Hamilton, 1962
Mountnorris, George Annesley, Earl of, *Analyses of new works of voyages and travels, lately published in London: Voyages and travels to India, Ceylon, the Red Sea, Abyssinia, and Egypt, in 1802, 1803, 1804, 1805 and 1806, by George, Viscount Valentia*. London: Macmillan, 1810
Mowl, Timothy, *Horace Walpole: The Great Outsider*. London: John Murray, 1996
Munro-Hay, S. C., *Excavations at Aksum: An Account of Research at the Ancient Ethiopian Capital Directed in 1972–4 by the Late Dr Neville Chittick*. London: British Institute in Eastern Africa, 1989
——*Aksum: An African Civilisation of Late Antiquity*. Edinburgh: Edinburgh University Press, 1991
Munro-Hay, S. C. (Stuart, C.), and Pankhurt, Richard (compilers), *Ethiopia*. Santa Barbara: Clio Press, 1995
Murray, Alexander, *Account of the Life and Writings of James Bruce of Kinnaird, Esq. F. R. S. author of the travels to discover the source of the Nile*. Edinburgh: 1808
Nimmo, William, Rev., *A General History of Stirlingshire*. Edinburgh: A. Bean, 1817
Notes and Queries, 25 October 1924
Nothling, F. J., *Pre-Colonial Africa: Her Civilisations and Foreign Contacts*. Johannesburg: Southern, 1989
Oliver, Roland, and Crowder, Michael, *The Cambridge Encyclopaedia of Africa*. Cambridge: Cambridge University Press, 1981
Oliver, Roland, and Fage, J. D., *The Cambridge History of Africa*. Cambridge: Cambridge University Press, 1975
Oppe, A. P., *English Drawings at Windsor Castle*. London: 1950
Packenham, T., *The Mountains of Rasselas*. London: 1959
Pankhurst, E. S., *Ethiopia. A Cultural History*. Woodford Green: Lalibela, 1955
Pankhurst, Richard, *An Introduction to the Economic History of Ethiopia, from Early Times to 1800*. London: 1960
——'An Eighteenth-Century Ethiopian Dynastic Marriage Contract between Empress Mentewab of Gondar and Ras Mika'el of Tegre'. London: *Bulletin of the School of Oriental and African Studies*, 1979
——*A Social History of Ethiopia: The Northern and Central Highlands from Early Medieval Times to the Rise of Emperor Tóewodros II*. Addis Ababa: Institute of Ethiopian Studies, Addis Ababa University, 1990
——*The Ethiopians*. Oxford: Blackwell, 1998
——, and Ingrams, Leila, *Ethiopia Engraved: An Illustrated Catalogue of*

Engravings by Foreign Travellers from 1681 to 1900. London: Kegan Paul International, 1988

Park, Mungo, *Travels in the Interior Districts of Africa.* New York: Arno Press, 1971

Parker, Ben, *Ethiopia. Breaking New Ground.* Oxfam Publications, 1995

Parkyns, Mansfield, *Life in Abyssinia: Being Notes Collected during Three Years' Residence and Travels in that Country.* London: 1853

Perham, Margery, and Simmons, J., *African Discovery.* Evanston: Northwestern University Press, 1963

Perruchon, J., *Vie de Lalibala, roi d'Ethiopie.* Paris: 1892

Pinkerton, John, *A General Collection of the best and most interesting voyages and travels in all parts of the world, many of which are now first translated into English.* London: 1808–14

Plant, Ruth, *Architecture of the Tigre, Ethiopia.* Worcester: Ravens Educational and Development Services, 1985

Playfair, Sir Robert Lambert, *Travels in the Footsteps of Bruce in Algeria and Tunis.* London: Smith, Elder & Co., 1877

——*The Scourge of Christendom.* London: Smith, Elder & Co., 1884

——*Murray's Handbook to Algeria.* London: John Murray, 1891

Pliny, *Natural History,* London: 1947–56

Plowden, Walter, *Travels in Abyssinia.* London: Longmans, Green, & Co., 1868

Poncet, Charles-Jacques, *A Voyage to AEthiopia, made in the years 1698, 1699 and 1700.* London: W. Lewis, 1709

Porter, Roy, *English Society in the Eighteenth Century.* London: Allen Lane, 1982

Pottle, F. A., *James Boswell: The Earlier Years 1740–1769.* London: Heinemann, 1966

Poulos, George, *Orthodox Saints: Spiritual Profiles for Modern Man.* Brookline: Holy Cross Orthodox Press, 1990–92

Prestage, Edgar, *The Portuguese Pioneers.* London: A. & C. Black, 1933

Pritchard, J. B., *Solomon and Sheba.* London: 1974

Purchas, Samuel, the Elder, *Hakluytus Posthumus; or, Purchas his Pilgrimes.* Glasgow: James MacLehose & Sons, 1905–7

Quirin, James Arthur, *The Evolution of the Ethiopian Jews: A History of the Beta Israel (Falasha) to 1920.* Philadelphia: University of Pennsylvania Press, 1992

Ramsay, Edward Bannerman, *Reminiscenses of Scottish Life and Character.* Edinburgh: Gall & Inglis, 1859

Reid, J. M., *Traveller Extraordinary. The Life of James Bruce of Kinnaird.* London: Eyre & Spottiswoode, 1968

Reith, J., *Life and Writings of Alexander Murray*. Dumfries: 1903

Rey. C. F., *In the Country of the Blue Nile*. London: Duckworth, 1927

——*The Romance of the Portuguese in Abyssinia*. London: Witherby, 1929

Rickman, John, *Journal of Captain Cook's last voyage to the Pacific Ocean, on Discovery; performed in the years 1776, 1777, 1778, 1779, illustrated with cuts and a chart, shewing the tracts of the ships employed in this expedition. Faithfully narrated from the original*. London: E. Newbery, 1781.

Robinson, John J., *Born in Blood: The Lost Secrets of Freemasonry*. London: Arrow, 1989

Runciman, Sir Steven, *A History of the Crusades*. Cambridge: Cambridge University Press, 1962–6

Russell, Alexander, *The Natural History of Aleppo*. Second edition revised, enlarged and illustrated with notes by Patrick Russell (republished). Farnborough: Gregg International Publishers, 1969

Sabah, Lucien, *La franc-maçonnerie à Oran de 1832 à 1914*. Paris: Aux Amateurs de Livres, 1989

Salt, Henry, *A Voyage to Abyssinia, and Travels into the interior of that country, executed . . . in the years 1809 and 1810. In which are included an account of the Portuguese settlements on the east coast of Africa . . . A concise narrative of late events in Arabia Felix, etc.* London: L. P. Bulmer, 1814

Sanceau, Elaine, *Portugal in Quest of Prester John*. London: Hutchinson, 1843

Scholes, Percy Alfred, *The Great Dr Burney*. London: Oxford University Press, 1948

Seward, Desmond, *The Monks of War: The Military Religious Orders*. Hamden: Archon Books, 1972

Simmons, Judy, *Fanny Burney*. London: Macmillan, 1987

Sinclair, Andrew, *The Sword and the Grail*. London: Century, 1993

——*The Discovery of the Grail: The True History*. London: Century, 1998

Smith, Edward, *The Life of Sir Joseph Banks*. London: 1911

Smout, T. C., *A History of the Scottish People, 1560–1830*. London: 1969

Soames, Jane, *The Coast of Barbary*. London: Jonathan Cape, 1938

Southey, Robert, *Selections from the Letters of Robert Southey*. London: Longman, Brown, Green, Longmans and Roberts, 1856

Steer, G. L., *Ceasar in Abyssinia*. London: 1936

Stevenson, David, *The Origins of Freemasonry*. Cambridge: Cambridge University Press, 1988

Tellez, Balthazar, *The travels of the Jesuits in Ethiopia: containing, I, The geographial description of all the kingdoms, and provinces of that empire* . . . *II, Travels in Arabia Félix* . . . *III, An account of the kingdoms of Cambate, Gingiro, Alaba, and Dancali beyond Ethiopia in Africk, never travelled into by any but the Jesuits* . . . *Illustrated with an exact map of the country, delineated by those fathers* . . . *The whole collected, and historically digested by F. Balthazar Tellez, of the Society of Jesus: and now first translated into English*. London: Printed for J. Knapton, A. Bell and J. Baker, 1710

The *Critical Review, or, Annals of Literature*. London: 1760–95

Topham, Edward, *Letters from Edinburgh in 1774 and 1775*. Edinburgh: Edinburgh University Press, 1971

Toy, Barbara, *In Search of Sheba*. London: 1961

Trimingham, J. S., *Islam in Ethiopia*. London: 1952

Ullendorf, Edward, *Exploration of Abyssinia*. Asmara: 1945

——*James Bruce of Kinnaird*. Aberdeen: Scottish Historical Review, 1953

——*Ethiopia and the Bible*. London: 1968

——*The Ethiopians. An Introduction to Country and People*. London: 1973

——*The Two Zions: Reminiscences of Jerusalem and Ethiopia*. New York: Oxford University Press, 1988

——, and Beckingham, C. F., *The Hebrew Letters of Prester John*. Oxford: Oxford University Press, 1982

Walpole, Horace, *Correspondence*. New Haven: Yale University Press, 1983

Ware, Timothy Richard, *The Orthodox Church*. Harmondsworth: Penguin Books, 1963

Waugh, Evelyn, *Remote People*. London: Duckworth, 1931

——*Waugh in Abyssinia*. London: Longmans, Green and Co., 1936

Whiteway, R. S. (ed.), and Castanhoso, Miguel de, *The Portuguese Expedition to Abyssinia in 1541–1543*. London: Hakluyt Society, 1902

Yayehe, Qes Asres, *Traditions of the Ethiopian Jews*. Ontario: 1995

Youngson, A. J., *The Making of Classical Edinburgh*. Edinburgh: Edinburgh University Press, 1966

Zaghi, C., *Luigi Balugani in Dizionario biografico degli Italiani*. Rome: 1963

INDEX